Organizational Behaviour:

A Critical Introduction

Fiona M. Wilson

Senior Lecturer, Department of Management,
University of St. Andrews

OXFORD
UNIVERSITY PRESS

OXFORD

UNIVERSITY PRESS

Great Clarendon Street, Oxford OX2 6DP

Oxford University Press is a department of the University of Oxford
It furthers the University's objective of excellence in research, scholarship,
and education by publishing worldwide in

Oxford New York

Athens Auckland Bangkok Bogotá Buenos Aires Calcutta
Cape Town Chennai Dar es Salaam Delhi Florence Hong Kong Istanbul
Karachi Kuala Lumpur Madrid Melbourne Mexico City Mumbai
Nairobi Paris São Paulo Singapore Taipei Tokyo Toronto Warsaw

with associated companies in Berlin Ibadan

Oxford is a registered trade mark of Oxford University Press
in the UK and certain other countries

Published in the United States
by Oxford University Press Inc., New York

British Library Cataloguing in Publication Data
Data available

Library of Congress Cataloging in Publication Data
Wilson, Fiona M. (Fiona Margaret), 1955–
Organizational behaviour: a critical introduction / Fiona Wilson.
p. cm.
Includes bibliographical references.
1. Organizational behaviour. I. Title.
HD58.7.W548 1999 302.3′5—dc21 99-24521

ISBN 0–19–878257–8

10 9 8 7 6 5 4 3 2 1

Typeset by Hope Services (Abingdon) Ltd.
Printed in Great Britain
on acid-free paper by
The Bath Press,
Bath

Acknowledgements

Thanks must be extended to Stewart Clegg who was instrumental and inspirational in helping design the course from which this book has developed. The reviewers, Chris Grey and David Wilson provided much support and enthusiasm at the proposal and later stages of the book which have motivated me in the writing. The interlibrary loan section of the University of St Andrews library were invaluable in helping access about 200 books and papers over an eighteen-month period in which the book was written.

Contents

Introduction

Work occupies a substantial proportion of most of our lives. It can be a symbol of personal value, provide status, economic reward, and a potential. It can also be regarded as a punishment. Work and employment structure our lives and shape inequalities of condition and opportunity.

Work can be divided into four types. The first is recognized and rewarded work which is paid. This takes the individual into a labour market to sell their skills, time, and energy to an employer like a university, a private or public company, or their family, if they work in their family business. The second type is reproductive labour and concerns the efforts involved in raising one or more children to adulthood. A third type of work is maintenance labour, the chores necessary to maintain yourself and other members of your family by cooking, paying the bills, food shopping, gardening, laundry, and so on. The fourth type is unpaid work, voluntary work for charities, churches and other religious groups, hospitals, political parties. Levels of voluntary activity are high and have risen significantly in recent years (Joseph Rowntree Foundation, 1991).

> **STOP**
>
> Where does student work fit in? What category would you need to add? Why isn't the work you do as a student defined as 'work'? Look at the contents pages of other management and organizational behaviour texts and see what kind of work is typically discussed.

Women do the lion's share of domestic, household work even when husbands are retired or unemployed. Husband's household labour is 'remarkably unresponsive' to decreases in their overall working hours, to increases in their wives' working hours, and to the fact that their wife is a high earner (Kynaston, 1996). Men's lives 'continue to be consistently enhanced by their appropriation of female labour' (Kynaston, 1996: 233). Little mention is made of this in books on work or organizational behaviour. The context in which work is defined as men's or women's work must be considered. The all-pervasive influence of culture and social structure on organizational behaviour needs to be explored.

The book is designed to challenge what constitutes organizational behaviour (OB). The meaning of the term is far from clear. Is it behaviour that occurs in some specified place and not in others or behaviour controlled by an organization (Weick, 1969: 25)? Should we only be interested in behaviour that happens within organizations? What happens within organizations affects what happens outside and vice versa. Organizational behaviour is seen here chiefly as being about the particular ways that individual's dispositions are expressed in an organizational setting and about the effects of this expression. While at work there is rest and play. What happens in rest and play, both inside and outside the organization, impacts on organizational life.

We also can gain insight into organizational behaviour by looking at less organized work, like work 'on the fiddle', and what work means to the unemployed. This book would ask you to question what organizational behaviour is and how it is influenced. What are the common characteristics to be found in organizations and what behaviour draws our attention? For you is it all about work, or do rest and play have a part too?

Textbooks on organizational behaviour usually included chapters on perception, personality, motivation, job satisfaction, job design, leadership, learning, and socialization. We seem to have accepted the litany of topics which fall under the heading of OB. Organizational psychology informs the discipline; the approach has a 'scientific' view, a mission to construct and validate theories which can explain and predict organizational behaviour. Science provides a justification for believing there is no problem with the status of knowledge. Knowledge produced through scientific methods is unproblematically true and scientists are potentially neutral agents in the process (Hollway, 1991). The individual is usually the unit of analysis. Theory construction in organizational psychology is based on a highly empirical-analytic form of science, rooted in the natural sciences. There is an unwillingness to self-reflect and critique the discipline (Steffy and Grimes, 1992). The bulk of the research does not focus on dynamic issues like organizational power, conflict, class, politics, and ideology. As a result there is a very tidy and sanitized view of what goes on in organizations, yet we all know that work issues and behaviour in organizations are much more than this. There is, as Sims *et al.* (1993) note, uncertainty, chaos, and confusion in organizing. There is control and resistance, work degradation and deskilling too. Workplaces are not peopled by high performing, highly committed individuals bound together in a common cause by a corporate mission enshrined within a strong organizational culture (Noon and Blyton, 1997). Workplaces are sites of inequalities, divided by class, levels of education, race, and gender. We need then a critical approach, taking a critical or radical view of contemporary behaviour in organizations, an approach which considers exploitation, repression, unfairness, and asymmetrical power relations.

Much of what we read in textbooks about work is about men and their work, how they are motivated, how they gain job satisfaction, are stressed, and so on. As Crompton (1989: 129) too has noted, much of the empirical research and theorizing on work, particularly in sociology, is derived from outdated studies of predominantly white male production workers. The theory of organizations and work is mainly a chronology of men's writings, research, and theory. Female management theorists, like Mary Parker Follett (Graham, 1995) and Simone Weil (Grey, 1996) have been written out of, or marginalized from, the history and development of management ideas. Classical theory comes from the intellectual 'fathers' like Weber. The fathers' ideas formed the foundation for the theory and research methods of organizational behaviour. Women's experiences are conspicuously absent from theory, methods, and data. Practically all organizational behaviour, analysis, and theory is about the male world. The topics that preoccupy it are topics which preoccupy men—power, leadership, technology, stress, the world of the (mainly male) manager and the work he does, and so on, with women only as adjuncts to men. If women are dealt with it is usually in a chapter thrown in as an extra, almost as beside the point or as an optional extra rather than as an intrinsic component of behaviour in organizations. Half the population of organizations are left at the edge or just tagged onto OB texts (Wilson, 1996). Very little in organizational behaviour texts deals with the nature, structure, and functioning of female-dominated jobs. Despite the fact that authors such as Richard Brown (1976) and Janet Wolff (1977) argued more than two decades ago that gender should figure more largely in organizational analysis, little progress has been made. A great deal of research focuses on men with no reference at all to women but when research is focused on women, it is almost always with reference to men. If comparisons are not made with men, the research is viewed as incomplete (Bernard, 1998). Research on women in their own right is not worthy of male attention.

A Personal Experience

A Ph.D. student recently had an experience where this view became a reality for her. She presented her research proposal and methodology—on women entrepreneurs (women who own and manage bed and breakfast establishments) to a group of academics and found that they did not think that she should limit her study to women. What about men who own and manage bed and breakfast establishments, they asked? Would the same question have been asked if she had designed her research on male managers or male entrepreneurs?

In 1995, I published a book *Organizational Behaviour and Gender* to try to begin to redress the balance. Gender though is not just about women, but also about men. Gender is more than an individual trait or set of roles. The differences between women and men are not essential to either sex. This book is written, as others like Grint (1991) have begun to do, to discuss women's work in balance with men's, to think about the implications of unpaid domestic work, to consider issues of ethnicity as well as gender. (If, when reading this book you think there is too much on women and work, ask yourself why this is the case when about half the population of organizations are female). Gender is systematically and inextricably tied to other inequality issues like race, sexual orientation, and class.

The issues of the racial and ethical foundations of organizational power and control are only just beginning to emerge in the literature (Reed, 1996). Race, like gender, offers itself as a kind of performance, a set of practices, and language. If we were to 'colour' organizational studies, we would need to think more about what colour means and take apart the grammars of race (black/white, African/American/Asian American, native/indigenous) to track racial identity and search ideological commitments (Ferguson, 1994: 93).

Another area from which OB could profitably draw is emotion and feeling. As Fineman (1996) notes, a scan of the indexes of textbooks on organizational behaviour and theory reveals few, if any, entries under emotions or feelings. Yet gripes, joy, drudgery, anger, anxiety, frustrations, glee, embarrassment, and tedium are part of the social creation and personal expression of work and organizational life. Activities like recruiting, firing, negotiating, and persuading are felt and shaped by feelings.

This book also asks you to look outside of what are normally thought of as organizations and how we usually think of work. What can be learnt from 'deviant' work, sex work for example? Everett Hughes, a sociologist, encouraged his students to look at 'dirty' or deviant types of occupations because they are interesting in their own right and because they can help highlight factors of general relevance to work experience which we might not notice in conventional work where we too easily take them for granted (Watson, 1997). Why is there so little mention of sex, violence, pain, and power in organizational life (Burrell, 1997: 52)? Gibson Burrell would say that organization studies tends to ignore or hide that which is thought to be unacceptable in polite company and management writers have acted like funeral directors or morticians, using cosmetics and 'rouge of excellence' to cover 'necrotic collapse' of organizational structures. There is plenty of research which reveals the difficulties, problems, and realities of organizational life, and plenty from outside organizations that could help inform our understanding about what happens in organizations, but so far little of it has appeared in mainstream management textbooks.

The book has been written as an alternative to the standard introductory texts in management. The purpose was to provide a fresh critical look at management and organizations, to uncover the issues and assumptions underlying the world of management and subject them to scrutiny. The emphasis here has been on exposing and discussing deep-seated features of organizational life like inequality, conflict, domination, subordination, and manipulation. It was written particularly for those people who acknowledge that there are few certainties about how to manage and many difficulties, uncertain tensions, irrationalities, and dilemmas to face in the mundane realities of work.

This book is designed to offer an introduction to a view of organizational behaviour which has a long history but, as yet, has not been included in many of the introductory texts. The style of writing is deliberately simple and straightforward in order to encourage students to grasp the basic ideas, arguments, and controversies before moving on to more complex levels of analysis and explanatory theory. Lecturers who want to use this book as a basis of their course design have some choices to make. They could lecture, using some of the sources here or from elsewhere, having the book as mandatory or supplementary reading, using the questions for further research and reading for tutorials assignments and exam questions. Or they could abandon the lecture/tutorial mode of teaching in favour of using the book as essential reading and the questions for further research as a basis for student projects for class, assignment, and exam. What was lecture time could be used for exercises like stress testing, or for excerpts from films or video as a means of getting attention for the subject. You choose.

References

Bernard, J. (1998) 'My Four Revolutions: An Autobiographical History of the ASA' in K. A. Myers, C. D. Anderson and B. J. Risman (eds.), *Feminist Foundations: Towards Transforming Sociology*. London: Sage, ch. 1.

Brown, R. (1976) 'Women as Employees: Some Comments on Research in Industrial Sociology', in D. L. Barker and S. Allen (eds.), *Dependence and Exploitation in Work and Marriage*. Harlow: Longman, ch. 2.

Burrell, G. (1997) *Pandemonium: Towards a Retro-Organizational Theory*. London: Sage.

Crompton, R. (1989) Review of Y. Gabriel (1988) *Working Lives in Catering*, in *Work, Employment and Society*, 3/1: 129–30.

Ferguson, K. (1994) 'On Bringing More Theory, More Voices, More Politics to the Study of Organization', *Organization*, 1/1: 81–100.

Fineman, S (1996) 'Emotion and Organizing', in S. R. Clegg, C. Hardy and W. R. Nord (eds.), *Handbook of Organization Studies*. London: Sage Publications, ch. 3.3.

Graham, P. (1995) (ed.) *Mary Parker Follett: Prophet of Management*. Boston, Mass.: Harvard Business School Press.

Grey, C. (1996) 'Towards a Critique of Managerialism: The Contribution of Simone Weil', *Journal of Management Studies*, 33/5: 591–611.

Grint, K. (1991) *The Sociology of Work: An Introduction*. Cambridge: Polity.

Hollway, W. (1991) *Work Psychology and Organizational Behaviour: Managing the Individual at Work*. London: Sage.

Joseph Rowntree Foundation (1991) *Nationall Survey of Volunteering*. Social Policy Research Findings, 22; York: Joseph Rowntree Foundation.

Kynaston, C (1996) 'The Everyday Exploitation of Women: Housework and the Patriarchal Mode of Production', *Women's Studies International Forum*, 19/3: 228, 232–3.

Noon, M., and Blyton, P. (1997) *The Realities of Work*, Basingstoke: Macmillan Press.

Reed, M. (1996) 'Organizational Theorizing: A Historically Contested Terrain', in S. R. Clegg, C. Hardy and W. R. Nord (eds.), *Handbook of Organization Studies*. London: Sage. ch. 1.1.

Sims, D., Fineman, S., and Gabriel, Y. (1993) *Organizing and Organizations*. London: Sage.

Steffy, B. D., and Grimes, A. J. (1992) 'Personnel/Organizational Psychology: A Critique of the Discipline', in M. Alvesson and H. Wilmott (eds.), *Critical Management Studies*. London: Sage, ch. 9.

Watson, T. J. (1997) *Sociology, Work and Industry*. London: Routledge.

Weick, K. E. (1969) *The Social Psychology of Organizing*. Reading, Mass.: Addison-Wesley Publishing Company.

Wilson, F. M. (1995) *Organizational Behaviour and Gender*. Maidenhead: McGraw Hill.

——(1996) 'Research Note: Organizational Theory: Blind and Deaf to Gender?', *Organization Studies*, 17/5: 825–42.

Wolff, J. (1977) 'Women in Organizations', in S. Clegg and D. Dunkerley (eds.), *Critical issues in Organizations*. London: Routledge and Kegan Paul, pp. 7–20.

I

The Meaning of Work

1

What Work Means

INTUITIVELY **WE KNOW** one of the prime reasons individuals give for working is to earn money. Most people will say that earning money is the prime reason they go to work. In a recent British survey (Rose, 1994) 68 per cent of respondents said they worked for the money to provide money for basic essentials or to buy extras and enjoy some economic independence from the primary earner in a household. Economic need may be contingent on family composition. It may be that the earnings of minority ethnic women are more important to their households than for many white households (Phizacklea and Wolkowitz, 1993; Westwood, 1988). In the survey 26 per cent (Rose, 1994) said they did not work for money but for 'expressive' reasons (intrinsic rewards like a sense of enjoyment, satisfaction, and a sense of achievement) so economic reasons are not a sufficient explanation for economic activity. Pakistani and Bangladeshi women record the lowest levels of economic activity despite living in the most disadvantaged households (Blackburn *et al.*, 1997).

Work is, then, more than a means towards the end of earning a living; people work for more than money. If work were purely a means to an economic end there would be no way of explaining the dislocation and deprivation individuals feel when they retire. Intrinsic reward is clearly important too, perhaps more so than money. More qualitative research, for example through individual interviews, shows similar findings. Respondents show that they are less concerned about earning than somebody wanting them 'for what I can do' (Sharpe, 1984: 78; see also Sayers, 1988).

People who win the pools or the lottery continue to work even if they hold jobs that could be described as dull, routine, and repetitive (Brown, 1954). If individuals are asked if they would continue working if they had enough money to live comfortably for the rest of their life, a majority will say they would continue to work (Gallie and White, 1993; Morse and Weiss, 1955). Men in middle-class occupations will point to the loss of interest and accomplishment they found in their jobs; those in working-class jobs typically mention the lack of activity they would experience (Morse and Weiss, 1955). Where the status of work is low, money will be stressed as the principal reward (Friedmann and Havighurst, 1954). At higher occupational levels intrinsic job components like opportunity for self-expression, interest-value of work, were more valued. At lower occupational levels, extrinsic job components like pay and security were more valued (Centers and Bugental, 1966). One explanation is in terms of Maslow's (1943) need hierarchy, where there are five sets of needs which people possess and as you satisfy most of the needs at one level you move up to seek satisfaction at the next. Physiological needs for food, drink, and sex are followed by safety needs, love needs, esteem needs, then finally the need for self-actualization, the desire to realize your ultimate potential. Individuals in lower level occupations are more likely to be motivated by lower order needs, physiological and safety needs, because these are not sufficiently gratified to allow needs at a higher order (self-esteem and self-actualization) to become prepotent. A more radical explanation might say that those in higher level jobs, with intrinsic job components, design jobs for those in lower levels and have no interest in designing them with the same intrinsic components.

Research from the USA shows that jobs in the new economy are very mixed in what they offer in terms of meaning. Reich (1991) calculated that just 20 per cent of the jobs in the new economy were intrinsically satisfying and economically rewarding. These jobs belong to the journalists, designers, architects, and lecturers whose work has creativity at its core as they communicate complex ideas. These are the 'fortunate fifth'. These jobs can be contrasted with the 25 per cent who regularly perform routine tasks and the 30 per cent who deliver a variety of mundane services. The recent growth in call centre jobs in Britain leaves you wondering how intrinsically satisfying they are.

Vecchio (1980) revisited Morse and Weiss's findings. While he also found that the majority of workers would desire to continue working, he also discovered a 39 per cent increase in the number of male workers who would stop working if given the opportunity. One explanation for this is that there has been a real decline in the perceived value and meaning of work. Alternatively it may be that a leisure ethic is replacing the traditional work ethic.

Classic studies of male workers demonstrate that the meaning of work is not confined to the workplace. Dennis *et al.* (1969) showed how the dangerous difficult conditions in mining created a male culture of mutual dependence which continued outside in leisure and other activities. The men defined themselves almost exclusively in terms of their work.

Dubin (1956) concerned himself with looking at the 'central life interests' of workers. Work was seen as a central life interest of adults in most societies and the capitalist system was seen to rest upon the moral and religious justification that the Reformation gave to work, as Weber (1930) pointed out. Dubin, however, found that for almost three out of four industrial workers, work and the workplace were not central life interests. People's life histories had their centres outside work; this was where they looked for human relationships, feelings of enjoyment, happiness, and worth. Yet, as Dubin notes, much management activity is directed at restoring work to the status of central life interest through human relations; management's efforts seem then to be at odds with reality.

STOP	Would money be cited as a principal reward for nurses (for example see Orzack, 1959)?

In spite of Dubin's findings, managements and researchers have sought to discover more about what work means to people and what can be done to increase productivity. Researchers moved on to dedicate themselves to trying to understand what motivated employees (for example, Herzberg, 1966, 1968). To do this, Herzberg in the USA looked at events in the lives of engineers and accountants, and their job attitudes. Both employee productivity and alienation were seen as a problem (Hackman and Oldham, 1975). It was thought that redesigning jobs to reduce problems of alienation and boredom would increase productivity. Job enrichment and job redesign were seen then as solutions. In order to measure and understand what happened to jobs when they were changed, in America Turner and Lawrence (1965) measured employee perceptions of task attributes. Based on that work, Hackman and Oldham (1975) developed the Job Diagnostic Survey (JDS). The theory underlying the tool was that experienced meaningfulness of work is enhanced by skill variety (using different skills and talents), task identity (doing a job from beginning to end with a visible outcome), and task significance (the degree to which the job has a substantial impact on the work or lives of other people). Hackman *et al.* (1975: 61) claimed that the JDS gauged the 'objective characteristics of the jobs themselves'. Similarly Sims *et al.* (1976) developed the Job Characteristics Inventory (JCI) while in Britain a Job Components Inventory was developed (Banks *et al.*, 1983) . The JDS and JCI would diagnose existing jobs as an input to planned job redesign.

Job redesign meant any attempt to alter jobs with the intent of increasing the quality of work experience and productivity such as job rotation, job enrichment, and socio-technical systems design. Typically changes involved providing employees with additional responsibilities for planning, setting up, checking their own work, and for making decisions about methods and procedures, for establishing their own work pace (within limits), and sometimes for relating directly with the client who sees the results of their work (Hackman, 1977). For example a basic job involved the assembly of a small pump used in a washing machine. The assembly line worker assembled a particular part of the job with five others on an assembly line. The job was redesigned so that each worker assembled a whole pump, inspected it, and placed his own identifying mark on it; workers were given more freedom to control their pace of work. As a result total assembly time decreased, quality improved and cost savings were realized (Hackman, 1977: 99). As job design became a quaint relic of the 1970s new initiatives emerged under new brand names like 'high performance work design' (Buchanan, 1987).

There were some serious problems with the measures of job characteristics (Aldag *et al.*, 1981; Salancik and Pfeffer, 1977; Stone and Gueutal, 1985). The job characteristics that were measured had been derived from a search of the literature, reflective thinking, and by trial and error. The dimensions then may or may not have coincided with the dimensions along which individuals generally perceive jobs to vary; they may just represent the idiosyncratic way in which Turner and Lawrence viewed jobs.

The questions for me now are 'Could job redesign have been "sold" to employers if it did not bring with it the promise of increased efficiency and productivity?' and 'Were employers really interested in what jobs meant to individuals with a view to increasing what they might mean and offer in terms of intrinsic rewards? Did employers have altruistic motives and were they interested in their employee's quality of work life?' Many are now disillusioned with the ideals of job design. For many teachers of organizational behaviour, job redesign is seen as a dated 1970s fad. Examples are to be found in the literature of new work designs which failed due to, for example, cost (Klein, 1982, cited in Clegg, 1984), because the role of supervisors was threatened (Cummings, 1978; Lawler *et al.*, 1973) or because changes were resented and opposed by other groups (Clegg, 1982). Complex job design may be exceptionally difficult to implement for a mixture of historical, economic, and psychological reasons (Clegg, 1984) so it is little wonder that few major initiatives of this kind have been attempted and survived.

The Issue of Anonymity

Hackman and Oldham (1975) recommend that employees take the Job Diagnostic Survey under conditions of anonymity. I discovered, from personal experience of consultancy work, how necessary this was when the managing director of the company where I had used a similar diagnostic instrument, to look at motivation and morale, asked me to identify the most disaffected employees so he could sack them. I did not comply with his request.

While some social scientists had much to say about how jobs should be redesigned and an international Quality of Working Life movement began in 1972 with a conference (Davis and Cherns, 1975), other social scientists, particularly sociologists and political scientists, were more critical of the job redesign movement (Blacker and Brown, 1978) and what it sought to achieve. One of these criticisms was that attempts to improve quality of working life amounted to little more than 'human relations' management (showing concern for employee's social needs, their personal problems, making them feel important) and a cosmetic activity to help managers increase collective endeavour (Blacker and Brown, 1980). John Child (1973: 243) noted that they may have the effect of increasing the employee's acceptance of a situation, while Alan Fox (1973: 219) spoke of how they did not address the principle of hierarchical rewards or the possibility of increases in intrinsic reward at the cost of efficiency. Job design could be described as a management control device. Instead of bringing fundamental change, job redesign only addressed marginal issues while the legitimacy of prevailing power structures and current business frameworks remained. Impartial science was claimed but poor research designs were used. The criteria used in evaluation studies were usually managerially rather than psychologically oriented as their emphasis was on organizational efficiency rather than individual's psychological growth (Blacker and Brown, 1978). While management had a definite interest is in seeing workers as thinking social beings with the potential to work together more productively, they also had an interest in limiting these potentials. Fineman (1996) says that the people presented are 'emotionally anorexic'. They may have dissatisfaction and satisfaction, be alienated or stressed, will have preferences, attitudes, and interests but these are noted are variables for managerial control. Managers had no wish to forfeit control and there were limits to what they could 'sensibly,' in their view, do (Nichols, 1976: 22; see also Thompson and McHugh, 1995: 251–8). This issue of managerial control is explored in Chapter 7 but we will turn our attention, in the next two chapters, to how managers have used 'rationality' to think about how work and jobs should be organized.

Questions for Further Research

1. 'In essence, work is a socially constructed phenomenon without fixed or universal meaning across space and time, but its meanings are delimited by the cultural forms in which it is practised' (Grint, 1991: 46). Discuss.

2. By looking at unemployment, we can understand more about what employment might mean to people. What can be learnt about what work means by looking at research on unemployment?

3. Some researchers , like Hakim (1991) and Coward (1992) have argued that women are less committed to their careers than men. Others (like Bradley, 1997; Spencer and Taylor, 1994; Demos in Walter, 1996) have shown strong attachment to the labour force among women. Read their findings and draw your own conclusion.

Suggestions for Further Reading

Noon, M., and Blyton, P. (1997) 'The Meaning of Work', *The Realities of Work*. Basingstoke: Macmillan, ch. 3.

Watson, T. (1997) 'Work: Meaning, Opportunity and Experience', *Sociology, Work and Industry*, 3rd edn. London: Routledge, ch. 4.

References

Aldag, R. J., Barr, S. H., and Brief, A.P. (1981) 'Measurement of Perceived Task Characteristics', *Psychological Bulletin*, 90/3: 415–31.

Banks, M. H., Jackson, P. R., Stafford, E. M., and Warr, P.B. (1983) 'The Job Components Inventory and the Analysis of Jobs Requiring Limited Skill', *Personnel Psychology*, 36/1: 57–66.

Blackburn, R., Dale, A., and Jarman, J. (1997) 'Ethnic Differences in Attainment in Education, Occupation and Lifestyle, in V. Karn (ed.), *Employment, Education and Housing among Ethnic Minorities in Britain*. London: HMSO.

Blacker, F. H., and Brown, C. A. (1978) *Job Redesign and Management Control*. London: Saxon House.

—— and —— (1980) 'Job Redesign and Social Change: Case Studies at Volvo', in K. D. Duncan, M. M. Gruneberg, and D. Wallis (eds.), *Changes in Working Life*. Chichester: Wiley, ch. 18.

Bradley, H. (1997) 'Gender and Change in Employment', in R. Brown (ed.), *The Changing Shape of Work*. Basingstoke: Macmillan, ch. 5.

Brown, J. C. (1954) *The Social Psychology of Industry*. Baltimore, Md.: Penguin.

Buchanan, D. (1987) 'Job Enrichment is Dead: Long Live High-Performance Work Design', *Personnel Management* (May): 40–3.

Centers, R., and Bugental, D. E. (1966) 'Intrinsic and Extrinsic Job Motivations among Different Segments of the Working Population', *Journal of Applied Psychology*, 50/3: 193–7.

Child, J. (1973) (ed.) 'Organisation: A Choice for Man', in *Man and the Organization*. London: Allen and Unwin.

Clegg, C. W. (1982) 'Modelling the Practice of Job Design', in J. E. Kelly and C. W. Clegg (eds.), *Autonomy and Control at the Workplace: Contexts for Job Redesign*. London: Croom Helm.

—— (1984) 'The Derivations of Job Designs', *Journal of Occupational Behaviour*, 5: 131–46.

Coward, R. (1992) *Our Treacherous Hearts*. London: Fontana.

Cummings, T. G. (1978) 'Self-Regulating Work Groups: A Socio-Technical Synthesis', *Academy of Management Review*, 3: 625–34.

Davis, L. E., and Cherns, A. B. (1975) *The Quality of Working Life*, i and ii. New York: Free Press.

Dennis, N., Henriques, F., and Slaughter, C. (1969) *Coal is Our Life*. London: Tavistock.

Dubin, R. (1956) 'Industrial Workers' Worlds: A Study of the "Central Life Interests" of Industrial Workers', *Social Problems*, 5: 138–42.

Fineman, S. (1996) 'Emotion and Organizing', in S. R. Clegg, C. Hardy and W. R. Nord (eds.), *Handbook of Organization Studies*. London: Sage, ch. 3.3.

Fox, A. (1973) 'Industrial Relations: A Social critique of Pluralist Ideology', in J. Child (ed.), *Man and Organisation*. London: Allen and Unwin.

Friedmann, E. L. and Havighurst, R. J. (1954) *The Meaning of Work and Retirement*. Chicago: University of Chicago Press.

Gallie, D., and White, M. (1993) *Employee Commitment and the Skills Revolution*. London: Policy Studies Institute.

Grint, K. (1991) *The Sociology of Work: An Introduction*. Cambridge: Polity.

Hackman, J. R. (1977). 'Work Design', in J. R. Hackman and J. L. Suttle, (eds.), *Improving Life at Work*. Santa Monica, Calif.: Goodyear, ch. 3.

Hackman, J. R. and Oldham, G. R. (1975) 'Development of the Job Diagnostic Survey', *Journal of Applied Psychology*, 60/2: 159–70.

——, —— Janson, R., and Purdy, K. (1975) 'A New Strategy for Job Enrichment', *California Management Review*, 17: 57–71.

Hakim, C. (1991) 'Grateful Slaves and Self-Made Women: Fact and Fantasy in Women's Work Orientations', *European Sociological Review*, 7/2: 101–21.

Herzberg, F. (1966) *Work and the Nature of Man*. New York: Staples Press.

—— (1968) 'One More Time: How Do you Motivate Employees?', *Harvard Business Review* (Jan.–Feb.), 46/1: 53–62.

Klein, L. (1982) 'Design Strategies in Theory and Practice', Paper presented at the 20th International Congress of Applied Psychology, University of Edinburgh.

Lawler, E. E., Hackman, J. R., and Kaufman, S (1973) 'Effects of Job Redesign: A Field Experiment', *Journal of Applied Social Psychology*, 3: 49–62.

Maslow, A. H. (1943) 'A Theory of Human Motivation', *Psychological Review*, 50: 370–96.

Morse, N. C. and Weiss, R. S. (1955) 'The Function and Meaning of Work and the Job', *American Sociological Review*, 20.

Nichols, T. (1976) 'Management, Ideology and Practice', in *People at Work*, Block 5, Unit 15. Milton Keynes: The Open University Press.

Orzak, L. (1959) 'Work as a Central Life Interest of Professionals', *Social Problems*, 7: 125–32.

Phizacklea, A., and Wolkowitz, C. (1993) *Homeworking Women: Gender, Racism and Class at Work*. London: Sage.

Reich, R. (1991) *The Work of Nations*. New York: Knopf.

Rose, M. (1994) 'Skill and Samuel Smiles: Changing the British Work Ethic', in R. Penn, M. Rose, and J. Rubery (eds.), *Skill and Occupational Change*. Oxford: Oxford University Press.

Salancik, G.R. and Pfeffer, J. (1977) 'An Examination of the Need-Satisfaction Models of Job Attributes', *Administrative Science Quarterly*, 22: 427–57.

Sayers, S. (1988) 'The Need to Work: A Perspective from Philosophy', in R. E. Pahl (ed.), *On Work: Historical, Comparative and Theoretical Approaches*. Oxford: Basil Blackwell.

Sharpe, S. (1984) *Double Identity: The Lives of Working Mothers*. Harmondsworth: Penguin.

Sims, H. P., Szilagyi, A. D., and Keller, R. T. (1976) 'The Measurement of Job Characteristics', *Academy of Management Journal* (June), 195–212.

Spencer, L., and Taylor, S. (1994) *Participation and Progress in the Labour Market: Key Issues for Women*, Dep. of Employment Research Series, no. 35. Sheffield: Dept. of Employment.

Stone, E. F., and Gueutal, H. G. (1985) 'An Empirical Derivation of the Dimensions along which Characteristics of Jobs are Perceived', *Academy of Management Journal*, 28/2: 376–96.

Thompson, P., and McHugh, D. (1995) *Work Organisations: A Critical Introduction*, 2nd edn. Basingstoke: Macmillan.

Turner, A. N., and Lawrence, P. R. (1965) *Industrial Jobs and the Worker*. Cambridge, Mass.: Harvard University Press.

Vecchio, R. P. (1980) 'The Function and Meaning of Work and the Job: Morse and Weiss (1955) Revisited', *Academy of Management Journal*, 23/2: 361–7.

Walter, N. (1996) 'Bringing out the Women in New Labour', *Guardian* (29 Feb.).

Weber, M. (1930) *The Protestant Ethic and the Spirit of Capitalism*. London: Allen and Unwin.

Westwood, S. (1988) 'Workers and Wives: Continuities and Discontinuities in the Lives of Gujarati Women', in S. Westwood and P. Bhachu, P. (eds.), *Enterprising Women: Ethnicity, Economy and Gender Relations*. London: Routledge: 103–31.

2

Rationalization and Rationality 1:
From the Founding Fathers to
Eugenics

EARLY MANAGEMENT THEORISTS (Babbage, 1989; F. W. Taylor, 1911; Ure, 1835) sought to apply 'rational' scientific practices to organization with the view of improving its performance. They mainly thought of organizations as machines while people were seen as too variable and unreliable. According to Ure (1835), for example, 'science now promises to rescue . . . business from handicraft caprice, and to place it . . . under the safeguard of automatic mechanism'. For Ure there were 'right mechanisms' for managing; one 'mechanism' would be for the manager to remove jobs which require dexterity from the workman, who cannot be relied upon, and place these jobs in the safe hands of mechanization so simple a child could supervise. Similar views can be found in both Babbage's and Taylor's writings. Frederick Winslow Taylor (1856–1915) believed that the best management was true science 'resting upon clearly defined laws, rules and principles' (1911: 7). The problems of production lay in the hands of management because they lacked knowledge on how to maximize production, the workers had a rationale for restricting output (the fear of underpayment or redundancy) and payment systems lacked sufficient incentive. All these problems could be solved by applying the principles of scientific management. For Taylor it was the manager's job to gather together all the traditional knowledge, which in the past was possessed by the workmen, and then classify, tabulate, and reduce this knowledge to rules, laws, and formulae which became a science.

'Experiments in Scientific Management'

The Spanish–American War in 1898 gave Taylor the opportunity to try his first experiment in scientific management at the Bethlehem Steel Company. With the war came an increase in the price of pig iron. The pig iron was in a field adjoining the works and needed to be moved inside to the furnaces. A railway was laid out to the field, an inclined plank placed against the side of the railroad 'car'. Each man was required to pick up a 'pig of iron' weighing about 92 lbs, walk up the inclined plank, and drop it in the car. About 12½ tons per man per day could be loaded by an average man, but it was found that the first-class men could handle between 47 and 48 tons. Four of the best pig iron handlers were picked from seventy-five. Then one was chosen to start the experiment, a man Taylor called 'Schmidt' and described as 'of the mentally sluggish type'. (Schmidt was in fact called Henry Knolle (Johnson and Gill, 1993) and had recently built his own house.) This man was offered $1.85 per hour instead of $1.25 if he followed another man's instructions on when to pick up the iron, when to walk, and when to rest; he managed to load forty-seven and a half tons of iron a day. He never failed to work at this pace and do the task set him during the three years Taylor was at Bethlehem. This 'science' being developed amounted 'to so much that the man who is suited to pig iron cannot possibly understand it, nor even work in accordance with the laws of this science, without the help of the those who are over him' (1911: 48). A fit pig iron handler should be 'so stupid and so phlegmatic that he more nearly resembles in his mental make-up the ox than any other type . . . He is so stupid the that the word "percentage" has no meaning to him . . . ' (1911: 59). In this way the man was selected, trained, and supervised. Seven out of eight pig iron handlers were thrown out of their jobs, but we are assured that they were given other jobs with the Bethlehem Steel Company.

Similar treatment is to be found in the second experiment to develop a science of shovelling. A first-class shoveller was found to do his biggest day's work with a shovel load of about 21 lbs. Eight or ten different kinds of shovels were provided at the Bethlehem Steel Company, one for each type of material depending on the weight of that material, for example a small one for ore (a heavy material) and a large one for ashes (a light material). Providing the different shovels prevented the shoveller, who previously owned their own shovel, from going from shovelling ore with a load of about 30 lbs per shovel to handling rice coal with a load, on the same shovel, of less than 4 lbs. Every day the shoveller would be given and would implement instructions for doing each new job; he would also be given feedback on his performance the previous day. Clerks planned the work the shovellers did. This time the work of 400 and 600 yard labourers was reduced to the work of 140.

Four duties emerge for the managers in developing the science. First they develop a science for each element of work which replaces the old rule-of-thumb. Secondly they scientifically select, then train the worker. Thirdly they cooperate to ensure that all the work is being done in accordance with the principles laid down, and fourthly they have an almost equal division of work and responsibility between manager and worker. The management take over all the work for which they are better fitted than the worker. They plan out the work at least one day in advance and each worker should receive a set of written instructions describing in detail the task they have to accomplish, the time it should take, as well as the means by which it should be done. When the worker has done the work right, within the specified time limit, they should receive an addition to their ordinary wages of between 30 and 100 per cent. A worker should never be asked, if the job has been scientifically studied, to work at a pace which could injure their health. With the scheme in place it was found that the workers and manager could profit considerably. The system was not designed to provide satisfying work but to maximize rewards and increase the division of labour.

Similarly Frank Gilbreth studied bricklaying, analysing the movement, speed, and tiring rate of the bricklayer (see F. W. Taylor, 1911). He developed the exact positions which the feet of the bricklayer should occupy in relation to the wall, the mortar box and pile of bricks. He studied the best height for the mortar box and brick pile then designed an adjustable scaffold to hold the materials. He asked that the bricks be sorted and packed in an orderly pile before being brought to the bricklayers, so that they were placed with their best edge up on a simple wooden frame; each brick could be lifted in the quickest time in the most advantageous position. He was thus able to reduce the motions of bricklayers from eighteen per brick to five. He also taught the bricklayers to pick up bricks with the left hand while at the same time taking a trowel full of mortar with the right hand. In this way 350 bricks per person per hour could be laid rather than the previous 120 bricks per hour. For this the standards and cooperation have to be *enforced;* the duty of enforcement lies with management. If the workforce agree to this enforcement, they receive higher pay.

While Taylor's 'men' were being scientifically selected and trained, 'girls' were working ten and a half hour days inspecting ball bearings for bicycles in another plant. Gradually their hours were shortened to ten, nine and a half, nine, then eight and a half hour days for the same pay. With each shortening of the day came an increase in output. The best workers were selected; some of the most intelligent, hardest working, and trustworthy girls were laid off because they did not perceive the fault and discard defective ball bearings fast, or accurately, enough. The honesty and accuracy of those remaining inspectors was checked. One anonymous lot from each of the inspectors was checked by senior inspectors. The chief inspector, in turn, checked the work of the senior inspectors. The inspectors were also kept in check by another method. Every two or three days a lot of balls was prepared by a foreman so it contained a definite number of perfect and defective balls; this was given to an inspector for checking and the inspector's accuracy was recorded. An accurate and daily record was kept of the quantity and quality of all the work. Temptation to slight the work or make false returns was, Taylor claimed, removed. The inspectors' ambition was 'stirred' by increasing the wages of those who turned out a large quantity of good quality while those who did indifferent work found their wages were lowered. Those who were slow or careless were discharged. The inspectors were seated so far apart that they could not conveniently talk whilst at work, but were given ten-minute breaks each hour and a half so they could leave their seats, walk around, and talk. This was found to be the best way to gain steady work without overexertion. Taylor believed, like the behaviourists, that feedback on performance was needed at regular intervals, like every hour. Profit sharing would only be mildly effective (1911: 94). As a result of these changes, 35 'girls' did the work formerly done by 120. The accuracy of the work at higher speed was two-thirds greater than at the former slow speed. In return the women's average wage was 80 to 100 per cent higher with an eight and a half hour day and a half-day holiday on a Saturday.

A psychologist might explain the roots of Taylor's thinking in terms of his upbringing. His youth was preoccupied with order, control, and parsimony, clearly rooted in the puritanical strictures of his family. Fastidious analysis was made of his sporting activities, country walks, sleeping position, and even his dancing (Fineman, 1996). It also has to be noted though that Taylor emerged in a particular climate and time of thinking about how to apply rational scientific practices to organization to increase performance.

From a job design perspective, Taylor's scheme rests upon the principle of the division of mental and manual labour. It also involved: (*a*) a general principle of the maximum decomposition of tasks; (*b*) the divorce of direct and indirect (setting up, preparation, maintenance) labour; (*c*) the minimization of skill requirements leading to minimum job learning time (Littler, 1985). These were the principles of job design accepted in the USA and, more slowly, in Britain. But not all economies accepted Taylor's ideas. A different pattern is to be found in Japan where factories depended on a tradition of work teams incorporating managerial and maintenance functions and few staff specialists, which allowed for considerable job flexibility, but according to Dore (1973) Taylor's time and motion studies were introduced there for a period around the First World War.

Taylor's work was carried out in union-free or weakly unionized plants, while the American Federation of Labour (AFL) initiated an anti-scientific management campaign (Grint, 1991). Within weeks of its first major implementation, a strike broke out in Watertown Arsenal. A full investigation by the House of Representatives found widespread malpractices and so Taylorist methods were banned from all arsenals, navy yards, and for 1916–1949, from all government-funded operations (Noble, 1974). The Society of Mechanical Engineers (despite Taylor being president) refused to publish the *Principles of Scientific Management* on the grounds that it was not scientific. Taylor was himself appalled at the strong hostility he witnessed amongst rank-and-file workers in response to his design of industrial organization (Stearns, 1989). Workers' feelings of anger, disaffection, humiliation, can breach organizational controls (Fineman, 1996).

Despite the problems inherent in Taylor's work design, Henry Ford adopted the principles of Taylorism for his car plants, having seen the system of mass disassembly in the Chicago meat packing plants before the First World War (Ackroyd and Crowdy, 1990; Burrell, 1997: 138). Ford had the wit to appreciate that the process of disassembly of animal carcasses in principle could be applied in reverse to the construction of complex products like cars. Here is an illustration of how the principles of mass assembly production were begun. He began with the little pieces and found that one man took twenty minutes to produce an electrical alternator. When the process was spread over twenty-nine operations, assembly time was decreased to thirteen minutes. Raising the height of the assembly line by 8 inches reduced this to seven minutes, while further rationalization cut it to five minutes (Sims *et al.*, 1993). The closely monitored, machine-paced, short-cycle, and unremitting tasks were combined with an authoritarian work regime.

In the early 1920s Ford's share of the car market was two-thirds. Fifteen years later, it had fallen to 20 per cent. According to Drucker (1989) Henry Ford tried to run his billion dollar business without managers. Henry Ford ran a one-man tyranny where he employed secret police who spied on Ford executives and informed him of any attempt on the part of executives to make decisions. When they seemed to acquire managerial authority or responsibility they were generally fired. Henry Ford demoted first-line supervisors regularly every few years so they would not become 'uppity' and forget they owed their job to him. Drucker believes that it was this absence of management that caused the fall of the Ford Motor Company. After the Second World War, Henry Ford's grandson (Henry Ford II) took over the company; he rebuilt management, though he had no business experience at all. He took most of his concepts of management and organization, along with his top managers, from his big competitor, General Motors.

Why would you pay a highly skilled worker to do a job from start to finish when you could split the job into component parts, assign each task to minimally qualified workers, and so reduce costs and increase output? Designing jobs so that each worker repeatedly performs a limited number of tasks in accordance to instructions provided by management increases efficiency, results in uniform products and gives management increased control. Management have no need to rely on the cooperation of workers to tell them how long a task takes, how many people are required to do a job, how much work can be completed in one shift. With less skilled jobs comes management's power to dictate wages, hours, and working conditions and greater interchangability of workers. The logic of routinization of work is simple, elegant, and compelling (Leidner, 1993). Routinization and detailed division of labour does, however, increase the possibility of a few people potentially disrupting a whole production process.

This routinization of work, deskilling of work, began in manufacturing industry. As clerical work grew, the principles were applied there so the thinking work was removed, leaving jobs lacking in variety and opportunities for decision-making (Braverman, 1974). For Braverman there were three principles of Taylorism:

1. the dissociation of the labour process from the skills of the workers
2. the separation of conception (the thinking about how work is done) from the execution (doing) of the work
3. the managerial use of the monopoly of this knowledge to control each step of the labour process and its mode of execution.

Following Marx, Braverman says that work under capitalism is geared to the creation of profit rather than the satisfaction of human needs, thus there is a conflict of interests between labour and capital. In these antagonistic conditions it is necessary for managers to secure maximum possible control over the labour process. (The labour process, as defined by Marx, has three elements—purposeful human activity directed to work, the materials on which work is performed, and the instruments of work). Braverman argues that the consequence of the extension of scientific management is degradation of the labour process, with jobs becoming increasingly specialized and routine. (For a critique of Braverman see Edwards, 1978; Grint, 1991: 190–5.)

The effect on workers is well documented; routinized jobs lack variety, job satisfaction, and meaning. A process of deskilling is complemented by the application of technology to the labour process. Watanabe (1990), for example, describes how labour was deskilled and degraded in the Japanese banking sector. Labour control was intensified and labour conditions deteriorated. The computer systems had bookkeeping skills, for example, so the work of a large mass of employees became routine and monotonous, punching computer terminal keys and so on. The work of middle management was also simplified as functions requiring judgement and discretion became almost unnecessary. Branch managers were placed under the unified and centralized control of head office by the use of computers so their authority was reduced and accountability increased. A polarization of labour occurred, a separation of mental and physical labour. Mental labour was concentrated in fewer employees such as top managers and systems analysts.

Managements did not always get their own way, however, as studies by Noble (1979), Buchanan (1985), Zeitlin (1983), and F. M. Wilson (1987) illustrated in the engineering industry. Taylorism could never be a universal set of specific practices. There was a defence from the 'doers' of work from the developing trade-union movement, as well as scepticism from some of the employers worried about labour unrest. Taylorism was never a universal practice and is inappropriate in some industries, like machine tools manufacture (Broadbent *et al.*, 1997: 4). But it did inform a management philosophy that managers had a right to manage and allowed a 'scientific' rationale for professional status and autonomy of mangers.

As we saw in the first chapter, numerous scholars documented the unintended and unfortunate consequences of the trend towards work simplification (e.g. Argyris, 1964; Blauner, 1964; Herzberg *et al.*, 1959; Walker and Guest, 1952). Routine non-challenging jobs often led to high employee dissatisfaction, increased absenteeism and turnover, and substantial difficulties in effectively managing employees who worked on simplified jobs (Hackman and Lawler, 1971). Researchers experimented with job enlargement and redesign to make jobs more meaningful and challenging. However, support for job redesign was hard to substantiate empirically. A major evaluative study of job redesign studies suggested missionary zeal, the publication of positive results only, and the employment of poor research designs (Blacker and Brown, 1978).

An understanding of job design requires a recognition of the strategic choices open to managers (Child, 1972; Monanari, 1979). Management, for example, have choices about the techno-structural arrangements, on the sort of technology in which to invest, and on the type of structures used to manage the organization. Despite the wide variety of choices available, job designers use a common set of criteria (Davis *et al.*, 1955; J. C. Taylor, 1979). They typically opt for a technology which minimizes the time required to perform the job, the skill level needed, the necessary training time, and the individual's contribution to the whole process. The choices usually made, then, seek to minimize immediate costs through specialization and routine. Management also have choices over the pattern of local control. When information processing requirements are low, then job holders are usually subjected to a relatively direct form of control (Clegg, 1984; Friedman, 1977). Economic and psychological values underpin the choices. The economic ones are Taylorist and include ease of training and replacing staff and the reduction of direct labour costs resulting from deskilling. The psychological value rests in the belief that individuals need close external control; the worker is seen as naturally lazy and unreliable (McGregor, 1960). These economic and psychological views may be widely held by both key decision-makers and job incumbents and represent a strong pressure for and expectation of the design of relatively simple, closely supervised jobs. Employing substitutable people in technologically simple jobs which are highly constrained and directly supervised goes a considerable way towards meeting the needs of managers to make their operations predictable and to maintain direct control over events.

Despite the limitations of Tayloristic job design and its negative effects, there are many benefits to be gained by the employer. Taylor's scientific management is very much in practice in many organizations. United Parcel Service employ industrial engineering managers who, for example, stipulate how fast their drivers walk; they are expected to walk at a pace of 3 ft per second. Until recently drivers were instructed in how to move in an effort to maximize efficiency. Packages were to be carried under the left arm and the driver stepped into the van with the right foot while holding the van's keys on the middle finger of the right hand. The rules about personal appearance include beards being forbidden, moustaches must not extend beyond the corner of the mouth, and the hair must not grow so long that it covers the top of the collar or the ear lobes. While this does not increase efficiency it does ensure, in the company's view, that employees look neat and clean (*Financial Times*, 16–17 August 1997, p. 7).

Neat and clean jobs may be found in the parcel delivery service but Taylor's principles are also found applied in less clean jobs, such as those to be found in a chicken factory. Here too work can be segmented into simple repetitive operations. Packing the chicken, for example, involves four people doing one of four tasks: inserting the giblets and tucking the legs in, bagging the chicken, weighing it, and securing the top of the bag. An employee in a chicken factory was found to be checking over 2,000 chickens an hour, 14,000 chickens a day. This involved checking that no chickens had been left with livers, hearts, or similar organs and, in the words of the employee, 'putting your hand in the backside of a chicken, feeling around then bringing anything out, dropping it in the bin, and then going on to the next' (see Noon and Blyton, 1997: 103). The employees found the work hard.

While scientific management has long been associated with behavioural problems at work, it has more recently become associated with inefficiencies arising from inflexibility. If you are producing a continuous, standardised product with homogeneous throughput for a mass market maybe it looks, for those who design work organization, like an extremely efficient way of organizing. Where there is no such mass market and a heterogeneous rapidly changing and unpredictable throughput (due to customer demand or product innovation) then what may be required is a more flexible committed, itinerant and skilled workforce capable of exercising discretion to cope with uncertainties and fluctuations in demand and technology. The mechanistic conception of people needs to be replaced with an alternative approach to human beings.

The Human Relations Movement

The roots of human relations are to be found in the nineteenth century in, for example, Emile Durkheim's (1858–1917) analysis of *anomie* (a pathology, a form of social breakdown; see Durkheim, 1984) and his concern about social solidarity and integration. The human relations movement began to emerge during the First World War and was concerned with the selection, testing, and classification of army recruits which required psychological testing. These developments ought to increase employees' productivity and personal satisfaction by easing difficulties rather than using sanctions (Lupton, 1971). The starting-point was a series of experiments at the Western Electric Company's Hawthorne plant in Chicago in 1924. First the relationship was investigated between lighting, temperature, humidity, frequency of rest breaks, and employees' productivity (Roethlisberger and Dickson, 1939). Two groups of employees were selected and isolated in another part of the plant. One group experienced changes in their working conditions while the other did not. The productivity of each group was monitored and it was found that output of the experimental group increased regardless of how illumination was manipulated. Even when lighting was reduced to the equivalent of a candle, output continued to increase. Output of the control group also steadily increased.

The second set of experiments was in the relay assembly rest room and looked in more detail at the effect of working conditions. Again, no matter what the researchers did, even lengthening the working day and reducing rest periods, productivity increased. The researchers explained this by saying that the employees had been made to feel special; they had been the centre of attention. This had increased their morale which led to the increase in productivity.

Later research in the early 1930s involved the detailed observation of a group of fourteen men in a seven-month period who worked in the bank wiring room. This time the men stayed in their normal work setting and a financial incentive scheme was introduced to reward group output. The men appeared to control their output, limiting it to what they thought was a 'fair day's work' for the pay they received. The group determined the maximum and minimum output norm. Any deviants were punished verbally and threatened with physical violence.

The studies are now famous for identifying the importance of social needs in the workplace and the way work groups can satisfy these needs by restricting output and engaging in all kinds of unplanned activities. In identifying the informal organization based on friendship and groups and unplanned interactions existing alongside the formal organization designed by management, the research dealt an important blow to classical management theory. The informal organization included the emotional, non-rational, and sentimental aspects of human behaviour in organizations, the ties and loyalties that affected workers, the social relations that could not be encompassed by the organization chart but shaped behaviour regardless. Other theorists who influenced the development of this perspective included Mary Parker Follett (Kanter, 1977).

The answer to problems of output restriction and resistance, according to Mayo (1949) writing on the Hawthorne research, was to develop managerial social skills so that the workers felt more disposed to work better with management. Morale and motivation could be improved if managers were better able to elicit cooperation through being more sensitive to

workers' social needs. Management was encouraged to intervene in the informal organization and build a new moral order which would 'create and sustain consent' (Thompson and
McHugh, 1990: 81).

The Hawthorne experiments have come under close scrutiny by researchers and been
found to be inadequate. Carey (1967) made it clear that these studies are replete with erro-
neous interpretations and do not demonstrate much of what everyone thought they did. For
example the conclusion that relaxed and friendly supervision causes higher productivity is
refuted by Carey who argues the opposite—because of higher productivity the managers became more relaxed. Further, the increase in productivity was caused by a simple change of
people in the work group. Two recalcitrant male workers were dismissed halfway through
the study and were replaced with two women who needed jobs to help with their financial
problems. It was their efforts and prodding that led to the increase in group output, and it
was only after this output increase that management relaxed their coercive style of supervision (Weick, 1969). Similarly R. Brown (1976) and more recently Acker and Van Houton
(1992) have noted how the Hawthorne studies produced questionable or incomplete interpretations of their results since they failed to consider adequately the gender dimensions of
organizational processes.

It is also interesting to note, as Kanter (1977) has done, that while the first thrust in management theory—planning and decision making—put the 'rational man' into management, the second thrust concerning motivation and morale (acknowledging the human
order behind the machine) did not significantly change this aspect of the management
image. The traits of the masculine ethic seen as necessary for effective management did not
change. Human relations theories may have made inroads adding a 'feminized' element to
the old masculine ethic, influencing new forms of organization using teams and project
management systems, yet the masculine ethic of rationality has dominated the spirit of
managerialism and gave the manager role its defining image. It told men how to be successful as men in the new organizational world. Such an image also provided a rationale for
where women belong in management. If they belonged it was in people-handling staff functions like personnel, at the 'emotional' end of management, excluded from the centres of
power (Kanter, 1977).

Rationality? Fitting Workers to Jobs?

Frederick Taylor argued that jobs and individuals should be matched. As employees are not
universally similar, in the interests of efficiency, jobs and workers should be matched in
terms of necessary skills and intelligence required. It has always been in employer's interests to fit workers to jobs but the First World War brought the issue into sharp relief. The
provision of munitions and people for the war forced the government of the time to intervene in the management of factories to accelerate efficiency. When the United States entered the war in 1917 the scale of activities changed and the army's Committee for
Psychology was established to place recruits, from the subnormal to officer material, using
psychological tests; they claim to have tested almost two million men. The Industrial Fatigue Board in Britain in 1918 was set up to investigate and promote mechanisms of efficiency; it looked at rest, working hours, ventilation, and lighting systems. Psychological

tests were also developed at this time so individuals could be tested and placed. C. S. Myers, founder and director of the National Institute of Industrial Psychology, began work in Britain in 1921. Industrial psychology has been dominated by the need to use psychometric testing to fit workers to jobs since this time. Wartime produced the technology for mass psychometric selection. While in the USA this generally tested ability, in Britain the tests were based on specific job needs to help select, for example, air pilots (see Hollway, 1991; Rose, 1988). 'Applied psychology thus achieved much favourable publicity, massive development funds and full respectability' (Rose, 1988: 92). After the war, selection tests were used more widely.

Social Darwinism, the application of Darwinist biology to society, provided the framework for a new psychology of individual differences. The relation of psychology of individual differences to psychometrics was 'symbiotic' (Hollway, 1991: 57); one fed off the other. Where psychometrics provided the method, the theory was individual differences. Darwinism had enabled theory in terms of populations rather than individuals. Social Darwinism at the turn of the century was concerned with improving the fitness of the race, genetic inheritance and national efficiency. Eugenics gave a new political salience to the question of individual differences.

Eugenics

Eugenics was the science of improving stock which takes cognizance of all influences that tend to give the more suitable races or strains of blood a better chance of prevailing speedily over the less suitable than they otherwise would have had (Hollway, 1991). Eugenics sees individual differences as largely determined by genetic inheritance. If an individual's performance is genetically determined, no attempt will be made to change it. You just need to group, place, and regulate individuals.

> **A Custom-Made Baby?**
>
> A French scientist claims to be able to guarantee the sex of your baby if you use his method. The method is called 'Rightbaby' and is sold for £199 (*The Scotsman*, 3 November 1997, p. 12). It offers what every consumer wants, choice. But can any engineered gender selection be natural or is this eugenics? Is it ethically acceptable? A value judgement is being made on the basis of gender. What do you think?

Eugenics has become a topical subject again since Scandinavian governments have been found to have executed a plan to purify the Nordic race through enforced sterilization. Those branded low class or mentally slow were sterilized. More than 60,000 women in Sweden were sterilized between 1935 and 1996 (*Guardian*, 30 August 1997, p. 14). The need for eugenics was also expressed in Britain by Bertrand Russell who suggested the state issue colour-coded procreation tickets. Those who reproduced without the ticket would be fined. H. G. Wells hailed eugenics as the first step towards the removal of detrimental types and the fostering of desirable ones.

Eugenics and the psychology of individual differences is derived from statistical theory of population distribution based on the normal curve. In Britain Cyril Burt was the most prominent representative of the psychology of individual differences, in particular the genetic determination of intelligence testing.

Intelligence Testing

Burt compared the IQ (Intelligence Quotient) scores of identical twins with less closely related siblings. He gathered a large set of data on identical twins who were raised separately. After Burt's death his work was closely scrutinised and carelessness and fraud was suggested. He had failed to indicate which tests of intelligence he was using and published his papers with co-authors who could not be located; the co-authors were unknown to the institutions listed as their place of employment and were unknown to members of the scientific community at that time. His findings showed identical correlation coefficients for twin samples; since IQ tests are not a precise tool it is unlikely that an identical IQ would be obtained even when testing the same person over time. These and other facts led to the uncomfortable conclusion that Burt had manufactured the data to support his belief that intelligence is largely inherited. Yet before being discredited, Burt influenced British social policies, for example, in schooling and the workplace.

While Burt was primarily an educational psychologist, he also worked with industrial psychologists to turn his attention to vocational guidance. In vocational guidance the measurement of general intelligence in children and the interests of employers come together to fit the person to the job. Burt claimed that the mental level of each child should be measured then the education most appropriate to that level should be given so that they are guided into a career 'for which his measure of intelligence has marked him out' (Burt, 1924: 71).

Burt testified to British government committees that children's intelligence levels were largely fixed by the age of 11 or so and were accurately measurable by standard tests given at that age. He helped produce the 'eleven plus' examination which streamed the top scoring minority into grammar schools or top streams at comprehensive schools and the rest into less challenging classes. It was virtually impossible for a child in a non-grammar secondary school to move and grammar school education was required for acceptance into university (Fancher, 1985).

Despite the assumption that IQ is static, Flynn (1987) is able to show data from fourteen countries indicating IQ gains ranging from five to twenty-five points in one generation. This increase suggests powerful environmental influences that affect performance in IQ tests. Howe (1998) shows how intervention can produce lasting change. Yet many write as if this was not the case (e.g. Murray, 1996). Other environmental factors likely to influence IQ differences are related to infant malnutrition or whether or not you have skipped breakfast (Spring *et al.*, 1992)!

The public assumes that intelligence testing is infallible and this has very negative consequences for those groups seen as 'genetically inferior' as 'proven' by 'science'. Intelligence tests have a very narrow focus on skills and tasks acquired in schooling; they do not test creativity or social intelligence (like the ability to know yourself or perceive the emotional states or social behaviour of others). Many treat intelligence as if it is inherited through genes and as unchangeable during life (see Fox and Prilleltensky, 1997: ch. 8 by Zack Cernovsky for a full discussion). Despite classical textbooks warning that it is unlikely that any test can be fair to more than one cultural group, numerous psychologists still misinterpret IQ scores from other cultures as indicating genetic inferiority of these groups. In the late 1960s a scientific discussion erupted on whether blacks were genetically less intelligent than whites. The issue became less popular in the 1970s when some researchers demonstrated, using the same logic and tests, that Asians in the USA on average scored more in intelligence than whites. It is difficult, if not impossible, to finds tests that are culture free (Hofstede, 1997).

Intelligence testing is so unreliable that even those who have been described as geniuses have been awarded low IQ scores. Cultural differences, for example, count for the ten-point gap in the IQ scores between white and black Americans. Yet in spite of this, there are still those like Christopher Brand, a psychologist at the University of Edinburgh, who continue to claim than it is a 'scientific fact' that white Americans and Asians are more intelligent than blacks. In the USA Hernstein and Murray (1994) in *The Bell Curve* have documented the alleged intellectual inferiority of African Americans. Not only did the result harm the research participants who had been given Standford-Binet or other tests, but weakened the available social support for people of colour by stigmatizing them as genetically inferior, thus strengthening the larger culture's racist attitudes (L. Brown, 1997).

There is no inherent quality of intelligence which can indicate high potential (Howe, 1997). Education and family background are better predictors of future success. Had George Stephenson, the nineteenth-century railway engineer, been given an intelligence test, he would probably have received a low score as he did not go to school, could not write his name, or do more than simple arithmetic by the age of 18. What intelligence tests have done is to set a threshold for entry into occupations which makes access to high-status jobs difficult for people with low scores. Large-scale research on army recruits from the Second World War found the median IQ scores increased and the range of scores decreased with occupational status. The median score for accountants was 128 with a range from 94 to 154 while the median scores for labourers was 88 with range of scores from 46 to 145 (Harrell and Harrell, 1945). If you accept that this is an accurate reflection of ability, it shows that some labourers have the intelligence to be accountants and vice versa!

> **STOP**
>
> Carol Vorderman, the TV presenter, known for being 'a brain with beauty', has an IQ of 157. In an interview she said: 'while I'm not stupid, I didn't get a particularly good degree—a third' (*Radio Times*, 1997). Is IQ a good predictor of degree result? What other factors contribute?

We all seem to know that a high IQ is about being clever, being good at thinking, good at solving abstract problems. According to Beloff (1992) we also assume that such power lies in the domain of men. Three separate studies how, compared with male self perceptions, females invariably underestimate their IQ. Further females project higher IQs on to their fathers than on to their mothers (Beloff, 1992; Higgins, 1987; Hogan, 1973). Young women students will, then, see themselves as intellectually inferior to young men. Women see themselves as inferior to their fathers and men as superior to their mothers. Issues of power, self-perception, gender, and IQ are clearly linked.

Vocational Guidance

Cyril Burt claimed that the results of the measurement of intelligence corresponded with existing forms of classification of the school population and could also justify the sorts of jobs which less intelligent adults should choose. The idea is that a world of industrial harmony and productivity can be created by making a fit between individuals and jobs. Misfits were those who, by virtue of being in the wrong job, did not match up to the new methods and speeds introduced into production (Hollway, 1991: 64). Vocational guidance for school leavers was of interest to industrial psychologists because if natural abilities and aptitudes could be measured, there would be no waste generated by those who found themselves in jobs which they did not 'fit'. As the vocational tests were applied almost entirely to mechanised jobs, all that was being tested would be aptitudes like finger dexterity and hand–eye coordination. These ideas were adopted by producers like the chocolate manufacturer, J. S. Rowntree, who believed that vocational selection would enable his company to reduce the number of cases in which work was experienced as monotonous. Automatic machinery would suit the lowest grade of worker. Rational scientific management practices could enable the employer to select the right worker for the job. From this basic assumption psychometric testing was developed. The 'science' produces a battery of methodologies and techniques for selecting the 'right person for the job'.

The Psychometric Testing Industry

It is estimated that 100,000 psychometric tests are taken each day in Western countries (*The Scotsman*, 1997). The tests are used to assist the recruitment process, for mid-career appraisal and outplacement. The two most well-known tests are personality tests: the 16PF and the Myers Briggs Type Indicator. The 16PF consists of sixteen factors measured through 186 multiple-choice questions.

In a recent review of managerial psychology, Smith and George (1994) note that non-work-related personality tests used as selection tools are poor predictors of job success and should be treated with caution. Despite this poor validity, personality tests remain in popular use. They are being used by management consultants to dupe clients and to satisfy the demand for assessment of personality. There is a world-wide abuse of personality testing going on, Smith and George believe.

Thompson and McHugh (1995: 246) note that personality test and inventories effectively perform the same function for an organization as stereotypes do for an individual or group. They help to sort a bewildering variety of information about a person into categories which can be more easily comprehended and evaluated. They aim to point to characteristics useful or damaging to the organization.

The psychometric testing industry is particularly apt at making sweeping claims, providing evidence, for example, of women's inadequacies as employees. Glenn Wilson says that the reason 95 per cent of bank managers, company directors, judges and university professors in Britain are men is because men are 'more competitive' and because 'dominance is a personality characteristic determined by male hormones' (1994: 62, 63). Women who do achieve promotion to top management positions 'may have brains that are masculinized' (1994: 65). Psychology is deeply implicated in the patriarchal control of women (Wilkinson, 1997). Women's alleged limited achievements are seen as due to biological differences, therefore unchangeable, or as a problem of social skills where the solution is assertiveness training. This locates women as the problem and says nothing about the social context, organizational structures, policies, or procedures that discriminate against women.

The underlying assumption behind personality testing is that managerial ability is related to personality factors. Those factors will not include the ability to hold down a job, run a household, and bring up children. It fulfils the expectations of existing managers—mainly white, male, middle-class, and middle-aged—about what makes a good manager (Hollway, 1984). The person unable or unwilling to make the correct responses automatically selects themselves out, regardless of managerial potential. The utility of psychometric testing is their cost-saving ability to predict who is capable or willing to be trained. The pragmatic psychology of Taylorism is at work here. If the person can do the job, as long as they have the 'right' personality, they will be a 'fit' employee.

Questions for Further Research

1. What are the advantages of scientific management according to Taylor? What disadvantages in employing scientific principles have been shown to exist?

2. Mary Parker Follett produced a prescription for a science of behaviour informed by the concerns of the human relations tradition (Thompson and McHugh, 1995: 104). How did she do this?

3. You have seen here the 'logic' of job design. Clegg (1984) shows how the processes of work simplification can be reversed. If you were a manager would you try to humanize work? Why or why not?

4. Read Smith and George (1994) and decide, from their review, what selection methods you might employ if you wanted to hire a manager.

5. What implications are there for managers to draw from the science of eugenics?

Suggestions for Further Reading

Braverman, H. (1974) *Labor and Monopoly Capital: The Degradation of Work in the Twentieth Century*. London: Monthly Review Press.

Fincham, R., and Rhodes, P.S. (1992) *The Individual, Work and Organization: Behavioural Studies for Business and Management*, 2nd edn. Oxford: Oxford University Press.

Hollway, W. (1991) *Work Psychology and Organizational Behaviour*. London: Sage.

Rose, M. (1988) *Industrial Behaviour*, 2nd edn. London: Penguin Business.

Thompson, P., and McHugh, D. (1995) *Work Organizations: A Critical Introduction*, 2nd edn. Basingstoke: Macmillan, ch. 8.

References

Acker, J. and Van Houton, D. R. (1992) 'Differential Recruitment and Control: The Sex Structuring of Organisations', in A. J. Mills and P. Tancred (eds.), *Gendering Organizational Analysis*. London: Sage, ch. 1.

Ackroyd, S. and Crowdy, P. A. (1990) 'Can Culture be Managed?', *Personnel Review*, 19/5: 3–13.

Argyris, C. (1964) *Integrating the Individual and the Organization*. New York: Wiley.

Babbage, C. (1989) *The Economy of Machinery and Manufactures*, 4th edn. (first published in 1832). London: William Pickering.

Beloff, H. (1992) 'Mother, Father and Me: Our IQ', *The Psychologist* (July), 309–11.

Blacker, F. H., and Brown, C. A. (1978) *Job Redesign and Management Control*. London: Saxon House.

Blauner, R. (1964) *Alienation and Freedom*. Chicago: University of Chicago Press.

Braverman, H. (1974) *Labor and Monopoly Capital: The Degradation of Work in the Twentieth Century*. New York: Monthly Review Press.

Broadbent, J., Dietrich, M., and Roberts, J. (1997) 'The End of the Professions?', in J. Broadbent, M. Dietrich and J. Roberts (eds.), *The End of the Professions? The Restructuring of Professional Work*. London: Routledge, ch. 1.

Brown, L. (1997) 'Ethics in Psychology: Cui Bono?', in D. Fox and I. Prilleltensky (eds.), *Critical Psychology: An Introduction*. London: Sage, ch. 4.

Brown, R. (1976) 'Women as Employees: Some Comments on Research in Industrial Sociology', in D. L. Barker and S. Allen (eds.), *Dependence and Exploitation in Work and Marriage*. Harlow: Longman, ch. 2.

Buchanan, D. A. (1985) 'Canned Cycles and Dancing Tools: Who's Really in Control of Computer Aided Machinery?', Paper presented to the 3rd Annual Labour Process Conference, Manchester.

Burrell, G. (1997) *Pandemonium: Towards a Retro-Organizational Theory*. London: Sage.

Burt, C. (1924) 'The Mental Differences between Individuals', *Journal of the National Institute of Industrial Psychology*, 11/2: 67–74.

Carey, A. (1967) 'The Hawthorne Studies: A Radical Criticism', *American Sociological Review*, 32: 403–16.

Child, J. (1972) 'Organizational Structure, Environment and Performance: The Role of Strategic Choice', *Sociology*, 6: 1–22.

Clegg, C. W. (1984) 'The Derivations of Job Designs', *Journal of Occupational Behaviour*, 5: 131–46.

Davies, L. E., Canter, R. R. and Hoffman, J. (1955) 'Current Job Design Criteria', *Journal of Industrial Engineering*, 6: 5–11.

Dore, R. P. (1973) *British Factory—Japanese Factory*. London: Allen and Unwin.

Drucker, P. F. (1989) *The Practice of Management*. Oxford: Heinemann Professional Publishing.

Durkheim, E. (1984) *The Division of Labour in Society*, trans. W. D. Halls. London: Macmillan.

Edwards, R. C. (1978) 'The Social Relations at the Point of Production', *Insurgent Sociologist*, 8: 2–3, 109–25.

Fancher, R. E. (1985) *The Intelligence Men: Makers of the IQ Controversy*. London: Norton.

Fineman, S (1996) 'Emotion and Organizing', in S. R. Clegg, C. Hardy and W. R. Nord (eds.), *Handbook of Organization Studies*. London: Sage Publications, ch. 3.3.

Flynn, J. R. (1987) 'Massive IQ Gains in 14 Nations: What IQ Tests Really Measure', *Psychological Bulletin*, 101: 171–191.

Fox, D., and Prilleltensky, I. (1997) (eds.) *Critical Psychology: An Introduction*. London: Sage.

Friedman, A. (1977) 'Responsible Autonomy versus Direct Control over the Labour Process', *Capital and Class*, 1 (Spring), 43–57.

Grint, K. (1991) *The Sociology of Work: An Introduction*. Cambridge: Polity.

Hackman, J. R. and Lawler, E. E. (1971) 'Employee Reactions to Job Characteristics', *Journal of Applied Psychology Monograph*, 55/3: 259–86.

Harrell, T. W. and Harrell, M. S. (1945) 'Army Classification Test Scores of Civilian Occupations', *Educational and Psychological Measurement*, 5: 229–39.

Hernstein, R. J. and Murray, C. (1994) *The Bell Curve: Intelligence and Class Structure in American Life*. New York: Free Press.

Herzberg, F., Mausner, B., and Snyderman, B. (1959) *The Motivation to Work*. New York: Wiley.

Higgins, L. (1987) 'The Knowing of Intelligence', *Guardian* (10 Feb.).

Hofstede, G. (1997) *Cultures and Organizations: Software of the Mind*. New York: McGraw Hill.

Hogan, H. W. (1973) 'IQ: Self Estimates of Males and Females', *Journal of Social Psychology*, 106: 137–8.

Hollway, W. (1984) 'Fitting Work: Psychological Assessment in Organizations', in J. Henriques *et al.*, *Changing the Subject: Psychology, Social Regulation and Subjectivity*. London: Methuen.

—— (1991) *Work Psychology and Organizational Behaviour: Managing the Individual at Work*. London: Sage.

Howe, M. (1997) *IQ in Question*. London: Sage.

—— (1998) 'Can IQ Change?', *The Psychologist* (Feb.): 69–72.

Johnson, P., and Gill, J. (1993) *Management Control and Organizational Behaviour*. London: Paul Chapman.

Kanter, R. (1977) *Men and Women of the Corporation*. New York: Basic Books.

Leidner, R. (1993) *Fast Food, Fast Talk: Service Work and the Routinization of Everyday Life*. Berkeley, Calif.: University of California Press.

Littler, C. R. (1985) 'Taylorism, Fordism and Job Design', in D. Knights, H. Wilmott, and D. Collinson (eds.), *Job Redesign: Critical Perspectives on the Labour Process*. Aldershot: Gower, ch. 2.

Lupton, T. (1971) *Management and the Social Sciences*. Harmondsworth: Penguin.

McGregor, D. (1960) *The Human Side of Enterprise*. New York: McGraw Hill.

Mayo, G. E. (1949) *The Social Problems of Industrial Civilisation*. London: Routledge and Kegan Paul.

Monanari, J. R. (1979) 'Strategic Choice: A Theoretical Analysis', *Journal of Management Studies*, 16: 202–21.

Murray, C. (1996) Murray's précis, *Current Anthropology*, 37 supplement (Feb.): S143–51.

Noble, D. F. (1974) *America by Design*. New York: Oxford University Press.

—— (1979) 'Social Choice in Machine Design: The Case of Automatically Controlled Machine Tools', in A. Zimbalist (ed.), *Case Studies in the Labor Process*. New York: Monthly Review Press, pp. 1–50.

Noon, M., and Blyton, P. (1997) *The Realities of Work*. Basingstoke: Macmillan Press.

Radio Times (1997) 'Why am I on TV so much? Probably because I'm cheap' (4–10 Oct.): 15–16.

Roethlisberger, F. J., and Dickson, W. J. (1939) *Management and the Worker*. Cambridge, Mass.: Harvard University Press.

Rose, M. (1988) *Industrial Behaviour*, 2nd ed. Harmondsworth: Penguin.

Scotsman, The (1997) 'Personality put to the test', (Nicky Cole) (24 Oct.): 1.

Sims, D., Fineman, S., and Gabriel, Y. (1993) *Organizing and Organizations*. London: Sage.

Smith, M. and George, D. (1994) 'Selection Methods', in C. L. Cooper and I. T. Robertson (eds.), *Key Reviews in Managerial Psychology: Concepts and Research in Practice*. Chichester: Wiley.

Spring, B., Pingitore, R., Bourgeois, M., Kessler, K. H., and Bruckner, E. (1992) 'The Effects and Non-Effects of Skipping Breakfast: Results of Three Studies', Paper presented at the 100th Annual Meeting of the American Psychological Association, Washington, DC, August.

Stearns, P. N. (1989) 'Suppressing Unpleasant Emotions: The Development of a Twentieth-Century American', in A. E. Barnes and P. N. Stearns (eds.), *Social History and Issues of Human Consciousness*. New York: NY University Press.

Taylor, F. W. (1911) *Principles of Scientific Management*. New York: Norton and Co.

Taylor, J .C. (1979) 'Job Design Criteria Twenty Years Later', in L. E. Davis and J. C. Taylor (eds.), *Design of Jobs*, 2nd edn. Santa Monica, Calif.: Goodyear.

Thompson, P., and McHugh, D. (1990) *Work Organizations: A Critical Introduction*. London: Macmillan.

—— and —— (1995) *Work Organizations: A Critical Introduction*, 2nd edn. Basingstoke: Macmillan, ch. 8.

Ure, A. (1835) *The Philosophy of Manufactures*. London: Charles Knight.

Walker, C. R. and Guest, R. H. (1952) *The Man on the Assembly Line*. Cambridge, Mass.: Harvard University Press.

Watanabe, T. (1990) 'New Office Technology and the Labour Process in Contemporary Japanese Banking', *New Technology, Work and Employment*, 5/1: 56–67.

Weick, K. (1969) *The Social Psychology of Organizing*. Reading, Mass.: Addison-Wesley Publishing Company.

Wilkinson, S. (1997) 'Feminist Psychology', in D. Fox and I. Prilleltensky (eds.), *Critical Psychology: An Introduction*. London: Sage, ch. 16..

Wilson, F. M. (1987) 'Computer Numerical Control and Constraint', in D. Knights and H. Wilmott (eds.), *New Technology and the Labour Process*. London: Macmillan.

Wilson, G. (1994) 'Biology, Sex Roles and Work', in C. Quest (ed.), *Liberating Women . . . from Modern Feminism*. London: Institute of Economic Affairs, Health and Welfare Unit, pp. 59–71.

Zeitlin, J. (1983) 'The Labour Strategies of British Engineering Employers 1890–1922', in H. Gospel and C. Littler, *Managerial Strategies and Industrial Relations*. London: Heinemann.

3

Rationalization and Rationality 2: Weber, McDonald's, and Bureaucracy

WHILE TAYLOR HAD been a theorist-practitioner, Max Weber (1864–1920) was a writer on sociology and politics. He described the process of rationalization underlying Western history, a trend where the traditional or magical criteria of action were replaced by technical, calculative, or scientific criteria. Weber's (1930) study of the rise of capitalism argued that the 'spirit of capitalism' owed a lot to the practices and thoughts of the Calvinist Church which, in turn, was enmeshed in logical, calculative thought, rationality that had spread from science, through politics and into the new Protestant church. Rationalization is a process whereby the means chosen to pursue ends can be determined by logical and rational calculation. The continuous drive towards greater rationalization and efficiency, according to Weber, is clear in every sphere of social, economic, and political life. With this process relations between people increasingly come to take the form of calculations about the exchange and use of the capabilities and resources. One key place where this happens is in bureaucracies.

All organizations make provision for their continuance to ensure they meet given aims. Bureaucracy helps them do this. Bureaucracies are enterprises or political parties or other organizations (like the Church) where people discharge functions specified in advance according to rules. Authority is wielded as tasks are allocated, coordinated, and supervised. Tasks are regulated through the organization's structure. The bureaucratic structure has become dominant in modern society, in the public and private sector.

Weber's starting-point is authority. The claims to legitimacy of authority come from three different sources:

1. Rational grounds where there is a belief in the rules and rights of those in authority to issue commands. This is legal authority.
2. Traditional grounds where there is a sanctity of tradition and legitimacy of status (traditional authority).
3. Charismatic grounds where there is devotion to sanctity, heroism, or character of an individual (charismatic authority).

With legal authority obedience is owed to the office whoever is in it; they have a right to issue commands. Legal authority is to be found in bureaucracy. In contrast a monarch or a feudal lord would have traditional authority and dynamic, influential characters would have charismatic authority. With legal authority and bureaucracy there is a levelling of status.

In Weber's view, what are the characteristics of bureaucracy? Modern officialdom functions in the following manner (adapted from Gerth and Wright Mills, 1948):

1. There is the principle of fixed and official areas of administration which are usually ordered by rules or regulations. Activities are distributed as official duties. The authority to give commands about these duties is distributed in a stable way and strictly delimited by rules concerning the coercive means which officials have. Only suitably qualified individuals are employed.
2. The hierarchy means that there is a firmly ordered system where those in lower office are under the command of those in higher office.

3. The management of the office is based upon written documents which are preserved in their original form. The officials, the office materials, and the files make up the bureau or office.
4. Specialized office management presupposes thorough and expert training.
5. When the office is fully developed, official activity demands the full working capacity of the official.
6. The management of the office follows general rules which can be learnt.

The official is in a vocation which requires work over a long period and for which the official needs to be qualified. Holding office is not to be exploited for, for example, rents or the exchange of services, as has been the case in the past. The official manages faithfully in return for security of employment. The job, at least in public authorities when Weber wrote, was held for life. Loyalty should be impersonal and functional, not personal, like that of the vassal or disciple; the official is not the personal servant of a ruler. The official enjoys social esteem. They are appointed by a superior authority. The official receives a fixed salary for the job and is set on a career within the hierarchical order.

Weber was keen to stress the technical advantages of bureaucratic organization. The decisive reason for the advance of bureaucratic organization has been its purely technical superiority over every other form of organization. There is precision, speed, lack of ambiguity, knowledge of the files, continuity, discretion, unity and uniformity, strict subordination, reduction of friction and of material and personal costs. All these are raised to the optimum in a strictly bureaucratic organization. There are calculable rules so there is a 'calculability' of consequences. Scientific management has a role to play in this process as it provides the ideal vehicle for the imposition of military discipline in the factory. Techniques such as Taylor's 'shop cards' specifying the daily routines of employees are ideal for this process of bureaucratization.

Business is discharged 'without regard for persons' (Weber, 1978: 226); the division of labour in administration is put into practice according to purely objective criteria. All love, hatred, and purely personal irrational and emotional sentiments are excluded. In contrast the lord of older societies was capable of being moved by personal sympathy, kindness, favour, or gratitude. With rationalization comes the use of calculative devices and techniques, formally rational means, the division of labour, sets of rules, accounting methods, money, technology and other means for increasing that rationality. There will, however, always be unintended consequences; bureaucracy could also manifest features which were 'materially irrational', for example individual freedom can be threatened by bureaucracy. Weber recognized that bureaucracy might become an 'iron cage' (1930: 181) and speculated that the domination of the official in modern society could become more powerful than the slave owner of eras past. Weber wrote on many topics, including the history of the piano and Freudianism (see Runciman, 1978), but is probably best known in management for his work on bureaucracy.

Since Weber wrote about the ideal bureaucracy, a good deal of work has focused on the dysfunctions of the bureaucratic form, the menace of bureaucracy, for example by Merton (1936) Gouldner (1954), and Selznick (1949). These writers, as well as questioning the perfection of the 'ideal type' discussed whether the opposition between organizational efficiency and the freedom of the individual was possible. The routine and oppressive aspects of bureaucracy were highlighted to show it as a 'vicious circle' that develops from the resistance of the human factor to the mechanistic rationalist theory of behaviour which is being imposed on it. The very resistance tends to reinforce the use of the bureaucracy. For example in Gouldner's view, impersonal bureaucratic rules evolve because they alleviate the tensions created by subordination and control, but at the same time they perpetuate the very tensions that bring them into being. They particularly reinforce the low motivation of the workforce that makes close supervision necessary.

As we have seen the ideal type of bureaucracy is governed by a formal set of rules and procedures which ensures that operations and activities are carried out in a predictable, uniform, and impersonal manner. Personal relationships are excluded from organizational life. Zygmunt Bauman (1989) shows the importance of bureaucratic organization to the death camps in Nazi Germany.

Bureaucracy in Pregnancy?

Pregnant women in the UK may see up to forty health care professionals on a 'production line' basis and may never see the same midwife twice. They are unlikely to know the names of those helping deliver the baby. If anything goes wrong with the delivery, the patient is likely to be even more distanced (Burrell, 1997: 145). What other elements of bureaucracy are likely to be witnessed during pregnancy and birth?

Can bureaucracy be devoid of emotion? We think of bureaucracy, organizational order, and efficiency as matters of rational, non-emotional activity. Cool clear strategic thinking should not be sullied by messy feelings. Good organizations are places where feelings are managed, designed, out or tamed. It is thought that emotions interfere with rationality (Fineman, 1996). But can organizations, and in particular bureaucracy, be free of emotion? Can you, for example, imagine a British political party free of all public embarrassment?

Recently writers (e.g. Acker, 1990; Brewis and Grey, 1994; Martin, 1990; Witz *et al.*, 1996) have suggested that while the rational-legal model presents itself as gender neutral, it actually constitutes a new kind of patriarchal structure. Ferguson (1984) too argues that bureaucracy is an organization of oppressive male power. Bureaucracy is both mystified and constructed though an abstract discourse of rationality, rules, and procedures ('discourse', as defined in the work of Foucault, refers to what is regarded as acceptable, both in terms of what is permitted to be said and thought, who can and cannot speak and with what authority, and also who is regarded as normal or abnormal). The reality of organizational life is constituted through discourses which have a 'normalizing' effect on individuals, defining what and who is normal, standard, and acceptable (Thomas, 1996). Bureaucracy is a construction of male domination. In response bureaucrats, workers, and clients are 'feminized' as they develop ways of managing their powerlessness that at the same time perpetuate their dependence.

Pringle (1989), using the case of secretaries, shows how the relationship between the boss and the secretary is the most visible aspect of a pattern of domination based on desire and sexuality to be found in modern bureaucratic structures. Secretaries seem to contradict the criteria of the ideal bureaucracy. For example they are far from being specialized as they can be called upon to do just about anything and there may be considerable overlap between their work and that of their boss; in bringing to bear the emotional, personal, and sexual, they represent the opposite of rationality, as discursively constituted. She argues that the concept of rationality excludes the personal, the sexual, and the feminine. The personal, sexual, and feminine are perceived as associated with chaos and disorder and in opposition to rationality; the concept of rationality is thus seen to have a masculine base.

Secretaries, Sex, and Work

While no one seriously believes that secretaries spend much time on their bosses' knee, sexual possibilities colour the way in which the boss-secretary relationship is seen. Outside of the sex industry, it is said to be the most sexualized of all workplace relationships (Pringle, 1989). Is Pringle right?

Pringle and others (e.g. Burrell, 1984, 1987; Hacker and Hacker, 1987) have questioned whether bureaucratic forms have banished sexuality from organizational life. While the complete eradication of sexuality from bureaucratic structures has been a goal which many top decision-makers have pursued, many managements content themselves with the incorporation and close containment of sexual relations in the non-work field. Human features, like love, comfort, and sexuality, have been gradually expelled from bureaucratic structures and relocated in the family. Faced with this curtailment, significant numbers of men and women have resisted, so acts of intimacy have taken place in the past and will continue to take place in the future (see Chapter 6 for more). This view stresses how male sexuality is routinely privileged within organizational practices as sexuality and power are intertwined in everyday social interactions.

Men, then, are more likely to match the requirements of bureaucratic organizations than women do. It is the male body, its sexuality, minimal responsibility in procreation, and the conventional control of emotions that pervades work and work organizations (Acker, 1990). Bureaucrats need to be highly controlled or regimented, lacking in desire, isolated in performance, and disassociated from self; this is 'the' male body being privileged (Witz *et al.*, 1996).

Rationalization and the Service Sector

More recently jobs in the service sector have expanded, challenging employers to rationalize workers' self-presentation and feelings as well as their behaviour (as we also see in Chapter 8). Employers may try to specify how a worker, such as a flight attendant, looks, how their hair should be styled and, in the case of women, how their make-up should look. Employers may try to specify what employees say, their demeanour, their gestures and even their thoughts. To do this they use scripts, uniforms, dress codes, rules, and guidelines for dealing with customers and co-workers, instructions about how best to think of the work and customers.

STOP Burger King have had a slogan—'You want it? You Got it!'—implying that the customer's wish was their command. What do you think would happen if you asked for your burger to be medium rare?

This routinization of human interaction is disconcerting but explicit rules have become a significant feature of employment contracts in many mass service industries. For example, the guidelines in personal appearance issued to Walt Disney World employees include 'Fingernails should not extend more than one-fourth of an inch beyond the fingertips' (Leidner, 1993: 9). These explicit rules include feeling rules (Fineman, 1995): 'First we practice a friendly smile at all times with our guests and among ourselves. Second, we use friendly courteous phrases. "May I help you" ... "Thank you" ... "Have a nice day" ... "Enjoy the rest of your stay" and many others are all part of our working vocabulary' (Walt Disney Productions, 1982: 6). The 'Magic Kingdom', also known as 'the smile factory' expects each member of staff, known as 'the cast' to show a constant smile even to those who are difficult, offensive, or threatening. They also have a system of staff surveillance but the cast seek out blind spots (a large rock, a concrete pillar) to have a rest, conversation, or smoke. The staff then resist these feeling rules by taking an illegitimate break (Van Maanen, 1991). They are also known to slap visitors hard across their chests with the seat belt of ride vehicles if they misbehave.

A Clean-Shaven Employee is Best?

Safeways has a preference for employing clean-shaven men. Perhaps they would like to consider the following story (*Scotland on Sunday*, 9 November 1997, p. 21).

An upper class woman employed a decidedly scruffy gardener who allowed a shadow of stubbly growth to appear on his chin. His employer did not like it but did not want to offend him by asking him to shave. She asked him one day how long he thought a person should go before shaving if they wanted to avoid looking scruffy. He looked at her thoughtfully and then replied 'I would say with a light growth like yours, every two days should be fine.'

Values and attitudes can be constructed and influenced through training programmes and corporate culture. Hochschild (1983) shows how recurrent training for flight attendants is aimed at reinforcing the 'inside-out' smile. She documents how flight attendants were trained to repeat 'I know just how you feel' to calm passengers furious over a missed connection or other failures of service. She also showed, in the case of flight attendants, that the result of regulating what she called 'emotion work' (the work of creating a particular emotional state in others, often by manipulating your own feelings) was that the attendants were alienated from their feelings, their faces, and their moods. Some showed signs of resistance by, for example, spilling a Bloody Mary over an offensive passenger's lap. Here is another story: 'A young businessman said to a flight attendant, "Why aren't you smiling?" She put her tray back on the food cart and said "I'll tell you what. You smile first, then I'll smile". The businessman smiled at her. "Good," she replied. "Now freeze and hold that for fifteen hours." ' (Hochschild, 1983: 127).

But the effect on the workforce is not always negative. Some will accept the tight scripting because it saves them having the make the effort of thinking of appropriate words to say or ways to act, the standards of good work have been clarified for them, the routines can act as shields against the insults and indignities a worker might have to accept from the public (Leidner, 1993: 5). Others will refuse to smile (Hochschild, 1983) or will insist on their right to the own style (Benson, 1986).

Most of us know how to behave with service workers in order to fit the organizational routines. We have been fitted into the routine of 'involuntary unpaid labor' (Glazer, 1984) when we serve ourselves petrol at the petrol station, gather up, bring, and unload groceries from our baskets in the supermarket and clear away our rubbish in fast food restaurants. We know not to order items in fast food restaurants that are not on the menu and we know to line up for service. The garish colours and plastic seats are designed to make sure we do not linger too long.

The Case of McDonald's

The routinization to be found at McDonald's shows a close links with the logic of Taylorism, maximizing managerial control of work and breaking work down into its constituent tasks which can be preplanned. The key to McDonald's success is its uniformity and predictability. Customers know exactly what to expect. McDonald's promises that every meal will be served quickly, courteously, and with a smile. It promises fast service, hot food, and clean restaurants. To do this it needs to use the principles of scientific management coupled with centralized planning, central designed training programmes, approved and supervised suppliers, automated machinery, meticulous specifications, and systematic inspections. As a result, 'a quarter-pounder is cooked in exactly 107 seconds. Our fries are never more than 7 minutes old when served.' Each restaurant aims to serve any order within sixty seconds (Beynon, 1992: 180). Customers are channelled through the restaurant by its layout and design and through the service routines and relatively restricted menu on offer.

About three-quarters of the outlets are owned by franchisees rather than the corporation, so owners retain control over pay scales, for example, but the company requires that every outlet's production methods and products meet McDonald's precise specifications. The regimentation covers food preparation, bookkeeping, purchasing, dealing with workers and customers and virtually every aspect of the business. The food production is the most visible aspect for the customer. A 'bible', an operations and training manual, demonstrates the proper placement and amount of ketchup, mustard, and pickle slices on each type of hamburger available. Lights and buzzers tell the crew when to take French fries out of the fat, the French fry scoops specify the size of portion and allow the worker to fill a bag and set it down in one continuous motion, specially designed ketchup dispensers squirt the correct portion of ketchup. Crew are also told in what sequence the products customers order are to be gathered, what arm motion is to be used in salting the batch of fries, and to double-fold each bag before presenting it to the customer. Only minor variations in the execution of its routines are allowed. Customers are referred to as 'guests' so that all customers are potentially treated with respect and courtesy.

How to Cook a Hamburger

Here is an example of the original McDonald's procedure for cooking hamburgers: Those grilling the burgers were instructed to put hamburgers down on the grill moving from left to right, creating six rows of six burgers. As the first two rows are furthest away from the heating element, they were instructed to flip the third row first, then the fourth, fifth, and sixth before flipping the first two (Love, 1986: 141–2). How would you feel if instructions as detailed as this were to be found in recipe books? Would you follow the instructions (*a*) in your own home, (*b*) for an employer?

There are rules about safety, hygiene, and uniform. All workers have to wear a clean uniform complete with hat and name tag. Brightly coloured nail polish, wearing more than two rings, and dangling jewellery are forbidden. Leidner (1993) shows how extensively these dress code rules stretched. For example one window worker always wore a piece of adhesive tape on his ear to hide a gold earring. While the tape was probably more offensive than the earring, management considered it less offensive.

Performance is rated and each worker is awarded stars (worn on a badge) which are linked to pay and promotion prospects. The performance rating is made on the basis of an assessment which lists criteria such as: 'Greeting the customer: 1. There is a smile   2. Greeting is pleasant, audible, sincere   3. Looks customer in the eyes' (from McDonald's 'Counter Observation Check List' quoted in Fineman, 1995). McDonald's training centre near Chicago is called Hamburger University. The 'university' is on a 'campus', the director is called 'the dean' and the trainers are 'professors'. The trainers work from scripts prepared for them. They try to produce managers 'with ketchup in their veins'. Crew, managers, and franchisees learn that there is a McDonald's way of doing business and that any diversion from this would be wrong. The full training programme requires between 600 and 1,000 hours of work and is required of all those who wish to own a McDonald's outlet.

While the routinization and extreme standardization is clear, McDonald's does favour some experimentation. When an employee produces a new idea, it can be adopted (the Egg McMuffin and the Big Mac are examples of employee ideas) but the corporation will experiment, test, and refine the idea before it is implemented in a uniform way. You will find that some products too differ depending on national or local context, despite the uniformity of approach. For example, in Spain there is (when I was last there in 1997) no vegetarian option.

Ritzer (1993) argues that fast food restaurants like McDonald's are the new model of rationalization which have replaced the bureaucratic structure. He talks of McDonaldization, defining it as 'the process by which the principles of the fast-food restaurant are coming to dominate more and more sectors of American society as well as the rest of the world' (1993: 1). He believes that McDonaldization affects education, work, travel, the family, and every other sector of society. The McDonald's model has proved to be irresistible. Four basic dimensions lie at the heart of McDonald's success:

1. Efficiency: it offers us the optimum method of getting from a state of being hungry to a state of being full.
2. It offers food and service that can be easily quantified and calculated. We feel that we are getting a lot of food for a modest amount of money. People think that it will take less time to go to McDonald's, eat the food, and return home than to prepare the food at home.
3. It offers predictability. We know that the burger we eat in one town will be the same as in another and that the one we order next week will be identical to the one we eat today.
4. Control is exerted over human beings, especially through the substitution of non-human technology for human. The humans do a limited number of tasks precisely as they are told to do them. Limited menus, few options and uncomfortable seats lead diners to do what management want them to do—eat quickly and leave. Technology replaces human labour where the soft drink dispenser shuts off when the carton is full, the programmed cash register eliminates the need for cashiers to calculate prices.

RATIONALIZATION AND RATIONALITY 2

The experience of working in a fast food restaurant is included in Gabriel's (1988) book on working lives in catering. He interviewed in three London outlets of one fast food company. Virtually all the staff were in their teens or early twenties and management were only slightly older. About one-third of the workers worked part-time and several were students; most lived with their parents and for many it was their first job. Few expected to stay for more than a year.

The jobs offered little intrinsic satisfaction and very few people found their jobs enjoyable. Most respondents spent most of their time in just one job like cleaning, sweeping, serving at the counter, or in the kitchen. To get through the day they had to fantasize. Nineteen of the twenty-six workers said they kept their minds on other things while they worked; only working on the till required concentration. Many had developed a contempt for the work they did ('crap jobs'). Some played games, like catching a girl's eye as she entered the restaurant and seeing if she joined your queue, some added personal touches to the burgers they put together and wrapped, or bent the rules of how many burgers to make in any one batch, to see if they could get away with it; breaking the rules, adding personal touches, and playing games broke the drudgery of work. As Burawoy (1981, 1985) notes, these games give some degree of control to workers and are tolerated by management because they enhance the efficiency of work. We are left wondering then, does increasing routinization really lead to efficiency or is a human relations view more appropriate?

There is a down side to the fast food industry, says Ritzer. For example, the fast food restaurant can be a dehumanizing setting in which to both eat or work. It can feel like dining or working on an assembly line. It minimizes contact among human beings. It serves food which is high in calories, fat, sugar, and salt content. It has run foul of environmentalists as well as nutritionists. It contributes to a homogenization around the world; diversity of food choice is being reduced or eliminated.

McDonald's did not, as Ritzer notes, develop in a historical vacuum; it had important precursors providing the principles of the assembly line, scientific management, and bureaucracy. Although the fast food restaurant adopts elements of these precursors, it takes a quantum leap in the process of rationalization. The basic dimensions of McDonaldization—efficiency, calculability, predictability, increased control through technology—are manifest not only in fast food restaurants but in a wide and increasing array of social settings throughout the world like shopping malls, home shopping, preprepared meals. They are also evident in factory farming (Ritzer, 1993: 103). Burrell (1997: 138) takes this point one stage further when he says that McDonald's is an organization dependent on the profitable death of cattle and chickens in profusion. Without automated death, the cost of the Big Mac would be higher. The Nazi concentration camps, he notes, relied upon the relative automation of death too (see also Bauman, 1989).

Ritzer (1998) has gone on to document the continuation, if not acceleration, of the rationalization process in a book called *The McDonaldization Thesis* and in another about credit cards (Ritzer, 1995). He argues that we have a 'new means of consumption' (1998: 1) in fast food restaurants, credit cards, tourism, shopping malls, superstores, home shopping television networks, and many more. Using Mannheim's thinking on rationalisation, Ritzer believes that McDonalized systems, through their rules, regulations, scripts, and so on, encroach upon and ultimately threaten the ability of people working with these systems to think intelligently. Central planning and considerable control exerted over franchisees, employees, and customers brings us back to a Weberian image of an iron cage of rationalization.

Ritzer says that this iron cage is currently being constructed, piece by piece, by the various organizations and institutions that follow the McDonald's model. It may be more escape-proof than Weber ever imagined.

Credit cards and fast food restaurants share some interesting similarities. Both represent radical change in society yet neither was highly innovative. Both rely heavily on advertising; both have been forced to engage in price competition and have tried to target teenage populations. While McDonald's rationalized the delivery of prepared food, the credit card rationalized the consumer loans business. Prior to credit cards, the process of obtaining a loan was slow, cumbersome, and non-rationalized. It now requires little more than the filling out of a short questionnaire. Credit bureaux and computerization mean that credit records can be checked and applications approved or rejected rapidly. The unpredictability of whether a loan will be approved has been greatly reduced. Credit card loans, like fast food hamburgers, are being served up in a highly rationalized assembly line.

There are also degrees of McDonaldization to be found in surprising areas of life. Academia might be one domain immune to it. But Ritzer believes that academia and even medicine and law have been influenced by McDonald's. For example, in the case of universities, parents and students are increasingly approaching the university as consumers in the same way that they approach other consumption items. They are looking for low price, convenience, efficiency, absence of hassle. Universities have responded by opening satellite campuses in suburban areas or smaller towns not well served by a central university. They provide plenty of parking space and advanced technology. Courses can now be transmitted by television, video, or video-conferencing. We confront a future of accelerating McDonaldization. McDonald's will remain powerful until the nature of society changes so dramatically that McDonald's is no longer able to adapt. Like scientific management, the assembly line, and bureaucracy, it leads to an ever more rational world.

A Thought

It could be argued that the last two chapters are misleading. Currently the book leads you to understand that there has been a linear development of management thinking from early theorists like Taylor and Babbage to the present day. An alternative view is presented by Tsoukas and Cummings (1997). They argue that we should abandon the idea that there is a development of thinking about organization and management that is underpinned by progression, that we are part of a continuous progress. Rather than seeing the history of management as a 'stairway to heaven' upwards and onwards, it should be viewed as a kaleidoscope, containing a number of discrete fragments, revealing a pattern, as Foucault (1966) did. The sequence of patterns from the kaleidoscope obeys no inner logic and conforms to no universal norm of reason. Fragments from the past will reappear now and again. What support do you find for this thought? Would you agree with Tsoukas and Cummings? What would be the rationale for presenting a non-linear view of management thinking?

Questions for Further Research

1. Why should management, thinking about rationalization, be seen as a kaleidoscope and not in a linear fashion?

2. Gabriel (1988) found that workers in the fast food industry said the main point of their job was to earn their own money. Why was this the case? If you have worked in the fast food industry, what was the main point for you?

3. Pringle (1989) says that her study of secretaries vividly illustrates the working of modern bureaucracy. How does she do this? Which of her arguments might you wish to disagree with?

4. Filby (1992) described the everyday life in a betting shop. The management tried, and partly succeeded, in using women's bodies and personalities to promote the product but the female employees 'turned the tables' (Thompson and McHugh, 1995: 152). How did they do this?

Suggestions for Further Reading

Joseph, M. (1989) *Sociology for Business*. Oxford: Polity Press in association with Basil Blackwell, ch. 4.

Thompson, P., and McHugh, D. (1995) *Work Organizations: A Critical Introduction*, 2nd edn. Basingstoke: Macmillan, ch. 2.

Class Exercise

Leidner (1993) found that McDonald's workers do not say that they are dissatisfied with their jobs. Ritzer (1998) says that this is a disturbing finding. If most of your life is spent in McDonaldized systems there is little or no basis for rebellion against your McDonaldized job because you lack a standard against which to compare and to judge such a job. More generally there is no basis for rebellion against the system or for seeking out an alternative. McDonaldization is an iron cage from which there is no escape and not even any interest in escape. Do you agree? Divide the class in two. One half should find arguments to support Ritzer and the other half to argue against.

References

Acker, J. (1990) 'Hierarchies, Jobs, Bodies: A Theory of Gendered Organisations', *Gender and Society*, 4/2: 139–58.

Bauman, Z. (1989) *Modernity and the Holocaust*. Cambridge: Polity.

Benson, S. P. (1986) *Counter Culture: Saleswomen, Manager and Customers in American Department Stores 1890–1940*. Urbana, Ill.: University of Illinois Press.

Beynon, H. (1992) 'The End of the Industrial Worker?', in N. Abercrombie and A. Warde (eds.), *Social Change in Contemporary Britain*. Cambridge: Polity.

Brewis, J., and Grey, C. (1994) 'Re-eroticizing the Organization: An Exegesis and Critique' *Gender, Work and Organization*, 1/2: 67–82.

Burawoy, M. (1981) 'Terrains of Contest: Factory and State under Capitalism and Socialism', *Socialist Review*, 11/4: 58, 83–124.

—— (1985) *The Politics of Production*. London: Verso.

Burrell, G. (1984) 'Sex and Organizational Analysis', *Organisation Studies*, 5/2: 97–110.

—— (1987) 'No Accounting for Sexuality', *Accounting , Organization and Society*, 12: 89–101.

—— (1997) *Pandemonium: Towards a Retro-Organizational Theory*. London: Sage.

Ferguson, K. E. (1984) The Feminist Case Against Bureaucracy. Philadelphia: Temple University Press.

Filby, M. (1992) 'The Figures, the Personality and the Bums: Service Work and Sexuality', *Work, Employment and Society*, 6/1: 23–42.

Fineman, S. (1995) 'Stress, Emotion and Intervention', in T. Newton (with J. Handy and S. Fineman), *Managing Stress: Emotions and Power at Work*. London: Sage, ch. 6.

—— (1996) 'Emotion and Organizing', in S. R. Clegg, C. Hardy, and W. R. Nord (eds.), *Handbook of Organization Studies*. London: Sage, ch. 3.3.

Foucault, M. (1966) *The Order of Things: An Archaeology of the Humanities*. London: Tavistock and Routledge.

Gabriel, Y. (1988) *Working Lives in Catering*. London: Routledge and Kegan Paul.

Gerth, H. H., and Wright Mills, C. (1948) *From Max Weber: Essays in Sociology*, trans. H. H. Gerth and C. Wright Mills. London: Routledge and Kegan Paul.

Glazer, N. Y. (1984) 'Servants to Capital: Unpaid Domestic Labor and Paid Work', review in *Radical Political Economics*, 16: 61–87.

Gouldner, A. (1954) *Patterns of Industrial Bureaucracy*. Glencoe, Ill.: The Free Press.

Hacker, B. C., and Hacker, S. (1987) 'Military Institutions and the Labor Process: Non-Economic Sources of Technological Change, Women's Subordination and the Organization of Work', *Technology and Culture*, 28: 743–75.

Hochschild, A. R. (1983) *The Managed Heart: Commercialization of Human Feeling*. Berkeley, Calif.: University of California Press.

Leidner, R. (1993) *Fast Food, Fast Talk: Service Work and the Routinization of Everyday Life*. Berkeley, Calif.: University of California Press.

Love, J. (1986) *McDonalds: Behind the Arches*. Toronto: Bantam.

Martin, J. (1990) 'Re-reading Weber: Searching for Feminist Alternatives to Bureaucracy', Paper presented to the Academy of Management in San Francisco.

Merton, R. K. (1936) 'The Unanticipated Consequences of Purposive Social Action', *American Sociological Review*, 1: 894–904.

Pringle, R. (1989) 'Bureaucracy, Rationality and Sexuality: The Case of Secretaries', in J. Hearn, D. L. Sheppard, P. Tancred-Sheriff, and G. Burrell (eds.), *The Sexuality of Organizations*. London: Sage.

Ritzer, G. (1993) *The McDonaldization of Society: An Investigation into the Changing Character of Contemporary Social Life*. Newbury Park, Calif.: Sage.

—— (1995) *Expressing America: A Critique of the Global Credit Card Society*. Thousand Oaks, Calif.: Pine Forge Press.

—— (1998) *The McDonaldization Thesis: Explorations and Extensions*. London: Sage.

Runciman, W. G. (1978) *Max Weber: Selections in Translation*. Cambridge: Cambridge University Press.

Selznick, P. (1949) *TVA and the Grass Roots*. Berkeley, Calif.: University of California Press.

Thomas, R. (1996) 'Gendered Cultures and Performance Appraisal: The Experience of Women Academics', *Gender, Work and Organization*, 3/3 (July): 143–55.

Thompson, P., and McHugh, D. (1995) *Work Organizations: A Critical Introduction*, 2nd edn. Basingstoke: Macmillan.

Tsoukas, H., and Cummings, S. (1997) 'Marginalization and Recovery: The Emergence of Aristotelian Themes in Organization Studies', *Organization Studies*, 18/4: 655–83.

Van Maanan, J. (1991) 'The Smile Factory', in P. Frost, L. F. Moore, M. R. Louis, C. C. Lundberg, and J. Martin (eds.), *Reframing Organizational Culture*. Newbury Park, Calif.: Sage.

Walt Disney Productions (1982) *Your Role in the Walt Disney World Show*. Orlando, Fla.: Walt Disney Productions.

Weber, M. (1930) *The Protestant Ethic and the Spirit of Capitalism*. London: Allen and Unwin.

—— (1978) *Economy and Society: An Outline of Interpretative Sociology*, ed. G. Roth and C. Wittich. Berkeley, Calif.: University of California Press.

Witz, A., Halford, S., and Savage, M. (1996) 'Organized Bodies: Gender, Sexuality and Embodiment in Contemporary Organizations', in L. Adkins and V. Merchant (eds.), *Sexualising the Social*, London: Macmillan, ch. 8.

The View from Below

WE EXPLORED BRIEFLY in the first chapter what work might mean to people, and we have looked at the rationality behind how work is organized and jobs allocated, but what do employees feel about work? How do they view their jobs? The concept of alienation forms, for many, a useful starting-point for understanding how people feel about work. Marx, in the *Economic and Political Manuscripts*, shows that there are various aspects to the experience. The work is external to the workers

> that is not part of his nature, that consequently he does not fulfil himself in his work but denies himself, has a feeling of misery, not of well being, does not develop freely a physical and mental energy, but is physically exhausted and mentally debased. A worker therefore only feels at home in his leisure, whereas at work he feels homeless. His work is not voluntary but imposed, forced labour. (Bottomore and Rubel, 1963: 177–8)

How is the experience of alienation and degrading work documented in research?

The Experience of the Assembly Line

An early account of concrete experiences of factory work can be found in the work of Simone Weil (see Grey, 1996) who worked in an electrical plant and a metalworking factory in Paris in 1934–5. The highly mechanized work was degrading, humiliating, and shaming for the individual. For example, she describes how she worked on a stamping press where the pieces were difficult to position, producing 600 pieces in less than three hours before having a half hour to reset the machine. She had to adapt to the 'slavery'. She felt disgust at being forced to strain and exhaust herself, 'with the certainty of being bawled out either for being slow or for botching, for the sake of these 56 centimes' (Weil, 1987: 159). Workers are oppressed, they are treated as means rather than as ends in themselves. The clearest manifestation of oppression is to be found, not in class, but in the organization of production, she says. Taylorism, bureaucratization, and management are all implicated in the development of forms of oppression.

A more recent experience of the assembly line is described by Michael Moore. 'This insane system known as the assembly line is designed to deny individuality and eliminate self worth', says Moore in the foreword to Ben Hamper's (1992) book *Rivethead*. This book is written by a journalist and tells his story of finding a job and working at General Motors' Truck and Bus Plant in Michigan. Initially he worked on an assembly line installing clips and screws inside rear wheel wells. Then he learnt how to spot weld so he could do his neighbour's job on the line too and they could 'double-up'—do two jobs for an hour or two and then have one or two hours' break. He complains about the monotony of the job (being faced with the same job every few minutes) in spite of being able to take these long breaks where he could read two newspapers, a magazine, and a good chunk of a novel each evening. In this world, 'workers suffer and cope through drink or madness'.

Some further realities of working on assembly lines in Britain and France are captured in accounts from researchers Ruth Cavendish and Robert Linhart. Ruth Cavendish's (1989) account of her seven-month experience of working in a motor components factory was so contentious that she had to go to considerable lengths to disguise the identity of the company. Ruth was an assembler and she learnt the job by sitting by a woman at a bench. The benches were at each side of a conveyor belt; each line had fifteen operators including two operators who sat at the end and mended incorrectly assembled or faulty products. The line produced 500 or 1,000 'sets' of assembled components each one or two days which meant each operator performed the same operation over and over 500 or 1,000 times. Sometimes Ruth would do up to five different jobs a day and was completely exhausted. She says that she had terrible pains in her neck and back and found it hard to keep up with the work on the line, but because the work kept coming, she had to keep on. Most days she worked so hard that she did not have time to look up or had to work extra fast so that she could have enough time between tasks to unwrap a piece of chewing gum or take a sip of tea. You could not blow your nose or flick hair out your eyes without losing valuable seconds. It was very hot and the ventilation was poor. The repetition of the work and being controlled by the speed of the line was hard to take.

The work and the speed of the line was set by management and was not negotiable. To keep the components moving at a steady pace, all the jobs on the line ought to have taken the same length of time, but some were harder to complete than others so there would be pile-ups of work. It took several weeks to become proficient in any one job and the best way to learn it was to have an experienced operator show you how to do it, how to hold the components, how to move your fingers, and which order to do the different operations so you could cut out unnecessary movements. If you could not keep up with the speed required, you were out. From that bench you could see all 200 staff on main assembly; you could see who was talking to whom, who went to the coffee machine or toilet, and how many times a day they went, who was late. The women were 'doing time'. Much of the language found in these accounts is similar to that used in prisons.

Linhart (1989) worked on the Citroen car assembly line. This time the line appeared to be slow moving and the operators were working at a resigned monotonous pace. The crash of a new car body arriving every three or four minutes marked out the rhythm of the work. Since the work moved, the workers also had to move in order to stay with the car. Each man had a well-defined area for the operations he had to perform, although the boundaries were invisible. If the man worked fast he had a few seconds to spare and could either take a very short break or intensify the effort to 'go up the line' to gain a little more time, working further ahead, outside his normal area, together with the worker at the previous position on the line. Gaining one or two minutes meant that he could smoke a cigarette. If, on the other hand, you worked too slowly, your work slipped back. By the end of the first day Linhart says his limbs were painful and he felt exhausted and anxious due to the repetition of the same movement over and over again. It was not unusual for a new recruit to give up after the first day 'driven mad by the noise, the sparks, the inhuman pressure of speed, the harshness of endlessly repetitive work, the authoritarianism of the bosses and the severity of the orders, the dreary prison-like atmosphere'. After five months in the plant, the management announced that the work shift would be extended by forty-five minutes to ten hours. This provoked a strike where Linhart was one of the organizers. After the strike there was a 'systematic persecution'; the management knew how to make each of the 'hard-liners' give in their notice, and succeeded in doing so.

These writers vividly describe the endless pressure and the continual fear of slipping behind with work. They want to do a good job; the control system hooks the worker into a manic concern for throughput (Littler, 1989). Few aspects of work provide intrinsic satisfaction but individuals become resigned to the daily drudge; these workers would not be in a strong position in a labour market.

Being a Machine Operator and Making Work Manageable

Forty-odd years ago (between 1944 and 1945) Donald Roy worked as a radial drill operator in a factory. He was a secret participant observer particularly interested in restriction of output, why workers did not work harder. Roy (1960) outlines how workers, who are subject to monotonous tasks, make their experiences bearable by adding meaning to their day. Work at the factory was tedious (simple machines operation) and for a twelve-hour day, six days a week. The group in which Roy worked had established a series of events for structuring the day. There was a 'banana time', followed by peach time and coke time. Various pranks were linked with the times. Ditton too (1979) describes the social construction of time and how the workers in a bakery broke the day up into 'digestible fragments to make it psychologically manageable' (1979: 160).

Some writers, following Marx, would argue that workers such as these are being exploited and alienated. There is a fundamental tension between the needs of capital and the needs of labour within capitalist economies. The worker is robbed of part of the value of the labour. 'In reality they (workers) are paid only the equivalent in monetary terms of the value they produce in part of the working day, say five out of eight hours' (Burawoy, 1979: 23). As well as being exploited economically, they are alienated from the products of their labour. Since they do not own or control the products of their labour, their needs and capacities are subordinated to the requirements of capital accumulation. The psychological consequence is that the worker feels a stranger to his or her work (Thompson and McHugh, 1990).

Burawoy (1979) worked as a machine operator at the engine division of Allied Corporation producing, among other things, agricultural equipment. This was the same plant Donald Roy had worked and researched in thirty years before. The central question for Burawoy was 'Why do workers work as hard as they do?' Why did he find himself actively participating in the intensification of his own exploitation and even losing his temper when he couldn't? He describes a series of games the operators played in order to achieve levels of production that earned incentive pay. The rules of the game were experienced as a set of externally imposed relationships, like informal alliances. The art of 'making out' (maximizing bonus pay in a piece-rate system) was to manipulate those relationships with for example, the foreman, superintendent, scheduling man, other operators, or truck drivers to the best of your advantage.

Truck drivers were responsible for bring the stock from the aisles, where it was kept, to the machine. Truck drivers could hold you up considerably if you hadn't befriended them, particularly at the beginning of the shift when they were in great demand. The foreman acted as a referee and expediter in the game of making out. The foreman could point out more efficient set-ups, help make special tools, persuade inspectors to pass work and so on, so the job could be done faster and you could earn more.

The shop-floor culture revolved around making out. Each worker was sucked into a distinctive set of activities and language which went with those activities. The pressure to make out could also lead to conflict between workers. The games workers play are not usually created in opposition to management but emerge out of struggle and bargaining. Management participates in the game by organizing it and enforcing the rules. The game is entered into for its 'relative satisfactions'. The satisfaction of that need reproduces consent and material wealth.

Burawoy (as Jermier *et al.*, 1994: 7 note) did not draw out the implications for understanding shop-floor resistance from this analysis. The game was, though, a way of testing self-esteem in which these factory workers became locked into practices that led to their own exploitation and subordination. Burawoy's account has been critiqued in some detail (Collinson, 1992; Knights, 1990; Thompson, 1990; Willmott, 1990). He is criticized for not investigating workplace subjectivity enough, for example, neglecting gender and sexual identity.

The Games

Burawoy has described the games that workers play as a way of making out and creating space outside managerial surveillance (see also Pahl, 1988). Stewart Clegg (1987) produces an interesting example of 'making out' in the 'inclemency rule'. Clegg worked on a building site. On construction sites in the UK joiners have an agreement that they do not have to work in 'inclement' weather. There is, though, no operational definition of how bad the weather has to be before it is called inclement. One day the worker unit leader decided it was inclement so the workmen downed tools, went to their hut, and brewed tea. After about ten minutes the site foreman came down and asked them to go back to work. It was drizzling lightly with rain. The first time this happened Clegg thought 'OK I know the joiners don't like getting wet and we don't work when it is raining.' But when it happened again a few days later, and the men downed tools, it was hardly raining at all. This went on several times over a period of two or three weeks. Clegg's explanation was that the joiners were using the inclemency rule to put pressure on incompetent managers to organize the job more effectively so that the materials and supplies the joiners needed to do the job were there on time and the joiners could increase their bonus. Since supplies were not arriving, the joiners were taking up slack time for 'inclemency'. They were putting pressure on management to increase control and thus more effectively exploit them.

Class and Gender

Focusing on issues of class and gender at work, Anna Pollert (1981) has described the differing situations and identities of men and women in a cigarette factory in Bristol. She talks about how the women were subject to a double burden of male oppression and capitalist exploitation. Women were pushed down, discriminated against, and unfree, much like blacks, immigrants, and other oppressed groups. She describes, in some detail, the lived experience of factory life and work in the home. The domestic background was a distinctive part of the women workers' consciousness. Women workers are workers in a man's world yet they also create their own. Women remain separate, they import their own world, and maintain a dual existence.

Similarly Westwood (1984) describes how home and work are part of the one world for women working in a company she calls Stitchco. Westwood is an anthropologist and was a participant observer for over a year working with the women on a wide variety of machines producing socks, tights, sweaters, and cardigans. Using a Marxist framework she begins with the point that that these women, formally free labourers, sell their labour power to employers for wages and so enter the world of social production and relations of exploitation in the workplace which give them a class position. But these women were also workers in the home, exploited through the gift of unpaid labour to men who were husbands and fathers. She and Cynthia Cockburn (1983) would argue that the sex-gender system and class structure are two interlocking systems from which women's subordination is generated and reproduced.

Westwood's book examines both the way in which women enter waged employment and become classed subjects and how working makes them a worker and a woman. Shop-floor culture offers, to women at work, a version of woman and they take upon themselves elements of this in ways which tie them more firmly to a 'feminine' destiny and the culture of femininity. Women in the labour market are affected by their domestic lives; being a woman counts. Women of colour are faced with an additional ideological hurdle of racism.

The factory employed over 2,000 workers; women made up nearly two-thirds of these workers. Nearly half the workers were Afro-Caribbean and Asian. The gendered division of labour was clear. While the men were knitters, mechanics, dyers, and top managers, the women worked in the finishing process, in personnel and white-collar jobs. The finishing jobs women did were low paid, repetitive, and based upon dexterity, which is conceived of as a natural attribute, not a skill; they joined fabric together, bar-tacked hems and operated button-sewing machines. A woman might sew side seams all day, every day, for weeks at a time. Unlike the assembly line that controlled the flow of work, the machinist was dependent on the supervisor to bring work to her. This could be an endless source of frustration and aggravation. The individual worker had no control over what she would do but tried to boost her speed on each operation in order to secure the highest rate for the job. The women disliked being moved between jobs but management looked for flexibility in the use of their labour power.

The work was physically tiring, noisy, and monotonous. Illness was a common response to the job. The women were expected to meet targets of production each day and had to work under tremendous pressure to earn a bonus. Monotony was eased though conversation, jokes, fierce quarrels, and passing sweets around. The women's work was domesticated by them. For example they used the phrases 'my machine' and 'my chair', adorned their machines with family photos or a picture of the current heart throb. A common practice was to wear slippers at work. They made aprons from company fabrics to protect their clothing. The aprons were embroidered and edged. These collusive practices reinforced a definition of woman that was securely tied to domestic work in the home. Engagements and weddings were major events to be celebrated by all. Like the women in Anna Pollert's study, these women brought the world of home to work.

The Experience of Catering Work

Researchers argue that little has been written on the class relations at the point of production. Helping redress the balance, like the other researchers in this chapter, Gabriel (1988)
documents working lives in catering. He says that catering workers frequently complain that
they are taken for granted and academic researchers who talk about the 'service sector' rarely
trouble themselves to find out what catering work is like. Even the public with whom the
catering workers come into daily contact seldom seems to register their existence. Work in
hotels and catering differs little in kind and quality from similar work in manufacturing, argues Wood (1992: 16).

Jobs in catering are low paid, have poor job security and union representation, and are
mainly done by part-time employees and women workers. Catering jobs have a sense of subservience which is not associated with other jobs. For many of the ancillary workers Gabriel
interviewed in a hospital kitchen, the job had become a prison; they felt trapped in their job
because they lacked training, because their command of English was limited, or because of
age, nationality, and background. In contrast the cooks in the hospital kitchen did not feel
trapped and expressed pride and achievement in their jobs. But cooks in a cook-freeze
kitchen were far less happy. The kitchen was a faithful adoption of Taylorist principles in
mass catering—splitting cooking from planning, making tasks simple and tightly controlled, and reducing the skill, initiative, and thinking required of cooks to a bare minimum.
There were pockets of resistance; for example, one of the supervisors started cooking curried
and vegetarian meals and used her initiative, ability, and skill. Like the workers in Anna
Pollert's study, domestic responsibilities dominated the women's thinking about work; the
main asset of the job was that the hours of work and holidays fitted with the schools.

The literature does not just document a single researcher's findings though. Wood (1992)
draws on a range of studies in the hotel and catering industry to construct a sociological account of employment there. He argues that the hospitality industry has attracted little research attention compared to manufacturing. Wood aims to relate what is known about
hotel and catering work to wider issues in industrial sociology led trends towards deskilling
and flexible working and trends in industrial conflict. He shows how hotel and catering work
is largely exploitative, degrading, poorly paid, unpleasant, insecure, and taken as a last resort
or because it can be tolerated in the light of family commitments and other constraints.
Some will value and enjoy their work in the industry but they are in the minority. How then
do people cope?

An in-depth study, using participant observation, by Paules (1991) of women who waited
at tables in a family-style restaurant in New Jersey demonstrates how the dictates of management can be resisted. She describes how these women protected and enhanced their position at work while absorbing the abuse of a hurried and often abusive public. The waitress's
subordination to her customers is proclaimed; she is directed to wear a uniform that recalls
a housemaid's dress and is prohibited from eating, drinking, and resting in public view. She
is to address each customer as sir or ma'am while the customers call her by her first name.
The greater part of her income comes from tips, conferred as gifts by strangers, as her wages
are below the national minimum wage. Despite this she is not passive and powerless. She can
boost tip income by increasing the number of customers she serves. This is accomplished by
securing the largest and busiest sets of tables, 'turning' the tables quickly (taking the order,

delivering the food, clearing, and resetting the table as fast as possible), and by controlling the flow of customers through the restaurant. In order to compete effectively with other waitresses, she does not take formal breaks. Waitresses had been known to refuse to serve customers who had not tipped them on an earlier occasion. She can resist the demands of management and customer either silently or with open confrontation.

Working-Class Kids, Working-Class Jobs: The Case of Care Assistants

Why do working-class individuals continue to enter working-class, gender-stereotyped jobs? Why do working-class boys look for heavy manual work (Willis, 1977) and trades like plumber, electrician, and forestry? Why do working-class girls still swarm towards traditional female occupations and rarely, for example, seek training as electricians, joiners, technicians, and computer operators? We might expect that new production patterns, new systems of education and training, coupled with the promise of lifting barriers to opportunity might have dislocated the processes of class and gender reproduction of careers. Yet little has happened to counteract the influence of class, race, and gender on career choice (Cockburn, 1987; Jones and Wallace, 1990; Mirza, 1992).

Bates (1993) explores the experiences of a group of young women who chose jobs in the field of institutional care. Careworkers, like many other female workers, find they are using a wide range of domestic skills. The work can be physically and emotionally demanding, involving a range of tasks from bed making, food serving, bathing, lifting the elderly, sitting with the dying, and laying out the dead. It is low paid and involves long and often socially inconvenient hours of work. Some of the tasks they have to do are stressful and traumatic, like dealing with violence, incontinence, and death. In order to cope they have been found to 'switch off' from their job (Bates, 1993). Swearing and being sworn at, getting a 'belt', and occasionally delivering one, were seen as given parts of a day's round. There was a perpetual tension between caring for and processing people. The limits to the caring came not from the women themselves but from the occupational culture and levels of resourcing. The girls expressed a pride in what they did, how they coped with death and their growing 'toughness' in becoming unflinching in the face of harsh facts of life. The paradox was that, despite the gruelling nature of the work, the girls came to accept it and even became enthusiastic. These jobs were not their initial choices at school (they would have preferred jobs like nursery nurse, beauty therapist, typist) but they failed to gain entry into the relevant courses or jobs so found themselves on a YTS 'Caring' course. The girls changed their definitions of themselves and their approach to the job in order to accommodate it in the light of labour market realities—high unemployment and job scarcity. They were able to challenge feelings of disgust, inferiority, and shame and convert them into feelings of pride and a job 'right for' them. Their family lives had exposed them to experiences such as care of the young or elderly, crowded conditions, demanding physical work, verbal and physical aggression, so they appeared to be the ideal candidates for care jobs.

Why Work at Home—the Experience of Homeworking

What is the reality of homeworking for individuals? Allen and Wolkowitz (1987) showed how it involved long hours, was punctuated by strict deadlines from employers, demanding family members, and was relied upon for a regular household income. A key factor in producing homeworking labour was women's responsibility for unpaid work, looking after young children and elderly relatives, coupled with the ideological constraints affecting women, such as a woman's rightful place is in the home. Racism in the labour market and discrimination against the disabled were other factors producing homeworking.

'Teleworking' has received a good deal of attention in the media. This media preoccupation is directed at largely professional jobs and the more boring data-entry clerk or women preparing your bills do not usually feature in these stories. Teleworking, Huws *et al.* (1990) showed, is only adopted by managers who see it as solving an immediate, concrete problem, such as the retention of valued staff or of cutting costs. The teleworkers do the work for equally practical reasons, such as having no alternative or for child-care reasons. The need to combine work and child-care was primary motive for Huws *et al.*'s predominately European female group. Similarly Christensen (1989) in a US sample of 7,000 women, found that values related to family, work, and money drove the initial decision to work at home. In contrast, Olson's (1989) largely US *male* sample gave work-related reasons. Over 50 per cent said the reason they first decided to work at home was to increase productivity; only 8 per cent said that it was to take care of their family.

Christensen (1989) directly challenges media images of homeworking involving computer-based work as offering freedom and independence. For example, she found that computers are not the central factor in the proliferation of homework; only one in four clerical workers and one in three professional workers were using them. A large number of clerical home-workers had the legal status of independent contractor but worked for only one employer and had little control over the amount and timing of their work. In some cases the women had worked in offices for the same company and the shift to home-based work mean the loss of employees status, rights, and benefits. She also showed that homework did not reconcile the tension between the need to earn money and the need or desire to care for children. The majority of women in the survey did not manage to work when their children were around or awake. Homeworking was stressful and isolating.

Phizacklea and Wolkowitz (1995) provide more recent evidence of the realities of home-working for a sample of thirty white English-speaking and nineteen Asian homeworkers in Coventry. The nine (all white) clerical workers were paid between £2.90 and £3.25 an hour but none of these workers received holiday leave and only one paid National Insurance so was eligible for the state sickness pay scheme. Despite the absence of employment rights, clerical homeworkers' levels of job satisfaction were comparatively high. They had relatively high earnings for homework, relatively low hours, and little variation in the flow of work.

The forty manual homeworkers in the survey were sewing or knitting machinists, dress-making, doing other forms of assembly and packing, or childminding. Manual homework was found to be sharply divided along ethnic lines. All the clothing assembly was done by Asian women. Fifteen of the nineteen Asian women either assembled whole garments or stitched pieces such as collars and cuffs; hourly earnings varied between 75p and £3.50. The white manual homeworkers were spread over a larger range of occupations, worked shorter hours than the Asian women, and had slightly higher average hourly earnings. The cultural stereotype is of Asian women homeworkers who work at home because their husbands want them to, so it was interesting that only 10 per cent of the Asian women said they preferred to work at home.

Further research showed how female homeworkers were segregated into female occupational ghettos; few women would be able to use homework as a way out. These workers did not have much access to the assistance offered to the self-employed. Perceptions of the disadvantages of homeworking were widely shared; there were more responses to the question about disadvantages of homeworking than advantages. The disadvantages included the low or unpredictable earnings, work-related health problems, and the inconvenience of working at home.

What then can we conclude about the view from below? The first point is that it is worth researching and understanding in order to gain insight into how employees feel and think about work. How they feel and react will be shaped by the context and content of what is being resisted so the nature of resistance will vary across space and time. The second is that most employees are not class-conscious revolutionaries about to overthrow managerial ownership or control. Nor are they passive docile automatons. What about the view from above, what is managerial work like? This is the subject of the next chapter.

Questions for Further Research

1. Burawoy says that the 'game' metaphor is more than an explanation; it is also a tool of critique (1979: 92). Discuss.

2. According to Burawoy, how does the capitalist labour process 'manufacture consent'?

3. What is the critique of Burawoy's account of worker subjectivity? (see Collinson, 1992; Knights, 1990; Thompson, 1990, Wilmott, 1990)?

4. Marx sees it as 'man's nature' to be 'his' own creator. Discuss (see du Gay, 1996: 11–15).

5. Hakim (1991) argues that women, particularly homeworkers, who willingly marry and accept the authority of husbands who have traditional views of women, should take the blame for their poor situation in the labour market. Some women gratefully accept slave status. Phizacklea and Wolkowitz (1995) argue against this view. How do both sides present the argument and with whom would you agree?

6. Anna Pollert (1981) asks 'Does it make any difference being a woman worker? Is work seen or felt differently from a man?' How does she answer these questions?

7. How does Westwood describe the linkages between home life and work in the factory?

8. Phizacklea and Wolkowitz (1995) say that researching homeworking is hard to do. Why?

9. How widespread is the 'electronic cottage' and does it offer increased autonomy or greater control over work? (See Huws *et al.*, 1990; Phizacklea and Wolkowitz, 1995; and other sources.)

10. What autonomy is to be found in waitressing work (see Paules, 1991, and other sources you can find)?

11. Hassard (1996) shows how important time is in the studies by Roy, Ditton, and Cavendish. Why is time so important?

12. How would you explain how working-class kids continue to get working-class jobs (see Bates, 1991; Mirza, 1992; Willis, 1977)? Why is it so inevitable? Can you find any research which demonstrates that this process is not inevitable?

Suggestions for Further Reading

Burawoy, M. (1979) *Manufacturing Consent: Changes in the Labour Process under Monopoly Capitalism*. Chicago: University of Chicago Press.

Cockburn, C. (1983) *Brothers: Male Dominance and Technological Change*. London: Pluto Press.

Littler, C. (1989) *The Experience of Work*. Milton Keynes: Open University Press.

Pahl, R. E. (1988) *On Work, Thirty Years of Making Out*. Oxford: Basil Blackwell, ch. 8 by M. Burawoy.

Westwood, S. (1984) *All Day Every Day: Factory and Family in the Making of Women's Lives*. London: Pluto Press.

Class Exercise

Divide the class up into small groups. Ask each individual to describe a job they have done using headings such as: features of the job I liked, features I disliked, the effect that the job had, what I learnt from doing that job.

References

Allen, S., and Wolkowitz, C. (1987) *Homeworking: Myths and Realities*. London: Macmillan.

Bates, I. (1991) 'Closely Observed Training: An Exploration of Links Between Social Structures, Training and Identity', *International Studies of Sociology of Education*, 1: 225–43.

—— (1993) 'A Job which is "Right for Me"? Social Class, Gender and Individualization', in I. Bates and G. Riseborough (eds.), *Youth and Inequality*. Buckingham: Open University Press, ch. 1.

Bottomore, T., and Rubel, M. (1963) *Karl Marx: Selected Writings in Sociology and Social Philosophy*. Harmondsworth: Penguin.

Burawoy, M. (1979) *Manufacturing Consent: Changes in the Labour Process under Monopoly Capitalism*. Chicago: University of Chicago Press.

Cavendish, R. (1989) 'Women on the Line', in C. Littler (ed.), *The Experience of Work*. Milton Keynes: Open University Press, ch. 8.

Christensen, K. (1989) 'Home Based Clerical Work: No Simple Truth, No Simple Reality', in E. Boris and C. Daniels (eds.), *Homework: Historical and Contemporary Perspectives on Paid Labour at Home*. Chicago: University of Illinois Press.

Clegg, S. (1987) 'The Language of Power and the Power of Language', *Organization Studies*, 8/1: 61–70.

Cockburn, C. (1983) *Brothers: Male Dominance and Technological Change*. London: Pluto Press.

—— (1987) *Two-Track Training: Sex Inequalities and the YTS*. London: Macmillan.

Collinson, D. L. (1992) *Managing the Shopfloor: Subjectivity, Masculinity and Workplace Culture*. Berlin: De Gruyter.

Ditton, J. (1979) 'Baking Time', *Sociological Review*, 27: 157–67.

Du Gay, P. (1996) *Consumption and Identity at Work*. London: Sage.

Gabriel, Y. (1988) *Working Lives in Catering*. London: Routledge and Kegan Paul.

Grey, C. (1996) 'Towards a Critique of Managerialism: The Contribution of Simone Weil', *Journal of Management Studies*, 33/5: 591–611.

Hakim, C. (1991) 'Grateful Slaves and Self-Made Women: Fact and Fantasy in Women's Work Orientations', *European Sociological Review*, 7/2 (Sept.): 101–21.

Hamper, B. (1992) *Rivethead: Tales from the Assembly Line*. London: Fourth Estate.

Hassard, J. (1996) 'Images of Time in Work and Organization', in S. Clegg, C. Hardy, and W. R. Nord (eds.), *Handbook of Organization Studies*. London: Sage, ch. 3.5.

Huws, U., Korte, V., and Robinson, S. (1990) *Telework: Towards the Elusive Office*. Chichester: Wiley.

Jermier, J. M., Knights, D., and Nord, W. R. (1994) 'Resistance and Power in Organizations: Agency, Subjectivity and the Labour Process', in J. Jermier, D. Knights and W. R. Nord (eds.), *Introduction to Resistance and Power in Organizations*. London: Routledge, pp. 1–24.

Jones, G., and Wallace, C. (1990) 'Beyond Individualization: What Sort of Social Change?', in L. Chisholm *et al.* (eds.), *Childhood, Youth and Social Change*. Lewes: Falmer Press.

Knights, D. (1990) 'Subjectivity, Power and the Labour Process', in D. Knights and H. Wilmott (eds.), *Labour Process Theory*. London: Macmillan, ch. 10.

Linhart, R. (1989) 'The Assembly Line', in C. Littler (ed.), *The Experience of Work*. Milton Keynes: Open University Press.

Littler, C. (1989) 'Introduction: The Texture of Work', in C. Littler (ed.), *The Experience of Work*. Milton Keynes: Open University Press.

Mirza, H. (1992) *Young, Female and Black*. London: Routledge.

Olson, M. (1989) 'Organizational Barriers to Professional Telework', in E. Boris and C. Daniels (eds.), *Homework: Historical and Contemporary Perspectives on Paid Labour at Home*. Chicago: University of Illinois Press.

Paules, G. F. (1991) *Dishing it Out: Power and Resistance among Waitresses in a New Jersey Restaurant*. Philadelphia: Temple University Press.

Pahl, R. E. (1988) *On Work, Thirty Years of Making Out*. Oxford: Basil Blackwell, ch. 8 by M. Burawoy.

Phizacklea, A., and Wolkowitz, C. (1995) *Homeworking Women: Gender, Racism and Class at Work*. London: Sage.

Pollert, A. (1981) *Girls, Wives and Factory Lives*. London: Macmillan.

Roy, D. (1960) 'Banana Time: Job Satisfaction and Informal Interaction', *Human Organization*, 18: 156–68; repr. in J. Hassard (ed.), *The Sociology of Time*. London: Macmillan, ch. 9.

Thompson, P. (1990) 'Crawling from the Wreckage: The Labour Process and the Politics of Production', in D. Knights and H. Wilmott (eds.), *Labour Process Theory*. London: Macmillan.

—— and McHugh, D. (1990) *Work Organizations*. Basingstoke: Macmillan.

Weil, S. (1987) *Formative Writings 1929–1941*. London: Routledge.

Westwood, S. (1984) *All Day Every Day: Factory and Family in the Making of Women's Lives*. London: Pluto Press.

Willis, P. (1977) *Learning to Labour*. Farnborough: Saxon House.

Willmott, H. (1990) 'Subjectivity and the Dialectics of Praxis: Opening the Core of Labour Process Analysis', in D. Knights and H. Wilmott (eds.), *Labour Process Theory*. London: Macmillan.

Wood, R. C. (1992) *Working in Hotels and Catering*. London: Routledge.

5

The View from Above:
Managers—What they Do and
How their Work is Described

IN ALL SOCIETIES people are involved in the complex and demanding work of organizing their lives, accomplishing ordinary tasks, and maintaining routines. We all manage; we manage our resources, our time, and sometimes others, but we are not called managers. Those who are called managers will be experts who are trained and employed to shape, organize, and regulate. They will be managing large, medium-sized and small production or service organizations—stores, hospitals, hotels, factories, voluntary organizations, cooperatives—so the job of manager will differ from organization to organization. Many people are managers without having the title of manager, for example nursing administrators, farmers, headteachers, prison governors, and bishops are all managers of people and resources. All are vested with formal authority within their organizations. Management is about having power and control over people while achieving a measure of voluntary compliance from them.

How then is management defined? Management can be defined as 'mental (thinking, intuiting, feeling) work performed by people in an Organizational context' (Kast and Rosenzweig, 1985). Stewart defines management as a level, a position of superordination above foreman and above first-level supervision (Stewart, 1994: 2). It is power and social context that differentiate managers from non-managers. As Grint (1995) notes, what managers do is little different from what anyone might do, but the context within which the act of management occurs differentiates the manager from the non-manager.

Henri Fayol, a French businessman, was one of first managers (along with others like Gulick and Urwick, 1937) to use his experience to theorize about the manager's job, to generalize about all managerial work (Fayol, 1949). He did this by describing the functions that all managers perform. They plan, organize, motivate, control, and coordinate. This very clear-cut traditional account of what managers do can still be found in current management textbooks. This view gives us the theory but is the everyday reality of what managers do like this?

Stewart (1994) believes that research to discover what managers actually did began in earnest in the 1950s, with a study by Carlson (1951) of the work of seven Swedish and two French executives over a four-week period. Managers are described as reactive socializers, not machine-like decision-makers, who, in Grint's (1995: 48) words 'fought fires with words and networks of colleagues and subordinates'.

Henry Mintzberg (1975) theorized having observed five chief executives work for a week. In *Mintzberg on Management* (1989) he describes how he used a stopwatch (much as Frederick Taylor had done before him) to observe in the course of one intensive week the activities of five chief executives of a major consulting firm, a well-known teaching hospital, a school system, a high technology firm, and a manufacturer of consumer goods. He says that if you ask a manager what they do they will most likely tell you that they plan, organize, coordinate, and control, giving you a traditional account in Fayol's terms. But if you watch them, do not be surprised if you cannot relate what you see to those four words. Where would the activity of presenting a gold watch to a retiring employee fit into those four Fayol categories, for example?

There are four myths, Mintzberg says, about managers' jobs which do not bear up under scrutiny:

1. The manager is a reflective, systematic planner.
2. The effective manager has no regular duties to perform.
3. The senior manager needs aggregated information which a formal management information system best provides.
4. Management is becoming a science and a profession.

Evidence suggests that managers work at an unrelenting pace. The work is characterized by brevity. For example half the activities engaged in by the five chief executives Mintzberg studied lasted less than nine minutes and only 10 per cent exceeded one hour. It is also characterized by variety and discontinuity. Chief executives are strongly oriented to action and dislike reflective activities. There are a number of regular duties to perform including negotiating, ceremonies (like presiding at special dinners), processing information that connects the organization with its environment. Managers favour telephone calls and meetings, not formal information systems. In two British studies, for example, managers spent an average of 66 and 80 per cent of their time in oral communication. This helps explain, at least in part, why managers are reluctant to delegate tasks—most of the important information they carry is in their heads and has not been recorded. Managers certainly do not, in Mintzberg's view, practise a science. They seek information by word of mouth, rely on what they call judgement and intuition and what Mintzberg would call ignorance. As a result the job of a manager is enormously difficult and complicated. They are overburdened yet cannot delegate. They are forced, then, to do tasks superficially. Scientific attempts to improve managerial work are impossible.

Mintzberg defines the manager as a person in charge of an organization or one of its subunits, which can include bishops, prime ministers, and vice-presidents. What all these people have in common is that they have all been vested with formal authority over the unit. From formal authority comes status which leads to various interpersonal relations. From these comes access to information. Information is used to make decisions and strategy. As a result of looking at managerial work and describing it, Mintzberg distinguishes between three main roles the manager plays: in interpersonal aspects, receiving and disseminating information (as a nerve centre for information), and as decision-maker. These three roles were then divided into ten subdivisions.

INTERPERSONAL ROLES	INFORMATIONAL ROLES	DECISIONAL ROLES
Figurehead	Monitor	Entrepreneur
Leader	Disseminator	Disturbance Handler
Liaison	Spokesperson	Resource Allocator
		Negotiator

As figurehead there are duties of a ceremonial nature like meeting local dignitaries. As the persons in charge, managers are responsible for the work of the people in their unit so are leaders. As a liaison they are making contact outside their vertical chain of command, spending as much time with peers and others outside their units (e.g. clients, suppliers, government officials) as with their own subordinates.

Due to interpersonal contact with those below in the hierarchy and a network of contacts, the manager is at the nerve centre of their unit. They will not know everything but will typically know more than their subordinates. This information needs to be processed. As a monitor they scan their environment for information (including gossip and speculation).

They share and distribute this information in the disseminator role. In their role as spokesman (Mintzberg doesn't use inclusive language) managers send some of their information to people outside their units, for example to consumer groups.

The manager also plays a major role in decision-making. As entrepreneur they seek to improve the unit and adapt it to changes in the environment. They seek and initiate new ideas. Some of the chief executives Mintzberg studied have as many as fifty development projects running at any one time. In the role of disturbance handler they are responding to pressures e.g. if a strike looms or if a major customer is declared bankrupt. They decide what resources go where, as resource allocator and as negotiator they find negotiations a way of life.

These roles are not easily separated and form an integrated whole. No role can be pulled out with the job left intact. Mintzberg believes that this description of managerial work should be more important to managers than any prescription that can be offered. Managers' effectiveness is significantly influenced by insight into their own work. Their performance is dependent on how well they understand and respond to the pressures and dilemmas of the job they do. Managers are challenged systematically to share their privileged information with subordinates, to step back to see the broader picture on offer, and to make use of analytical inputs. They need to control their time carefully.

Kotter (1982) conducted a detailed analysis of what twenty general managers did and how they spent their time. He compared his data with those of Mintzberg in the US (1975) and Stewart (1979) in the UK. All three agree that managers' work is largely reactive rather than proactive and is varied, fragmented and frequently interrupted. This research gives a different picture of the hectic day that contrasts with the theorist's view of a manager who plans, organizes and controls. The research also shows how important interpersonal skills are for managers. Successful managers spend time establishing informal networks, creating or being involved in cooperative relationships with people. Most managers spend three-quarters or more of their time with others (Stewart, 1997). The emphasis is on frenetic, disjointed activity, using informal methods of disseminating and collecting information, and a realization of the paramount importance of people skills. As Alimo-Metcalfe (1992) notes, these skills are difficult to measure and simulate in situation where you wish to judge if a manager has these skills. Equally difficult to measure are the necessary political skills. Studies of British and American managers have shown how they spent nearly all of their time with other people, trying to find out what is happening, trying to persuade others to cooperate, and less often trying to decide what ought to be done. They need to know how to trade, bargain and compromise. The more senior they are, the more political will be the world in which they live (Stewart, 1997).

Studies have repeatedly shown that managerial activity is high on oral communication (see also Kanter, 1977). Gowler and Legge (1996) go beyond this assertion to say that such verbal activity involves the use of rhetoric, that is the use of a form of word delivery which is lavish in symbolism and involves several layers or textures of meaning. Managers use a rhetoric of bureaucratic control that is highly expressive, constructing and legitimizing managerial perogative in terms of a rational, goal-directed image of organizational effectiveness. This rhetoric is political. Not only do managers spend most of their time talking, they generate a culture, in an anthropological sense, which is maintained and transmitted from one generation to another. Meaning may be generated through rituals, myths, magic, totemism, and taboo, in the same way as is documented in distant cultures by social anthropologists. This talk, especially the rhetoric, may be the way in which social control is maintained.

The issue of social control arises again when we look at the hours managers are required to work. Pahl (1995) notes the consistent patterns of long work hours and few holidays which characterize managerial work. Watson's (1994) participant observation study of managers shows how long work hours, especially in the evening, were seen as a measure of commitment to the organization. Male managers in particular deliberately stayed at work late in the evening, wasted time, artificially extended meetings ,and criticized managers who left at 7.15 p.m. Similarly Coyle (1995) notes the long hours mangers worked in the five UK organizations where she conducted research (see Collinson and Collinson, 1997). Surveys have shown how mangers are working increasingly long hours. Austin Knight UK (1995) found that 45 per cent of senior male managers said they were working more than fifty hours a week. An Institute of Management survey (1995) showed that 60 per cent of respondents stated that their workload had 'greatly increased' over the past two years. The Institute's 1996 survey showed that 80 per cent of respondents confirmed an increase in their workload over the past year. As a result most were experiencing signs of stress. Many managers now experience job insecurity and uncertainty. Fear of redundancy can create an imperative to appear visibly committed to the job to maximize limited promotion opportunities. Such presenteeism has been found to be highly gendered—it is more likely to be recognised by women but practised by men (Simpson, 1998).

While many similarities can be found in managerial jobs, there can also be differences. Kotter (1982) found the jobs of the general managers he studied differed. He also found that managers did their jobs differently, as also noted by Stewart (1982) who showed how each manager does his or her job in their own way, choosing, for example, to be outward focused, spending much time with people outside the organization building business, or inward looking, spending most of their time developing relations with and managing their own staff. Johnson and Gill (1993) believe that there is little consensus about what managers' everyday activities are. This is made worse because management is not an undifferentiated, homogeneous occupational group. But there must be some consensus to be found. Grint (1995) concludes that in Britain, at least, management seems to be mainly concerned with talk and manic attempts to stamp out numerous 'fires'. They dash from one emergency to the next, resolving short-term problems and crises whilst keeping production going. The typical manager's day involves 'keeping the show on the road, and managing to keep one's head above water when all around are losing theirs to stress' (1995: 66).

Drucker (1989) does not describe what the manager does but describes what a manager should do. He says, for example that managers should put economic performance first, as they can only justify their existence and authority by economic results. The ultimate test of management is business performance. Their second function is to make a productive enterprise out of human and material resources; the transmutation of resources requires management. The third and final function of management is to manage workers and work. In practice managers discharge these three functions in every action. His is a very practical approach to management, a guide for those working in management.

In a similar prescriptive vein, Kanter (1987) examined the conditions that support innovation and change, coupled with the experiences and activities of the innovators that bring this about. She looked at how people acquire and use power in empowering organizations and how this contributes to innovation and the mastery of change. She used ten core research companies and found that to manage effectively, corporate entrepreneurs need to work through participative teams to produce small changes that will add up later to big ones.

They need 'power skills' to persuade others to invest information, support, and resources in new initiatives driven by an entrepreneur. They need the ability to manage the problems associated with the greater use of teams and participation and an understanding of how change is designed and constructed in an organization.

A power approach to manager and management would say that the distinguishing feature of the professions is their ability to gain societal recognition as professions. This approach emerges from the Chicago School of symbolic interactionists who argue that professions are essentially the same as other occupations. There is no precise and unique definition of professions; it is just a title claimed by certain occupations at certain points in time. Professional rewards are sufficient for people to want and to strive for professional status.

Has there been a revolution in management and what interests do managers serve? Some, like Burnham (1945), have argued that a managerial revolution has come about. Specialist knowledge and skills of managerial experts have become crucial to the successful running of increasingly large and complex businesses and bureaucracies. The dominance of owners of wealth is undermined and a new class of professional salaried managers exercises control. The counter-argument is that the criteria of performance under which managers operate are oriented to ownership interest. The more successful managers tend to be those who internalize profit-oriented values and priorities. Corporate profits are prerequisites for high managerial income and status (Zeitlin, 1989). The ownership of wealth and control of work are closely related; both managers and owners play their parts in the same 'constellations of interest' (Scott, 1979; see also Watson, 1997).

We saw earlier how Mintzberg questions the view that management is becoming a profession. Is it a profession now? What would the characteristics of a profession be? The taxonomic approach would say that a profession possesses specialized skills, the necessity of intellectual and practical training, and the perceived collective responsibility for maintaining the integrity of the profession as a whole via a professional body (see Dietrich and Roberts, 1997: 23). This is done through, for example, barriers to entry and occupational closure.

STOP | Does management have these attributes?

Is management a profession? During the 1980s British management education and training became a matter for public concern, debate, and action as a number of reports (Constable and McCormick, 1987; Handy, 1987; Mangham and Silver, 1986) showed that the range and quality of provision of education and training fell well below that of America, Europe, and Japan (Reed and Anthony, 1992). British management was, in some areas, a 'spurious elite' (Handy *et al.*, 1988: 168). British managers were embedded in a centuries-old technique and culture of rule which emphasized stability at the expense of innovation and compromise at the expense of confrontation (Fox, 1983: 33). They seemed to lack the entrepreneurial zeal and basic technical competence of managerial elites in other countries. British management relied on a model of status rather than occupational professionalism. They lacked developmental, educational and training opportunities. While other professionals, in law, medicine, accountancy, and architecture, for example, spent up to seven years in apprenticeship and further study, British managers did nothing to apply the procedures of professionalism to management. As the practice of management is so diversified and bereft of occupational organization and control, they cannot generate effective professional authority and closure.

Management and Men

It is interesting to note (as Collinson and Hearn, 1996 have done) how Mintzberg uses 'manager' and 'he' interchangeably; he remains silent about the inherently gendered assumptions he makes about management. Drucker does the same. His book *The Practice of Management* (1989) is aimed 'at being a guide for men in major management positions . . . For younger men in management—and for men who plan to make management their career' (1989: preface). What does this tell us about who should be successful in management?

Most managers are men and men are associated with organizational power, yet male domination of management is a subject which has received little scrutiny (Collinson and Hearn, 1996). Management has been portrayed as a masculine concept, about controlling, taking charge, and directing. Journalistic profiles of male executives and 'captains of industry' present heroic macho images emphasizing struggle, battle, a willingness to be ruthless, brutal, a rebellious nature, and an aggressive, rugged individualism (Neale, 1995). Managers were frequently depicted as masculine, abrasive, and highly autocratic 'hard men' who insisted on the 'divine right of managers to manage' (Purcell, 1982).

> **STOP** Is this inevitable? Does management need to be dominated by men? See Collinson and Hearn (1996) and Wensley (1996).

Kanter (1977) has studied men and women in management. She notes how the 'masculine ethic' can be identified as part of the early image of managers in the writings of Taylor, Weber, and Chester Barnard. This masculine ethic elevates the traits assumed to belong to some men to necessities for effective management: a tough-minded approach to problems, analytic abilities to abstract and plan, a capacity to set aside personal, emotional considerations in the interests of task accomplishment, and a cognitive superiority in problem-solving and decision-making. These characteristics supposedly belonged to men, but then, practically, all managers were men. However, when women tried to enter management jobs, the masculine ethic was invoked as an exclusionary principle.

Middle Management

There are some gloomy views of middle management. There are a number of reasons why middle managers may be frustrated disillusioned individuals, according to Dopson and Stewart (1990).

1. They are in the middle of a long hierarchy and may have been bypassed by top management's efforts to increase employee involvement.
2. They have to cope with conflicting expectations of those above and below them in the

hierarchy. They are squeezed between the demands of the strategies they cannot influence and the ambitions of independent-minded employees (Kanter, 1986). They can get caught in crossfire between departments and customers or suppliers.

3. They have lost technical expertise to administrative tasks.
4. There is career disillusionment among middle managers. They can no longer expect lifetime careers, they express frustration, dissatisfaction, and powerlessness; their numbers have been cut in large companies in response to increased competition and the need for flatter hierarchies. Some commentators have talked about the 'end of the career' in management (Handy, 1989; Osterman, 1996).

This gloomy view is counteracted by a number of writers who show that information technology has led to a reshaping of middle managers' role rather than to its decline. For example, Dopson and Stewart (1990) found that a smaller number of middle managers had a greater responsibility for a wider range of duties for which they were clearly accountable. They were described as more important than in the past because they are in slimmer flatter organizations, have more responsibility, and are seen by top management as having a major role in implementing change. Most managers were positive about the changes and how their jobs had changed. Middle managers found themselves closer to top management and strategic decisions. They had their own clear area of responsibility with more control over resources and could more legitimately take decisions within their own areas. The traditional career model for managers has to be revised (McGovern *et al.*, 1998).

The Reality for the Woman Manager

Women managers experience unique sources of stress related to their minority status and gender; these pressures result in higher levels of overall occupational stress compared to their male counterparts (Davidson, 1996; Davidson and Cooper, 1992). Women managers experience strain coping with discrimination, prejudice, and sex stereotyping; there is a lack of role models, they feel isolated, they have to cope with being the 'token woman' and with higher work/home conflicts.

> **STOP** When I talk to male and female students about the prejudice faced by women at work, they tend to deny that this is the case. Why do you think this is so?

Since the 1980s there has been talk of a glass ceiling preventing women managers progressing. Lack of family-friendly employment policies, poor access to training, the pattern of career development, and informal barriers contribute to this glass ceiling. Gregg and Machin (1993) note that only 8 per cent of top UK executives are female and the number of females drops dramatically as you move to the top of the hierarchy. A survey of British management salaries (Institute of Management, 1994) recorded a fall in the number of women managers from 10.2 per cent in 1993 to 9.8 per cent in 1994. This downward trend has also been noted in the USA, other countries in Europe, and in Australia (Fagenson, 1993). Women managers earn less than men in the same jobs, with the largest pay gaps found at the extreme top of the hierarchies.

Wajcman (1996) studied the attitudes and experiences of men and women managers and showed how women who made it into senior positions were in most respects indistinguishable from men in equivalent positions. They had similar backgrounds, attitudes, and worked the same long hours. However, this was not enough to guarantee success as their career progression was still blocked. The most commonly cited barrier was the senior management 'club', the prejudice of colleagues, lack of career guidance, and family commitments. She concludes that it is men who have the power to define what constitutes occupational success and men who dominate it.

Double Jeopardy—the Reality for the Black and Ethnic Minority Woman Manager

The American literature on women managers has been accused of making African-American women managers invisible (Nkomo, 1988). The double jeopardy faced by African-American women managers helps secure their position at the very bottom of the managerial hierarchy. In the US white women hold 38 per cent of the executive administrative and managerial positions while women 'of color' represent only 5 per cent (Hite, 1996).

If you are young, female, and black in Britain the chances are slim that you will find a job to reflect your academic ability or potential (Mirza, 1992). Ethnic minority women are under-represented in the professional field compared to white women (Bhavnani, 1994). Yet little research has been devoted to the plight of the black and ethnic manager woman in Britain (Davidson, 1997). Davidson, in her study of thirty black and ethnic minority managers, shows how these women face the double negative effects of sexism and racism. These women had fewer, if any, role models and were more likely to feel isolated. They had to contend with stereotypical images based on gender and ethnic origin and were more likely to experience performance pressure. As one noted 'I feel under enormous pressure to perform well. White people always seem to be looking to me to fail. If I fail, though, I let down all black women' (1997: 46). They have greater home/social/work conflicts, particularly with regards to the family and black community. As a result, 80 per cent reported negative psycho-social and health outcomes which were related to sexism and racism at work.

> **STOP** How often have you opened a book on management and seen any reference to race?

Bhavanani (1994) notes how there is some evidence from local government which suggests that the segregated patterns of black women's professional areas actually block access into senior management positions. For example, black women in education were given opportunities to use their background as relevant experience but when they attempted to move out of these areas their work experience become a barrier to parity of status. There is also evidence that black staff employed at managerial level in local government are primarily recruited for directing services towards black users. There may then be new forms of resegregation emerging.

Similarly, racism is likely to be experienced by black male managers, yet there is little research evidence on this. There have been attacks on the army and prison service recently for discriminating on grounds of race. There are, for example, only nine black prison officers in the grade of principal officer in Britain's gaols yet one in five inmates are from ethnic minorities. Of more than 28,000 officers only 2.5 per cent are from ethnic minorities and only six are at junior governor level. (*Observer*, 10 August 1997).

Hotel Management

Hotel management: is it the same as or different from other management? Research into the occupation of hotel management is fairly recent, most taking place in the 1980s. Hotel management has been found to be notoriously insular (Wood, 1992: 80). Those training in hotel and catering management are generally separated off from those studying management or business. Hotel and catering trainees are usually required to do periods of industrial placement as a form of pre-entry socialization. Two-thirds of hotel managers have been found to have had no work experience outside the hotel industry (Baum, 1989; Guerrier, 1987). Formal qualifications do not seem to affect the position on entry, promotion prospects, or career patterns, for example most managers find themselves in very junior positions at first in spite of qualifications. Most managers will have to move jobs in order to gain experience of specific functions and different types of hotels.

Hotel managers engaged in a larger number of activities than their counterparts in other industries, saw less of their peers, and were rarely involved in group situations. They spent less time alone because of time spent directly supervising staff and due to customer contact. Generally they dislike sitting behind a desk and see the important job as being out and about in the hotel. Like other managers they work long hours. In Mintzberg's terms, hotel managers place emphasis on leadership and entrepreneurial roles (Wood, 1992).

Managers in luxury international hotels are required to deliver a highly standardized service, controlled and maintained with the help of volumes of operating manuals. Coupled with this they need to provide an 'authentic' (non-routinized and individualized) service in a variety of cultural contexts to gain competitive advantage (Jones *et al.*, 1997). How do they ensure that rules are followed, standards maintained, staff act consistently, yet provide a non-routinized and individualized service? Various methods are used which include customer feedback and careful selection and training of employees who have internalized 'appropriate' corporately determined values. Well trained, socialized and informed employees can be empowered to make good decisions. Jones *et al.* (1997) give us the case of 'Americo', a multinational hospitality company. Here empowered employees are asked to 'do whatever it takes' to ensure that every guest leaves satisfied. The company advertises this aim by showing a waiter on night duty driving round town to find a favourite night-time drink and a porter retracing a guest's journey on a tram to retrieve a lost wallet. But creating these empowered employees was not a simple task for managers if employees had already been socialized to accept a more directive management style or where employees felt they were being asked to take on duties that managers were paid to have. Empowerment also meant less need for as many layers of management so some lost their jobs.

Managers are always faced with dilemmas, for example like the ones posed here by the need to standardize and customize, control and empower. For managers then there is no best way to manage, 'only partial routes to failure' (Hyman, 1987: 30). Managers face complexities in their social and organizational worlds. With management we have a highly structured order permeated by relational networks that, in Reed's (1989: 93) words, 'simultaneously sustain undermine the viability of the former'. Whether managers are able or willing to overcome the obstacles that stand in the way of constructing a more meaningful and satisfactory work environment remains to be seen.

Questions for Further Research

1. Middle management work is a moving, complex picture. How can it best be researched?

2. How rational is management (see Grint, 1995)?

3. What are the differences in the findings from Stewart, Kotter, and Mintzberg on what managers do?

4. How would you decide on the attributes of a successful manager in any job?

5. There is an abundance of contradictions to be found in the culture of organizations. How does Aktouf (1996) describe the contradictions he found and what examples have you seen in your own experience?

6. What is it about management behaviour that makes it masculine? What are the parallels to be found in shop-floor behaviour (see Collinson, 1992)?

7. How do men master themselves (see Hollway, 1996)?

8. 'Representing management as a predominantly technical activity creates an illusion of neutrality' (Alvesson and Wilmott, 1996: 12). Discuss.

Suggestions for Further Reading

Reed, M. (1989) *The Sociology of Management*. London: Harvester Wheatsheaf.

Thompson, P., and McHugh, D. (1995) *Work Organizations: A Critical Approach*. Basingstoke: Macmillan, ch. 4.

References

Aktouf, O. (1996) 'Competence, Symbolic Activity and Promotability', in S. Linstead, R. Grafton Small, and P. Jeffcutt (eds.), *Understanding Management*. London: Sage, ch. 4.

Alimo-Metcalfe, B. (1992) 'Different Gender—Different Rules', in P. Barrar and C. L. Cooper (eds.), *Managing Organizations*. London: Routledge, ch. 11.

Alvesson, M., and Wilmott, H. (1996) *Making Sense of Management: A Critical Introduction*. London: Sage.

Austin Knight UK (1995) *The Family Friendly Workplace*. London: Austin Knight.

Baum, T. (1989) 'Managing Hotels in Ireland: Research and Development for Change', *International Journal of Hospitality Management*, 8/2: 131–44.

Bhavnani, R. (1994) *Black Women in the Labour Market: A Research Review*. Manchester: Equal Opportunities Commission.

Burnham, J. (1945) *The Managerial Revolution*. Harmondsworth: Penguin.

Carlson, S. (1951) Executive Behaviour: *A Study of the Workload and Working Methods of Managing Directors*. Stockholm: Strombergs.

Collinson, D. L. (1992) *Managing the Shopfloor: Subjectivity, Masculinity and Workplace Culture*. Berlin: De Gruyter.

—— and Collinson, M. (1997) 'Delayering Managers: Time-Space Surveillance and its Gendered Effects', *Organization*, 4/3: 375–407.

—— and Hearn, J. (1996) (eds.) M*en as Managers, Managers as Men*. London: Sage.

Constable, J., and McCormick, R. (1987) *The Making of British Managers*. London: British Institute of Management.

Coyle, A. (1995) *Women and Organizational Change*, Research Discussion Series,14. Manchester: Equal Opportunities Commission.

Davidson, M. J. (1996) 'Women in Employment', in P. Warr (ed.), *Psychology at Work*. London: Penguin.

—— (1997) *The Black and Ethnic Minority Woman Manager: Cracking the Concrete Ceiling*. London: Paul Chapman.

—— and Cooper, C. L. (1992) *Shattering the Glass Ceiling: The Woman Manager*. London: Paul Chapman.

Dietrich, M., and Roberts, J. (1997) 'Beyond the Economics of Professionalism', in J. Broadbent, M. Dietrich and J. Roberts (eds.),*The End of the Professions? The Restructuring of Professional Work*. London: Routledge, ch. 2.

Dopson, S., and Stewart, R. (1990) 'What is Happening to Middle Management?', *British Journal of Management*, 1: 3–16.

Drucker, P. F. (1989) *The Practice of Management*. Oxford: Heinemann Professional Publishing.

Fagenson, E. (1993) (ed.) *Women in Management*. Newbury Park, Calif.: Sage.

Fayol, H. (1949) *General and Industrial Management*. London: Pitman.

Fox, A. (1983) 'British Management and Industrial Relations: The Social Origins of a System', in M. Earl (ed.), *Perspectives on Management*. Oxford: Oxford University Press.

Gowler, D., and Legge, K. (1996) 'The Meaning of Management and the Management of Meaning', in S. Linstead, R. Grafton Small and P. Jeffcutt (eds.), *Understanding Management*. London: Sage, ch. 2.

Gregg, P., and Machin, S. (1993) *Is the Glass Ceiling Cracking? Gender Compensation Differentials and Access to Promotion Among UK Executives*, National Institute of Economic and Social Research, Discussion Paper 50. London: NIESR.

Grint, K. (1995) *Management: A Sociological Introduction*. Cambridge: Polity.

Guerrier, Y. (1987) 'Hotel Managers' Careers and their Impact on Hotels in Britain', *International Journal of Hospitality Management*, 6/3: 121–30.

Gulick, L., and Urwick, L. (1937) *Papers on the Science of Administration*. New York: Columbia University Press.

Handy, C. (1987) *The Making of Managers*. London: London Manpower Services Commission, National Economic Development Council, and British Institute of Management.

—— (1989) *The Age of Unreason*. London: Business Books.

—— Gordon, C., Gow, I., and Randlesome, C. (1988) *Making Managers*. Oxford: Pitman.

Hite, L. M. (1996) 'Black Women Managers and Administrators: Experience and Implications', *Women in Management Review*, 11/6: 11–17.

Hollway, W. (1996) 'Masters and Men in the Transition from Factory Hands to Sentimental Workers', in D. L. Collinson and J. Hearn (eds.), *Men as Managers, Managers as Men*. London: Sage, ch. 2.

Hyman, R. (1987) 'Strategy or Structure? Capital, Labour and Control', *Work, Employment and Society*, 1/1: 25–55.

Institute of Management (1994) *The 1994 National Management Salary Survey*. London: Institute of Management.

Institute of Management (1995) *Survival of the Fittest: A Survey of Managers' Experience of and Attitudes to Work in the Post Recession Economy*. London: Institute of Management.

—— (1996) *Are Managers Under Stress?* London: Institute of Management.

Johnson, P., and Gill, J. (1993) *Management Control and Organizational Behaviour*. London: Paul Chapman.

Jones, C., Taylor, G., and Nickson, D. (1997) 'Whatever it Takes? Managing "Empowered" Employees and the Service Encounter in an International Hotel Chain', *Work, Employment and Society*, 11/3: 541–54.

Kanter, R. (1977) *Men and Women of the Corporation*. New York: Basic Books.

—— (1986) 'The Reshaping of Middle Management', *Management Review*, 19–20.

—— (1987) *The Change Masters: Corporate Entrepreneurs at Work*. London: Unwin Books.

Kast, F. E., and Rosenzweig, J. E. (1985) *Organization and Management: A Systems and Contingency Approach*, 4th edn. New York: McGraw Hill.

Kotter, J. P. (1982) *The General Managers*. London: Free Press.

McGovern, P., Hope-Hailey, V., and Stiles, P. (1998) 'The Managerial Career after Downsizing: Case Studies from the "Leading Edge" ', *Work, Employment and Society*, 12/3: 457–77.

Mangham, I., and Silver, M. (1986) *Management Training: Context and Practice*. London: Economic and Social Research Council.

Mintzberg, H. (1975) *The Nature of Managerial Work*. New York: Harper and Row.

—— (1989) *Mintzberg on Management*. New York: Free Press.

Mirza, H. S. (1992) *Young, Female and Black*. London: Routledge.

Neale, A. (1995) 'The Manager as Hero', Paper presented at the Labour Process Conference, Blackpool, Apr.

Nkomo, S. M. (1988) 'Race and Sex: The Forgotten Case of the Black Female Manager', in S. Rose and L. Larwood (eds.), *Women's Careers: Pathways and Pitfalls*. London: Praeger.

Osterman, P. (1996) (ed.) *Broken Ladders: Managerial Careers in the New Economy*. Oxford: Oxford University Press.

Pahl, R. (1995) *After Success: Fin-de-siecle Anxiety and Identity*. Cambridge: Polity.

Purcell, J (1982) 'The Rediscovery of the Management Prerogative: The Management of Labour Relations in the 1980s', *Oxford Review of Economic Policy*, 7/1: 33–43.

Reed, M. (1989) *The Sociology of Management*. London: Harvester Wheatsheaf.

—— and Anthony, P. (1992) 'Professionalizing Management and Managing Professionalizing: British Management in the 1980s', *Journal of Management Studies*, 29/5: 591–613.

Scott, J. (1979) *Corporations, Classes and Capitalism*. London: Hutchinson.

Simpson, R. (1998) 'Presenteeism, Power and Organizational Change: Long Hours as a Career Barrier and the Impact on the Working Lives of Women Managers', *British Journal of Management, Conference Issue*, 9 (special issue): 37–50.

Stewart, R. (1979) *Managers and their Jobs*. London: Macmillan.

—— (1982) *Choices for the Manager*. Maidenhead: McGraw-Hill.

—— (1994) *Managerial Behaviour*, Templeton College Management Research Paper. Oxford: Templeton College.

—— (1997) *The Reality of Management*, 3rd edn. Oxford: Butterworth Heinemann.

Wajcman, J. (1996) 'Women and Men Managers: Careers and Equal Opportunities', in R. Crompton, D. Gallie and K. Purcell (eds.), *Changing Forms of Employment: Organizations, Skills and Gender*. London: Routledge, ch. 12.

Watson, T. (1994) *In Search of Management*. London: Routledge.

—— (1997) *Sociology, Work and Industry*, 3rd edn. London: Routledge.

Wensley, R. (1996) 'Isabella Beaton: Management as "Everything in its Place" ', *London Business School Strategy Review*, 7/1: 37–46.

Wood, R. C. (1992) *Working in Hotels and Catering*. London: Routledge.

Zeitlin, M. (1989) *The Large Corporation and Contemporary Classes*. Cambridge: Polity.

6

The View from Outside: Sexuality, Deviancy, Normality, Emotionality, and Feelings

IN AN EARLIER CHAPTER we looked at the view from below, at the perspective of some employees. In the last chapter we saw the view from above, the manager's reality. But what insights can be gained by taking a more external view, if we take a step outside the organization and look back in? In this chapter we look back into organizations and also concentrate on issues which are normally treated as if they are external to organizations—sexuality, emotions, 'deviancy', and feelings.

Sexuality in Organizations

What about bureaucracy and sexuality—do they mix? We saw earlier how in bureaucracies women are strangers in a male-defined world. There is evidence of women managers being perceived as threats to male self-image (Cockburn, 1991; Sargent, 1983). Women may play down their sexuality in order to 'blend in' (Sheppard, 1989). In this chapter we look further into the issue of sexuality and how it is pertinent to understanding organizational behaviour. Issues of emotionality, sexuality, and intimacy are currently missing from descriptions of organizational life (Brewis and Grey, 1994), they are seen as belonging to a private sphere. Women and sex are not welcome in the public sphere. Women, characterized as inherently passionate, sexual beings, are thought not to function as well as men in the rational public sphere as they are overly prey to their basic emotions. Popular myth says that women are too neurotic to be able to cope with public positions of responsibility and are more suited to 'instinctive' roles like caring for the young or infirm, or in supportive, helping, administrative roles.

Sexuality here refers to sex roles, sexual preference, sexual attractiveness, and notions of masculinity and femininity in organizations. It is sexuality that marks men and women out as different and also marks out differences between groups, for example, gay men and lesbian women. Some professions have been sex typed as male. The legal profession is one good example of where this has happened. Male lawyers (with a few exceptions) and the professional bodies in England fiercely resisted the entry of women into the profession for three reasons (Podmore and Spencer, 1982). First, they are a very conservative profession who oppose change. Secondly, and most importantly for our purposes here, the men felt that professional standards would be dangerously compromised by the entry of women into the profession. Maleness was one of the attributes of professionalism; maleness was part of the profession's character so that the admission of women was seen as threatening the very identity of the institutions. Men lawyers referred to stereotypes which portrayed women as emotional, illogical, and irrational. Women were seen as successful only if they suppressed the feminine side of their characters. This would mean 'unsexing' women, which would be deplored by the male legal establishment. So women should be excluded. The third reason was that they wished to exclude the competition women would present. Women in the profession feel that their careers have been shaped and fashioned by their gender; for example they find themselves channelled into particular types of work seen as fit for females, desk-bound work like conveyancing and divorce work. Women tend to be excluded from higher status and more remunerative work (particularly company and commercial law) as they are thought, by men, to be less effective in these areas (Podmore and Spencer, 1982).

Social norms are often personified in sexual stereotypes. For instance a commonly held belief is that female bar staff should be attractive, warm-hearted, easy-going women, providing a shoulder for men to cry on, capable of taking and giving a joke. Such consensual objectivity has a reality independent of fact. The barmaid who is not attractive, is embarrassed by *risqué* humour, or unsympathetic to the cries for sympathy fails to comply with criteria for membership of the group 'barmaid' and is unlikely to be ignorant of that failure (Breakwell, 1979).

Rosemary Pringle in her book *Secretaries Talk* (1989) shows how femininity and secretarial work are closely tied. Though most secretaries were men until the late nineteenth century and they retained a presence in secretarial work until the Second World War, secretarial work is currently seen as quintessentially feminine. Moreover, all women are assumed to be capable of secretarial work: 'typing is seen as something every woman can do—like washing up!' (secretary in Pringle, 1989: 3). Men may perceive any woman in an office as the secretary and expect her to perform secretarial service in the absence of a secretary. Secretaries are also represented almost exclusively in familial or sexual terms as wives (e.g. office wife), mothers, spinster aunts, mistresses, and *femmes fatales*. The image is often of the 'sexy secretary' and the 'mindless dolly bird'. It is virtually impossible to talk about secretaries without making a set of sexual associations. Images of secretaries sitting around filing their nails or doing their knitting reinforce the idea that they do little work.

The Sex Stereotype and Emotions

Sexuality and emotions are clearly brought into work. Women are often required to display the sex stereotype in order to be effective in their work. Arlie Russell Hochschild (1983) was among the first scholars to show how extensively individuals, particularly employed women, are expected to manage their emotions; she uses the metaphor of a 'managed heart' to underscore the emotional control the women were required to exhibit. With this research we have a new angle on the experience of work and the view from below. We saw earlier in Chapter 3 how Hochschild has described emotion work. Hochschild's (1983) study of US airline flight attendants shows how the attendants were trained to display an emotional commitment to the welfare and comfort of airline passengers; they were required to show a caring, courteous, friendly, and efficient front even when passengers were rude or arrogant. There were rules for grooming and personal attitudes. Customers had to be met with warmth and smiles; the smiles were to be 'inside-out' ones, felt and meant. Cabin crew at Delta Airlines were socialized during their training to believe, not only that they had to make customers feel cosseted and valued, but they had to genuinely experience positive regard for them and suppress both negative behaviour and negative emotions. This is 'emotional labour' for the flight attendants, particularly when it involves the semi-institutionalized expectation of flirting expected between (mainly) female air stewardesses and male airline passengers, reflected in advertising like 'We really move our tails for you to make your every wish come true' (Continental Airlines) or 'Fly me, you'll like it' (National Airlines) (see Hochschild, 1983: 93). The response to the client was, then, manufactured by the company for the employee. 'Professionalism' requires this behaviour.

There is, however, a cost attached to this labour; the labour 'affects the degree to which we listen to feeling and sometimes our very capacity to feel' (Hochschild, 1983: 21–2). She goes on to imply that many, perhaps most, women have had the kinds of training she observed among Delta flight attendants who were taught 'that an obnoxious person could be reconceived in an honest and useful way'. Such lessons were part of their 'anger desensitization' (1983: 25).

Showing and Hiding Feelings

Research has also shown how men are often reluctant to admit to vulnerability or fear at work. Prison officers, for example, view requests for help from colleagues as a show of professional weakness. Asking for help was tantamount to admitting you were not 'man enough' for the job. Asking for help, showing fear or emotion was not occupationally acceptable (Carter, 1996). Can you think of other occupations where this might be the case?

Managing Emotions and the Image of Professionalism—the Case of Prostitutes

Professionalism is also important for sex workers, prostitutes. Prostitution has been described as the mutually voluntary exchange of sexual services for money or other consideration (COYOTE, 1988: 290) but though others might argue that prostitution is always by force, is always a violation against women and an outrage to their dignity (e.g. Barry, 1991, quoted in Van der Gaag, 1994). Others argue that a firm distinction must be made between 'free choice' prostitution and all forms of forced and child prostitution (e.g. Delacoste and Alexander, 1988). Free choice prostitution can be regarded as sex work and a form of work like any other.

Sex workers generate future business by adopting an equivalent professionalism to that found in other jobs. For example, both flight attendants and sex workers have been found to separate the realms of experience into private and public domains (McKeganey and Barnard, 1996). Publicly they are required to act in order to present a certain 'face'; privately they can let this go. Publicly flight attendants' faces and feelings help to make money, although not directly for themselves. Prostitutes' faces and bodies are a resource to make money for themselves.

Maintaining the public image requires the individual to distance themselves from the clients in some way. The most visible strategy the prostitute uses to distance themselves from clients is explicitness. From the outset they make clear that they are sexually available but at a price. Negotiation and contract are central concerns for prostitution. Prostitution is governed by unwritten 'rules' but as the 'rules of the game' are not fixed for clients there are three considerations: what the prostitute is prepared to do, the nature of the client's request, and the amount of money on offer. All these have to be negotiated and agreed. Throughout the process of initial negotiation the women adopt an assertive business-like stance in the hope of securing client compliance and so they can dictate the terms and conditions of the sale. A large part of the rationale for this resides in an acute awareness of the potential dangers of providing sex to men who for most part are total strangers. Once the deal has been negotiated, additional income is dependent on the skill of the prostitute and level of *naïveté* of the client; extra charges are incurred by the client for 'extras' like touching (McKeganey and Barnard, 1996).

While the prostitutes describe themselves as being in charge of the encounter with the client, the client will similarly feel they are in charge. As the client has the money, they have the power. The business relationship is 'managed' so that both parties feel they have control (McKeganey and Barnard, 1996). The 'rules of the game', the unwritten code of conduct adopted by one group of prostitutes, are described by Sharpe (1998). These women claimed never to accept business without insisting their clients used condoms. Information about whether the vice squad were patrolling, information about punters (particularly 'funny punters'), attacks, violent incidents, or strangers 'on the patch' (new prostitutes, new police in the vice squad, media people, and researchers) was exchanged but the women never mixed socially beyond the boundaries of the patch. Most of the prostitutes developed a territorial affiliation and the 'poaching' of someone else's patch or customers was not appreciated or tolerated. The newcomer had to stand her ground and the war of attrition was played out until she was accepted or tolerated. The patch had a well-established internal market which controlled and regulated prices. If an individual moved her prices to attract more business she laid herself open to retribution from the others, at least verbal abuse and at worst a severe beating (Sharpe, 1998).

Karen Sharpe (1998) noted that negotiations with the clients also followed 'rules'. Once it was ascertained what service the client required, he was informed of the prices and where the business would take place. Then the prostitute made the decision whether to accept or decline the business. Prices were invariably non-negotiable and the women always took the money first. Condoms were always provided by the women; if a hotel room was used, the cost would be met by the client. Again being in control was a major issue for the women— being in control of the situation, the client, the location, and what their children understood, were all important for these women.

Feeling in Control—the Stripper

Strippers too express the feeling of being in control. The women describe themselves as powerful 'It's your show, you're higher than everyone else on that stage and you feel in control' says Ninon. Melissa (a student at Oxford who works in the same show) says 'It's the only sexual relationship I've had where I feel completely in control'. (*Scotland on Sunday*, 3 August 1997, p. 4)

'When I am on stage I am a sex goddess, I'm revered by every man in the room. I'm all powerful, they all want me but they can't have me' (Melissa Butler, quoted in the *Sun: Guardian*, 28 August 1997)

It is not only relationships with clients that sex workers manage. Relationships between prostitutes and police, for example, have to be managed too. For example to reduce the chances of being arrested by the police they use 'the courtesy of the road' which means, if the police come along, the prostitutes will move, walk off, or even just look in the opposite direction (McKeganey and Barnard, 1996). Sharpe (1998) found that an unwritten rule with the police was that the women would not start working on the patch until six o'clock in the evening. If they came out before this they were immediately arrested and charged.

Unwritten Rules

All jobs have unwritten rules attached to them. For example, when I worked as a hospital cleaner as a temporary worker, I found that temporary cleaners were given all the worst jobs to do, like cleaning up sewage from a broken ceiling pipe. Temporary cleaners could only use the cleaning equipment (floor polishers, etc.) when not needed by those with permanent cleaning jobs. What jobs have you done and what unwritten rules applied?

Images of stereotypical femininity in contemporary culture are associated with the good wife and mother, the good girl, reliable, passive, nurturing, often fragile, gentle, and emotional. Some prostitutes claim to challenge these stereotypes for all women by resisting the pressure to conform to the stereotype of being the good girl and by bringing into the public sphere and to many men the services women would usually perform in private for one man. They insist that prostitution is work and a service that anyone can offer or seek and that they should have the same rights and liberties as other workers (ONeill, 1997).

O'Connell Davidson (1995) describes some of the many similarities between sex workers and other self-employed individuals. One of the most difficult aspects of the prostitutes business is the flow of custom and therefore cash. About 90 per cent of the men break their appointments so it is difficult to control or reliably predict demand. One way to do this is to build up a regular clientele who more generally do keep the appointments they make. Some control can also be achieved over the nature and volume of demand through pricing systems, skills and specialisms. The prostitute called Desiree in O'Connell Davidson's study catered for men who were better off, came to her premises, and had diverse and demanding requirements in terms of skill, equipment, and props. The clients were prepared to pay higher prices for these services than they would pay to a street prostitute. She plans and controls all aspects of her business: where and when to advertise, who to employ and tasks they are assigned, the pricing system, the services on offer, the hours and days of business. She also exercises a great deal of control over the details of transactions with clients and has a clearly defined split between her private and public self.

Issues concerning 'being in charge' or in control in both the public and private world seem to be important in managing sexuality in organizations. An interesting example of who is in charge can be found in some research by Martin (1990). Taking the example of an TV interview with a chief executive of a very large multinational organization she shows how organizational practices can break down the separation between the individual's public and private life. In this interview the chief executive talks of how a young woman is important to the launch of a new product the next day. In order for her to be prepared for the launch she had arranged to have a Caesarean section for the birth of her child. The company had 'insisted' she stay at home and her involvement with the product launch was going to be maintained and televised on closed circuit television.

Feelings

We have seen how traditional organizational theory has stressed the functional and how managers try to shape worker behaviour to organizational objectives using an armoury of rules, regulation, and inducements. The view is of a 'passionless organization' (Fineman, 1994). Organizational theory needs to account for the process and interaction of emotions, felt and displayed, emotions as diverse as pride, jealousy, love, hate, happiness, despair, anger, grief, joy, fear, and excitement. Feelings connect us with our realities and provide internal feedback on how we are doing, what we want and what we might do next. We work over our feelings, have feelings about feelings, and are guided by previous experience and social scripts, for example asking ourselves: 'How should I really feel about what is happening? Should I be feeling upset? Why do I feel angry? Some people are going to feel intrinsic pleasure from aesthetic work such as dancing, designing, painting. Surgeons, computer programmers, and mathematicians are reputed to report similar feelings of deep involvement in work (Fineman, 1996). Being in organizations involves us in worry, envy, hurt, sadness, boredom, excitement, and other emotions. Even if you feel dull indifference to work, this is still feeling. We will look at feelings again, and the management of feeling and emotion a later chapter on organizational culture. First we will look at managerial power and control.

Questions for Further Research

1. Performing emotional labour can be a stressful experience. How (see Handy, 1995;Hochschild, 1983)?

2. Rosemary Pringle (1989) found that the secretaries in her sample were mostly married to men of a similar class background to their bosses but this did not mean that the secretary was a social equal of either the boss or the husband. Why not? Discuss.

3. Sex workers' work is similar and dis-similar to other paid work. How (see Scambler and Scambler, 1997)? What insight does the study of prostitution as work give us when we consider other types of work?

Suggestions for Further Reading

Noon, M., and Blyton, P. (1997) *The Realities of Work*. Basingstoke: Macmillan, ch. 7.

Thompson, P., and McHugh, D. (1995) *Work Organizations: A Critical Approach*, 2nd edn. Basingstoke: Macmillan, ch. 5.

References

Barry, K. (1991) *The Penn State Report on Sexual Exploitation, Violence and Prostitution*. Paris: Coalition Against Trafficking in Women /UNESCO.

Breakwell, Glynis (1979) 'Women: Group and Identity?', *Women's Studies International*, 2: 9–17.

Brewis, J., and Grey, C. (1994) 'Re-Eroticizing the Organization: An Exegesis and Critique', *Gender, Work and Organization*, 1/2 (Apr.): 67–82.

Carter, K. (1996) 'Masculinity in Prison', in J. Pilcher and A. Coffey (eds.), *Gender and Qualitative Research*. Aldershot: Avebury, ch. 1.

Cockburn, C. (1991) *In the Way of Women: Men's Resistance to Sex Equality in Organizations*. London: Macmillan.

COYOTE (1988) 'COYOTE/National Task Force on Prostitution', in F. Delacoste and P. Alexander (eds.), *Sex Work: Writings by Women in the Sex Industry*. London: Virago.

Delacoste, F., and Alexander, P. (1988) (eds.) *Sex Work: Writings by Women in the Sex Industry*. London: Virago.

Fineman, S. (1994) 'Organizing and Emotion: Towards a Social Construction', in *Towards a New Theory of Organizations*. London: Routledge, ch. 4.

—— (1996) 'Emotion and Organizing', in S. R. Clegg, C. Hardy. and W. R. Nord (eds.), *Handbook of Organization Studies*. London: Sage, ch. 3.3.

Handy, J. (1995) 'Rethinking Stress: Seeing the Collective', in T. Newton, *Managing Stress*. London: Sage, ch. 4.

Hochschild, A. R. (1983) *The Managed Heart: Commercialisation of Human Feeling*. Berkeley, Calif.: University of California.

McKeganey, N., and Barnard, M (1996) *Sex Work on the Streets: Prostitutes and their Clients*. Buckingham: Open University Press.

Martin, J. (1990) 'Deconstructing Organizational Taboos: The Suppression of Gender Conflict in Organizations', *Organization Science*, 1/4: 339–59.

Newton, T. (1995), with J. Handy and S. Fineman, *Managing Stress: Emotions and Power at Work*. London: Sage.

O'Connell Davidson, J. (1995) 'The Anatomy of "Free Choice" Prostitution', *Gender, Work and Organization*, 2/1: 1–10.

O'Neill, M. (1997) 'Prostitute Women Now', in G. Scambler and A. Scambler (eds.), *Rethinking Prostitution: Purchasing Sex in the 1990s*. London: Routledge, ch. 1.

Podmore, D., and Spencer, A. (1982) 'Women Lawyers in England, the Experience of Inequality', *Work and Occupations*, 9/3: 337–61.

Pringle, R. (1989) *Secretaries Talk: Sexuality, Power and Work*. London: Verso.

Sargent, A. G. (1983) *The Androgynous Manager*. New York: AMOCOM.

Scambler, G. and Scambler, A. (1997) (eds.) *Rethinking Prostitution: Purchasing Sex in the 1990s*. London: Routledge.

Sharpe, K. (1998) *Red Light, Blue Light: Prostitutes, Punters and the Police*. Aldershot: Ashgate Publishing.

Sheppard, D. (1989) 'Organizations, Power and Sexuality: The Image and Self Image of Women Managers', in J. Hearn, D. L. Sheppard, P. Tancred Sheriff, and G Burrell (eds.), *The Sexuality of Organization*. London: Sage.

Van der Gaag, N. (1994) 'Prostitution: Soliciting for Change', *The New Internationalist*, 252 (Feb.): 4–7.

II

Power, Control and Resistance

7

Management Power, Surveillance, Control, and Technology

UNDER THE MEDIEVAL guild structure, masters held the power over those who were employed. Power clearly derived from ownership and control of the means of production and was supported by the power of surveillance. Knowledge was important as power was derived from knowledge, from 'mastery' of the skills. The organization's status hierarchy and knowledge hierarchy coincided (Offe, 1976). Increasing size and complexity of organizations brought about by the concentration of capital into larger units, and the bringing together of different production processes meant that the unity of status and knowledge hierarchies became disrupted. Hardy and Clegg (1996) believe that modern organizations passed by the guild structures and as organizations grew larger, skills became increasingly fragmented and specialized and positions became more functionally differentiated. It was unlikely that any one person would have sufficient knowledge of all the processes to be able to control them in an adequate manner. Power was centralized. Modern organizations were designed to function as if they were a unitary organism. Power is structured into the organization design so that some will have more power than others. Obedience to those with power is central. But how is power defined and understood?

Management Power

Power has been defined by Weber (1978) as the ability to get others to do what you want them to do, even if this is against their will, or to get them to do something they otherwise would not (Dahl, 1957). Weber, like Marx (1976) argued that power was derived from owning and controlling the means of production but went on to say that it was also derived from the knowledge of operations as much as ownership. Organizational members will use creativity, discretion, and agency as power, some more than others. From the employer's viewpoint the employee represents the capacity to labour which must be realized as efficiently as possible. Standing in the way of this realization is the power of employees who may be more or less willing to work under managerial discretion and control. Managerial control can be increased or tightened through the hierarchy and discipline of the manager, and through rules and bureaucracy.

How much power do workers have to resist managerial power and control? One of the early studies on this was by Crozier (1964) who looked at bureaucracy and power relations in a French state-owned tobacco company. The male maintenance worker's job was to fix machine-breakdowns reported by the mainly female production workers. The production workers were paid on a piece-rate system and had been effectively deskilled. Their jobs and the workflow was tightly planned and control. The main uncertainty was machine stoppages. Machine stoppages were usually caused by the difficulties in conditioning the raw material and stoppages led to a decrease in the bonus the production workers could earn, so the production workers needed the machines to function and were dependent on the efficient working of the maintenance workers. The maintenance workers thus had a high degree of power over the production workers because they controlled the source of uncertainty. Comparable problems seemed to be handled better in other factories. The maintenance workers kept the maintenance and repair problems a secret and their skill as a rule of thumb skill, completely disregarding all blueprints and maintenance directions which they were able to make 'disappear from the plants' (1964: 153).The maintenance workers were able then to maintain relative autonomy, privilege, and power through their skills and knowledge. While the rationale of bureaucracy is the elimination of power relationships and personal dependencies, unintended results are yielded.

Uncertainty, control, and power were linked as concepts. A theory of strategic contingency arose from the work of Hickson *et al.* (1971); central to this theory were four subunits connected by the major task element of the organization, coping with uncertainty. The balance of power between the subunits was dependent on how the units coped with uncertainty. The most powerful units were those least dependent on the other subunits and coping with the greatest systematic uncertainty. (For a critique see Clegg and Hardy, 1996.) But this view assumes a unitary, cohesive organization, whereas the units are likely to be hierarchical with problems of consent and dissent.

How do managers and other elites bring about political quiescence and perpetuate the status quo? Bachrach and Baratz (1963) would say that they are in a position to use power to prevent decisions being taken over issues where there would be a conflict of interests, when they limit decision-making to 'safe' issues. Power is exercised when they devote their energies to creating or reinforcing social and political values and institutional practices that limit the issues considered, by, for example, agenda setting.

Lukes (1974) considers that Bachrach and Baratz do not go far enough so provides us with a radical view of power. Lukes asks us to look at latent unobservable conflict and the role of ideology in shaping perceptions and preferences contrary to the real interests of those who hold them. Luke's radical concept is that 'A exercises power over B when A affects B in a manner contrary to B's interests' (Lukes, 1974: 34). Power could be used to prevent conflict by shaping people's perceptions and preferences so that they accept their role in the existing order of things. Power helped sustain the dominance of elite groups and reduced the ability of subordinate interests to dissent.

More recently theorists have looked at disciplinary practices, the micro techniques of power used in organizations, following in the steps of Foucault (1977). These are ways in which both individuals and groups become socially inscribed and 'normalized' through routine aspects of organizations. In studying managerial power this would mean that we would look at the 'rules of the game', which both constrain and enable action (Clegg, 1975) and how the disciplinary gaze is put into action in organizations. An example of the disciplinary gaze might be an appraisal system. (Employee appraisal is a process where current performance in a job is observed and discussed order to add to that performance.)

The Disciplinary Gaze?

At the University of St Andrews staff are requested, if they make private calls, to prefix the number they dial with 77. They are subsequently issued with an itemized personal bill which they are required to pay. The bill lists the numbers dialed and the names of the people or organizations called and the cost of the call. If this is how private calls are logged, could this be the same for all other calls university staff make?

The rule systems that made up Weber's bureaucracy are reinterpreted under the auspices of disciplinary practices. Power is embedded in the everyday life. Central to disciplinary practices is surveillance—personal, technical, bureaucratic, legal—seeking increasingly to control the behaviour and dispositions of the employee. Discipline is both a system of correction and a system of knowledge. Power then is much more than negation and repression of the actions of others. 'Rather than A getting B to do something B would not otherwise do, social relations of power typically involve both A and B doing what they ordinarily do' (Isaac, 1987). From a manager's point of view, this means that managers have a right to manage.

Control and Surveillance

Wherever there is a need for efficiency, effectiveness, and coordination, structures of control will be found. Hierarchical control is often seen as tainted (Jermier, 1998). As with power, we are uncomfortable discussing struggles for control. But processes of control are integral to the way organizations operate. We have been made aware of the excesses of control in the writings of novelists like George Orwell and Aldous Huxley. Their writings were designed to horrify, shock, and provoke thought and discussion.

Although all organizations use a mix of strategies of control, some scholars have argued that specific strategies have become popular in specific historical periods. For example, Edwards (1979) argued that managerial practices moved away from widespread use of coercive control in the late nineteenth century towards technological control (like the assembly line) and then on to bureaucratic control in the mid-twentieth century. Each shift was precipitated by changes in the nature of work and the climate of labour relations. More recently it has been argued that we make more use of post-bureaucratic control with advanced technology and of instilling emotions, values, and world-views congruent with the interests of more powerful parties (Wilkinson and Wilmott, 1995).

Teamwork and surveillance are two ways in which this can be done. New information technologies increase the scope and reach of workplace surveillance and never before have employees been subjected to such intense scrutiny and monitoring (Sewell, 1998). For example, new technology has allowed for the close monitoring of the activities of supermarket checkout operators, telesales staff, and long-distance truck drivers. Zuboff (1988) has talked about the 'information panopticon'. (The panopticon was originally a model of prison design devised in the eighteenth century where inmates were kept in single cells constructed in a ring surrounding a central watchtower. Inmates would be constantly visible from the observation tower.) Elite groups exercise control using computer-based production and information technology; armed with the new technology they consolidate better quality information (Robey, 1981).

While teamwork may be about empowering workers, devolving responsibility, and reversing repressive workplace control structures, it can also mean intensifying attention. Instead of an individual exercising a degree and influence over their own work, they can now influence the work of others in their team through suggestion, demonstration, and exhortation. Life in teams can be stressful as individuals are subject to intense peer pressure to conform to group norms (see Barker, 1993, for an example). Those who stand out as either good or bad workers will receive the scrutiny of their peers and then be subjected to sanction or reward or other forces determined by the team. Teamwork does not necessarily descend into tyranny though as McKinlay and Taylor's (1996) discussion of 'Pyramid' shows.

The Case of 'Kay Electronics'

At Kay Electronics (see Sewell and Wilkinson, 1992) teams comprised twelve to forty members who were assembling printed circuit boards (PCBs). As the PCBs progressed they were subjected to electronic tests and the test results were relayed to a central inventory control database. At the start of each day the team members had yesterday's quality performance information displayed above their workstations in the form of 'traffic lights'. A red card signified that a team member had exceeded acceptable quality limits. A green card signified they had made no quality errors at all and an amber card signified that the operator had made some errors but they remained in an acceptable range. This display of management information unambiguously identifies for all those team members who are above average or good workers as well as those who are below average. As a result teams are likely to normalize their productive effort at the level of better performers. Persistent poor workers, identified by regular red cards, would be removed by management from the line, counselled, and retrained; repeated unsatisfactory performance would lead to dismissal. A persistent green card could mean that an individual was worthy of closer attention because they may have made some kind of innovation in the work process.

Managerial Prerogative

Managers have a right to manage, they have the prerogative (Storey, 1983). The boundaries of managerial prerogatives or rights give management its distinctiveness and are hotly defended. Justification for this comes from the fact that owners or managers have control over capital assets, they are supported by law, and managers should be left to manage as they see fit. Securing legitimation promotes willing compliance for their rules, policies, and decisions. Golding (1980) believes that the maintenance of prerogative depends on it not being overtly recognized or challenged; the belief in the rule of manager's right to control is 'blissful clarity'(1980: 772). It seems to go unchallenged because of employee socialization and the tendency to accept most aspects of the status quo. Managerial control may be impossible without a prerogative that in some way legitimates the right to control (Johnson and Gill, 1993). That prerogative and managerial control will extend, for example, to decision-making over technical change.

Technology

Technology is not just about machines—computers, washing machines, telephones, and so on—but also social relations. These technologies encourage some forms of interaction. There is little point in defining technology as devices and machines. As Kramarae (1988) noted, defining technology in this way would be like describing housework in terms of dust cloths and cleaning fluids without reference to the social systems which determine who it is who dusts and cleans. Technology can be described as 'the application of scientific and other knowledge to practical tasks by ordered systems that involve people and organizations, living things and machines' (Pacey, 1983) or the transformation of science into a means of capital accumulation (Noble, 1977; 1984). Technology is, then, a human, political and social activity.

Technology is usually thought of as a masculine invention and activity. It is often assumed that women have not been very involved in the invention of technology. For example, there were no women among the qualified engineering professionals responsible for the food processor or the washing machine (Cockburn and Dilic, 1994). However, many inventions have been made by women (see Trescott, 1979; Warner, 1979). Household technologies like refrigerators and washing machines were originally designed and manufactured for commercial laundries, hotels, and hospitals but have been scaled down for family use. These technologies, sold as 'labour saving' devices have not made the household easier to run or freed women for other activities (Cowan, 1983). As the equipment has been introduced into the homes of families who could afford it, cleaning standards have been raised and it is still women who are doing the repetitive tasks. But what about factory technology?

Technology and power have been drawn together in research on the 'labour process', work initiated by Braverman (1974). Here power and technology were combined through the intermediary concept of control. Power was originally seen as exercised in a 'zero-sum' power game in which one party profits at the expense of another. The classical cases were documented by Marglin (1974) and Gorz (1972). Marglin cites the case of cotton and wool merchants who constructed a role for themselves using technology to control the activities of their workers rather than just to enhance productivity. A very different technology would be developed if maximum control had not been the main aim (Gorz, 1972). Technology can have a major impact on work tasks, using judgement, discretion, decision-making, and so reduce or eliminate the individual's opportunities for resistance (Beynon, 1974; Nichols and Beynon, 1977). More recent examples include Watanabe (1990), who describes how labour was deskilled and degraded in the banking sector (whose work was described in Chapter 2), and Knights and Sturdy (1987), who argued that there had been a massive increase in routine work in the insurance industry and a polarization of skills.

However, it would be wrong to believe that technology always deskills jobs. Zeitlin (1983) shows how the introduction of new technology in the British engineering industry during the period 1890–1920 increased the margin of workers' control. Employers remained heavily dependent on skilled labour and vulnerable to craft militancy during boom periods. But the marginal gains by skilled employees were short-lived. Managerial intentions towards deskilling have been limited as Buchanan (1986), Wilson (1987), and others have shown. When Computer Numerically Controlled Machines are introduced new demands are made on the workforce—programmes need to be debugged and the production process monitored; workers' knowledge and skills prove to be essential. How long management is dependent on skills following the introduction of new technology is probably related to products, processes, and the configuration of power (Clegg and Wilson, 1991). The locus of control cannot always be moved from workers to managers during technical change nor from managers to workers. Control ultimately does lie with management, though it may be resisted by workers.

The Latest Technology 'Fad'—Business Process Engineering (BPR)

BPR represents the latest in a series of managerial 'recipes' which advocate the use of techni-cal/organizational changes. BPR has been described as 'the fundamental rethinking and radical design of business processes to achieve dramatic improvements in critical, contemporary measures of performance, such as cost, quality, service, and speed' and as 'a manifesto for revolution' (Hammer and Champy, 1993: 32). It is the most recent in a long line of management innovations adopted by a wide spectrum of industry and commerce in Britain and the USA.

The distinctiveness, for Knights and McCabe (1998), of BPR is that it focuses upon radical change and is a process-based approach to the organization of work. The process is facilitated by the increased use of information technology. The implementation of new information technology is usually the main push for transforming the organization and is closely associated with BPR. BPR can include teamworking, empowerment, flatter hierarchies, and a customer orientation; the novelty rests in packaging these together to 'transform' organizations (Grint *et al.*, 1996).

While BPR is widely discussed amongst management practitioners and proponents, they have widely different perceptions as to what BPR means. For some practitioners within the UK financial service industry, for example, it means short-term cost savings; for others it promises a radical future of change (McCabe *et al.*, 1994). Examples of effective implementation are rare (Willcocks and Grint, 1997). The claims and promises of BPR are also being challenged by academics (e.g. Grey and Mitev, 1995). While practitioners may think that BPR presents the radically new, discontinuous future and recommend 'don't automate, obliterate', calling for organizational politics to be cast aside, Willcocks and Grint (1997) say that BPR is an inherently risky and political process.

Technology and Surveillance

Employers have always monitored the performance of their employees but in the last twenty years surveillance at work has increased with the introduction of information technology. This is to be found particularly in high-volume service operations like call centres such as those used in direct banking and insurance sales, where it is used to ensure work is being done. It has been described as 'the technological whip of the electronic age' (Fodness and Kinsella, 1990). Calls are listened to by those who are monitoring levels of service quality and data collected on performance levels, like number of calls received or made. Those who are being monitored know their work is being seen but do not often know what information is being generated about them and their performance.

Kirsty Ball and David Wilson (1997) describe two case studies of the technology of surveillance, in a debt collection department in a building society and in a credit card division of a bank. In the debt collection department work varied according to the complexity of the accounts in question and the length of time they had been in arrears. In the case of the credit card division the main activity was the inputting of credit card sales vouchers onto the computer system to charge the correct amounts to the customer. In both cases manager and supervisors could see what each operator and team had produced in a day. The performance statistics were a great source of stress to the operators as the calculation of them were secret. They would be given feedback on their performance and, in one company, if they persistently fell short of their targets, they were sacked.

Strike over 'Spy' Scheme

Road maintenance workers went on strike in Dundee when 'spy' devices, satellite global positioning system devices, were planned to be installed in every maintenance vehicle. These devices can plot staff movements to within 10 metres. The location of the vehicles can be determined on a computer screen equipped with a street map at the company headquarters. The workers protested as they said the plan showed lack of trust from managers. The managing director said that no member of staff should have anything to fear but he conceded there was an element of management control: 'It will let us know that the workforce is where it is supposed to be and identify inappropriate or unauthorized use of vehicles.' (*The Scotsman*, 12 October 1998)

Understanding organizations as political systems is a productive image which helps us understand more of the nature and functioning of organizations. Seeing organizations as political systems draws attention to the ways in which they can serves as sites where different values, forms of knowledge, and interests are articulated and embodied in decisions, structures, and practices. As political systems organizations use power and control; in so doing they provide meaning and personal identity as well as goods, services, and income. The issue of control is central to this book and is picked up again in the next chapter on organizational culture.

Questions for Further Research

1. Sewell (1998) says that discipline can be maintained through teamwork and peer group scrutiny. Surveillance and teamwork are an unexpected combination. How are surveillance and teamwork combined?

2. Struggles for control are viewed with embarrassment or ignored, according to Jermier (1998). Why is this the case?

3. Search for research that would help you argue that the panopticon is as diverse in its use as the contexts in which it occurs (see Ball and Wilson, 1997).

3. There is no system of managerial control that can completely eliminate the discretion of the employee. Discuss.

Suggestions for Further Reading

Clegg, S., and Wilson, F. (1991) 'Power, Technology and Flexibility in Organizations, in J. Law (ed.), *A Sociology of Monsters: Essays on Power, Technology and Domination*. London: Routledge.

Hardy, C., and Clegg, S. R. (1996) 'Some Dare Call it Power', in S. R. Clegg, C. Hardy, and W. R. Nord (eds.), *Handbook of Organization Studies*. London: Sage.

Johnson, P., and Gill, J. (1993) *Management Control and Organizational Behaviour*. London: Paul Chapman.

Thompson, P., and McHugh, D. (1995) *Work Organizations: A Critical Introduction*, 2nd edn. Houndmills, Basingstoke: Macmillan Business Press, chs. 4 and 5.

References

Bachrach, P., and Baratz, M. S. (1963) 'Decisions and Nondecisions', *American Political Science Review*, 57: 641–51.

Ball, K., and Wilson, D (1997) *Computer Based Monitoring and the Electronic Panopticon: A Review of the Debate and Some New Evidence from the UK*, Working Pape. Birmingham:, Aston Business School.

Barker, J. R. (1993) 'Tightening the Iron Cage: Coercive Control in Self Managing Teams', *Administrative Science Quarterly*, 38: 408–37.

Beynon, H. (1974) *Working for Ford*. Harmondsworth: Penguin.

Braverman, H. (1974) *Labor and Monopoly Capital: The Degradation of Work in the Twentieth Century*. New York: Monthly Review Press.

Buchanan, D. A. (1986) *Canned Cycles and Dancing Tools: Who's Really in Control of Computer Aided Machining?*, Working Paper Series, 1 (Mar.). Glasgow: University of Glasgow, Department of Management Studies.

Clegg, S. R. (1975) *Power, Rule and Domination*. London: Routledge.

—— and Wilson, F. (1991) 'Power, Technology and Flexibility in Organizations', in J. Law (ed.), *A Sociology of Monsters: Essays on Power, Technology and Domination*. London: Routledge.

Cockburn, C., and Furst-Dilic, R. F (1994) (eds.) *Bringing Technology Home: Gender and Technology in a Changing Europe*. Buckingham: Open University Press.

Cowan, R. S. (1983) *More Work For Mother: The Ironies of Household Technology from the Open Hearth to the Microwave*. New York: Basic Books.

Crozier, M. (1964) *The Bureaucratic Phenomenon*. Chicago: University of Chicago Press.

Dahl, R. (1957) 'The Concept of Power', *Behavioral Science*, 20: 201–15.

Edwards, R. C. (1979) *Contested Terrain: The Transformation of the Workplace in the Twentieth Century*. New York: Basic Books.

Fodness, K., and Kinsella, S. (1990) *Stories of Mistrust and Manipulation: The Electronic Monitoring of the American Workforce*. Cleveland, Ohio: National Association of Working Women.

Foucault, M. (1977) *Discipline and Punish: The Birth of the Prison*. Harmondsworth: Penguin.

Golding, D. (1980) 'Establishing Blissful Clarity in Organizational Life: Managers', *Sociological Review*, 28/4: 763–83.

Gorz, A. (1972) 'Technical Intelligence and the Capitalist Division of Labour', *Telos*, 12: 27–41.

Grey, C., and Mitev, N. (1995) 'Reengineering Organizations: A Critical Appraisal', *Personnel Review*, 24/1: 6–18.

Grint, K., Case, P., and Willcocks, L. (1996) 'BPR Reappraised: The Politics and Technology of Forgetting', in W. J. Orlihowski, G. I. Walsham, M. R. Jones, and J. I. Degross (eds.), *Information Technology and Changes in Organizational Work*. London: Chapman and Hull.

Hammer, M. and Champy, J. (1993) *Reengineering the Corporation: A Manifesto for Business Revolution*. London: Nicholas Brealy.

Hardy, C. and Clegg, S. R. (1996) 'Some Dare Call it Power', in S. R. Clegg, C. Hardy and W. R. Nord (eds.), *Handbook of Organization Studies*. London: Sage, ch. 3.7.

Hickson, D. J., Hinings, C. A., Lee, C. A., Schneck, R. E., and Pennings, J. M. (1971) 'A Strategic Contingencies Theory of Intraorganizational Power', *Administrative Science Quarterly*, 16/2: 216–29.

Isaac, J. C. (1987) *Power and Marxist Theory: A Realist View*, Ithaca, NY: Cornell University Press.

Jermier, J. M. (1998) 'Introduction: Critical Perspectives on Organizational Control', *Administrative Science Quarterly*, 43: 235–56.

Johnson, P., and Gill, J. (1993) *Management Control and Organizational Behaviour*. London: Paul Chapman.

Knights, D., and McCabe, D. (1998) 'When "Life is but a Dream": Obliterating Politics through Business Process Reengineering?', *Human Relations*, 51/6: 761–98.

Knights, D., and Sturdy, A. (1987) 'Women's Work in Insurance: Information Technology and the Reproduction of Gendered Segregation', in M. J. Davidson and C. L. Cooper (eds.), *Women and Information Technology*. Chichester: Wiley.

Kramarae, C.(1988) 'Gotta Go Myrtle, Technology's at the Door', in C. Kramarae (ed.), *Technology and Women's Voices: Keeping in Touch*. London: Routledge and Kegan Paul.

Lukes, S. (1974) *Power: A Radical View*. London: Macmillan.

McCabe, D., Knights, D., and Wilkinson, A. (1994) *Quality Initiatives in Financial Services* (Research Report available from D. McCabe). Manchester: Financial Services Research Centre, Manchester School of Management, UMIST.

McKinlay, A., and Taylor, P. (1996) 'Power, Surveillance and Resistance', in P. Ackers, C. Smith, and P. Smith (eds.), *The New Workplace and Trade Unionism*. London: Routledge, pp. 279–300.

Marglin, S. A. (1974) 'What do Bosses Do? The Origins and Functions of Hierarchy in Capitalist Production', *Review of Radical Political Economics*, 6: 60–112.

Marx, K. (1976) *Capital*. Harmondsworth: Penguin.

Nichols, T., and Beynon, H. (1977) *Living with Capitalism*. London: Routledge and Kegan Paul.

Noble, D. (1977) *America by Design: Science, Technology and the Rise of Corporate Capitalism*. New York: Alfred A. Knopf.

—— (1984) *Forces of Production*. New York: Alfred A. Knopf.

Offe, C. (1976) *Industry and Inequality*. London: Edward Arnold.

Pacey, A. (1983) *The Culture of Technology*. Cambridge, Mass.: MIT Press.

Robey, D. (1981) 'Computer Information Systems and Organization Structure', *Communications of ACM*, 24: 679–87.

Sewell, G. (1998) 'The Discipline of Teams: The Control of Team-Based Industrial Work through Electronic and Peer Surveillance', *Administrative Science Quarterly*, 43: 397–428.

—— and Wilkinson, B. (1992) 'Someone to Watch over Me: Surveillance, Discipline and the Just-in-Time Labour Process', *Sociology*, 26: 271–89.

Storey, J. (1983) *Managerial Prerogative and the Question of Control*. London: Routledge and Kegan Paul.

Trescott, M. M. (1979) *Dynamos and Virgins Revisited: Women and Technological Change in History*. Metuchen, NJ: Scarecrow Press.

Warner, D. (1979) 'Women Inventors at the Centennial', in M. M. Trescott (ed.), *Dynamos and Virgins Revisited*. Metuchen, NJ: Scarecrow Press.

Watanabe, T. (1990) 'New Office Technology and the Labour Process in Contemporary Japanese Banking', *New Technology, Work and Employment*, 5/1: 56–67.

Weber, M. (1978) *Economy and Society: An Outline of Interpretive Sociology*, ed. G. Roth and C. Wittich. Berkeley, Calif.: University of California Press.

Wilkinson, A., and Willmott H. (1995) (eds.) *Making Quality Critical: New Perspectives on Organizational Change*. London: Routledge.

Willcocks, L., and Grint, K. (1997) 'Re-inventing the Organization? Towards a Critique of Business Process Re-engineering', in I. McLoughlin and M. Harris (eds.), *Innovation, Organizational Change and Technology*. London: International Thomson Business Press, ch. 4.

Wilson, F. M. (1987) 'Computer Numerical Control and Constraint', in D. Knights and H. Wilmott (eds.), *New Technology and the Labour Process*. London: Macmillan.

Zeitlin, J. (1983) 'The Labour Strategies of British Engineering Employers, 1890–1922', in H. Gospel and C. Littler (eds.), *Managerial Strategies and Industrial Relations*. London: Heinemann.

Zuboff, S. (1988) *In the Age of the Smart Machine*. New York: Basic Books.

8

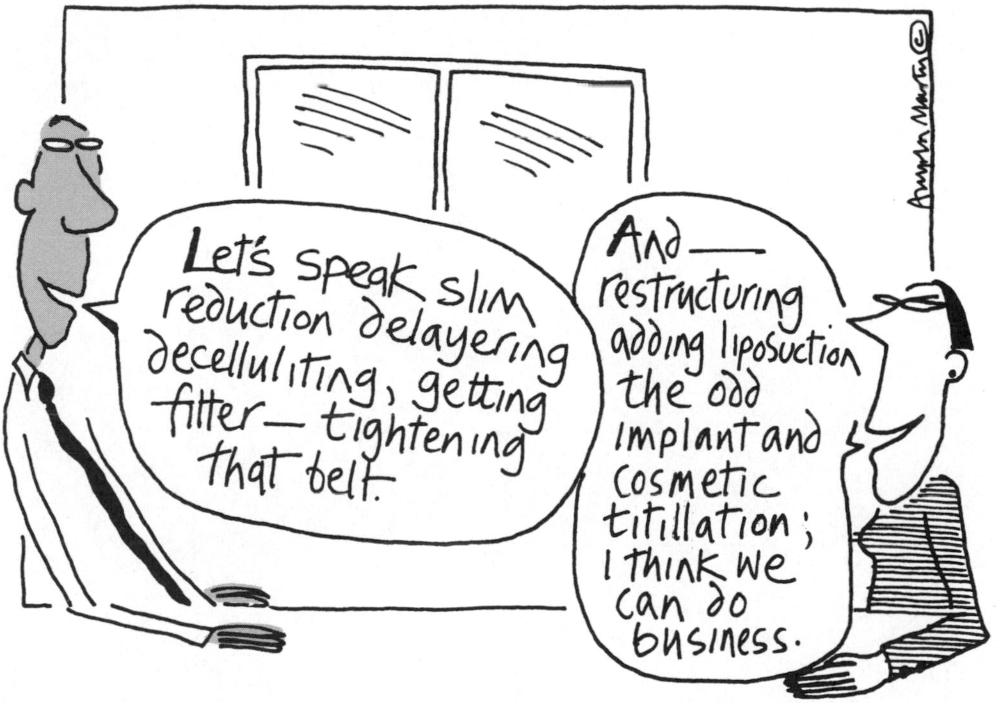

Organizational Culture and Control

CULTURE IS A POPULAR explanatory concept frequently used to describe a company, a rationale for people's behaviour, as a guideline for action, a cause for condemnation or praise, or a quality that makes a company 'what it is' (Kunda, 1992). Organizational culture is defined by Hofstede (1991: 262) as 'the collective programming of the mind which distinguishes the members of one organization from another'. Since the late 1970s a vast body of literature has looked at the importance of organizational culture for organizational outcomes (Smircich and Calas, 1987). For some the emphasis has been on improving efficiency, growth, and success (e.g. Ouchi, 1981; Peters and Waterman, 1982). Peters and Waterman, in looking for excellence in organizational culture, place considerable emphasis on the importance of positive reinforcement, rewarding desirable behaviour. At IBM a senior manager adopted the practice of writing out a cheque as a reward for achievements he observed as he wandered about the organization. It is thought that positive reinforcement is practised in many Japanese, British, French organizations often 'with considerable influence on employee motivation and performance' (Morgan, 1986). Well-known examples of companies who claim to have changed their culture are British Airways, who attempted to change the emphasis on flying routes to an emphasis on company service, and Nissan, who claimed they achieved an entirely new sentiment and identification from their labour force (Ackroyd and Crowdy, 1990).

Interest in culture was sparked by Japanese business success, which was thought to arise from competitive advantage secured through national and corporate culture (Ouchi, 1981; Pascale and Athos, 1982). Through the 1970s Japanese industry managed to establish a solid reputation for quality, reliability, value, and service—attributes that others wished to emulate. A large and profitable literature has capitalized on the idea that culture can be diagnosed and changed to improve organizational effectiveness. Deal and Kennedy (1982: 15) claim, for example, that with a strong culture 'a company can gain as much as one or two hours of productive work per employee per day'. The prescriptive view shows how organizational culture can be designed and managed through the 'hearts and minds' of employees. The ideal employees are those who have internalized the organization's goals and values and no longer require rigid control. The trend has been towards a 'normative control' (Etzioni, 1961), an attempt to direct the efforts of employees by controlling the underlying experiences, thoughts, and feelings that guide their actions (Kunda, 1992: 11). Inherent conflict can be transformed into cooperation in the interests of both employee and employer. Through education, personal development, growth, and maturity employees become better, healthier people, saved from alienation and conflict. As Johnson and Gill (1993: 33) note, it is not clear whether the organizations Deal and Kennedy and Peters and Waterman observed developed in the way they have through chance and spontaneity (social control) or through conscious intent (administrative control).

It has to be acknowledged that employees are not passive objects of control (Goffman, 1961). They may accept, deny, react, reshape, rethink, acquiesce, rebel, or conform and create themselves within constraints imposed on them. Research, for example on employee values and norms reflected in everyday practices (like restriction of output), shows direct conflict with the aims and objectives of management (Lupton, 1963; Roy, 1960). Hofstede

(1998) believes that there are no shared values at the core of an organization's culture. While there is little doubt that practices are designed according to the values of the founder and significant top managers, this does not mean that all members of the organization share these values. Organizations can be composed of various subcultures which may be mutually antagonistic. These subcultures can compete overtly and covertly as different groups of organizational members seek to establish or impose their distinctive meaning systems and definitions of reality. There may be various sites of culture embedded in the various groups that make up the organization, creating subcultures or even counter-cultures (Smircich, 1983*a*; see Smircich, 1983*b*, for how networks of meaning can be researched). As Smircich (1983*a*) argues, organizations can only change those variables they 'have', like payment and information systems, mission statements and corporate image. They cannot change what an organization 'is', the common values and beliefs which emerge from people's shared experiences. Individuals act out their work roles relying on customary definitions and understandings. These meanings are themselves embedded in class, regional, and national cultures. There will be distinctive patterns and connections which will be beyond the capacity of influence, never mind managerial control.

When and if we do find occupational cultures, shared values, and norms of behaviour, how can they best be described and researched? Stephen Barley (1991) argues that few organizational researchers have actually bothered to study the deep structure of a work setting; instead they have focused on symbols like stories, myths, logos, heroes, and so on, while failing to reveal the core of the system that lends a culture its coherence. He looks at the occupation of funeral directors and analyses the meanings of funeral directors activities, offering a seamlessly integrated interpretation of what may have otherwise appeared as disparate tasks. Closing the corpse's eyes, making the bed, opening the windows and curtains of the death room to allow fresh air to remove any odours, and embalming the body are all ways of making death seem lifelike. The strategic arrangement of the room is intended to reconstruct the room to how it would have looked before it became a death room. The corpse's features are posed to make it look as though it is having a restful sleep. Peaceful sleep will appear familiar and natural to the mourners so they are less likely to disrupt a smooth-flowing funeral. No emotionally disruptive hint of ambiguity or conflict is allowed to mar the funeral directors' choreographed presentation of a lifelike death. Barley (1991) provides us then with some insight and understanding of how the occupational culture created by the undertakers serves their purposes and makes their job easier.

For other researchers the focus has been on describing, but not prescribing, the relationship between culture and ideological and discriminatory practices (e.g. Collinson, 1987, 1992; Mills, 1988). One way of examining the culture of an organization is to look at its corporate image to see what and who is valued in the organization. A corporate image is the mental picture the clients, customers, employees, and others have of an organization. The impression is the combination of unconscious, unintended, conscious, and intended factors that arise. The source of this impression could be annual reports, advertisements, or in-house magazines. Clues to the culture of an organization can be found in its norms, its values, and its rituals. You can also look at the language of an organization, the metaphors, myths, and stories which are in common use or at the ceremonies, symbols, physical artefacts, taboos, and rites. (For example, the informal use of military, athletic, and sexual language in the workplace produces a subtle separation between men and women and alienates those who do not participate in the use of sexual language: Bates, 1988; see also Wilson,

1992). Culture is a characteristic of the organization, not of individuals, but is manifested in and can be measured from the verbal and non-verbal behaviour of individuals. Traditionally, organizational culture has been studied through case-study description, often involving participant observation (Hofstede, 1994). While these studies provide interesting insights, the problem is that different researchers might arrive at different conclusions.

Looking at occupational cultures tells us more. Occupational cultures consist of ideologies (emotionally charged, taken-for-granted beliefs) and cultural forms (mechanisms for affirming and expressing those beliefs). Ideologies tell members what they ought to do (Trice, 1993). Culture is a major carrier of social order. Cultures and subcultures bind people emotionally. Charismatic leaders are thought to be able to manage emotion.

The Language of Redundancy

In the early 1980s I interviewed a manager, in a declining industry, who talked of his fear that so many individuals would be made redundant that the organization would become 'anorexic' and too thin to function when an upturn in business came about. Some academics use metaphors of slimming to talk of delayering and redundancy. For example, Burrell (1992) talks of 'corporate liposuction' where senior managers have to 'slim down' the 'bulky' middle layers of the organization. What metaphors have you heard used recently to describe an organization and events?

Kunda (1992) provides us with a very detailed study of one organization and its culture, an example of successful culture management. He concentrated on how the culture was 'engineered', exploring, describing, and evaluating the reality behind the rhetoric of corporate culture. The company he looked at was called Tech Engineering, an intense and complex environment. The rhetoric was taken seriously by management and considerable time and energy was expended on embedding the rules, prescriptions, and admonitions of the culture into the fabric of everyday life. The company was portrayed as morally sound, organic, and undifferentiated. He describes how social reality was formed around key words and strong images. Relentless repetition was the rule and the ideological formulations were to be found in the ready-made words of wisdom, platitudes posing as insight and found in public places, in the mail, in workshops, and used in decoration—it became constant background noise. Metaphors characterizing Tech as a social entity were based on imagery of the family or analogies with moral institutions: religious or scientific. The ideal state was one of self-control and self-discipline. Many members managed to maintain a sense of freedom but they also experienced a pull that was not easy to resist, an escalating commitment to the corporation and its definitions of reality, coupled with a systematic and persistent attack on the boundaries of their privacy.

Breaking the Boundaries of Personal Time at Work?

An investment bank treats all their employees, from clerk to partner, to lunch. The employees each order up a very good lunch, from a menu, and it is delivered to their desks. What is the impact of this on the employee's behaviour? The effect on the employee is that they feel they have to sit at their desk at lunch-time, eat lunch, and carry on working. It is very hard for them to say, well, I think I'll take some time out now, having been given a gift of lunch.

While an organization may wish to engineer a culture, or a working atmosphere, it is not always totally successful in inducing harmonic relationships. Aktouf (1996) provides us with some excellent examples of how competence and promotability was displayed by charge-hands and workers in two breweries in Canada and Algeria where he worked as a participant observer. He looks at the signs and indicators that made middle and lower level employees look competent. They had to demonstrate that they had something extra or different from ordinary workers, for example, by being zealous and doing more work, by being ruthless, and by keeping their distance from other workers. There are some interesting omissions from the list of necessary attributes; for example, technical competence was not mentioned as an attribute necessary for being a foreman. Less surprisingly, the workers' idea of an 'ideal' foreman was found to be the exact opposite of that of management's.

A career-minded employee had to learn to use the language of the power holder and adhere to their values, for example to talk about costs, productivity, rates, and so on, when dealing with superiors, particularly if senior managers were around. The required non-verbal symbolic activity included adopting behaviour which conformed to management prescriptions (like zeal in observing rules and quotas) and doing everything possible to help management, from 'seeing with the master's eye' to outright spying. Even more enlightening are the names given to promotion candidates, like 'blockheads', 'shit eaters', 'brown noses', and 'limp wrists' in Montreal, and to 'traitors', 'lickers', 'porters', and 'yes-men' in Algiers.

An earlier study of symbolism is by Thompson (1983), who reports on his work in a slaughterhouse. He documents the workers' interaction as they cope with the danger, strain, and monotony of their jobs, as well as the consumer-spending norms that trap them in their jobs. Non-verbal gestures were the primary form of communication in this work culture. Knives were used to beat against the tubs to communicate time. As managers had refused to install a clock in the work area the gesture symbolized the workers' efforts to regain the control that management had taken from them. These gestures cannot free them from their oppressive jobs, though, or help them escape from the alienation of a consumer society.

Ackroyd and Crowdy (1990) also look at the case of slaughterhouse men and raise questions about how much control management had over the work culture. Much of the culture could not be explained by (and was highly resistant to) management action. The precise nature of the division of labour was not decided by management. The work cycle and therefore the pace of the line varied with the kind of animal being processed. The men worked fast and hard, habitually aiming to finish available batches of animals in the minimum time. Toughness and strength were the heroic qualities of the culture. Typically they worked without a break until the work was done. Though meal breaks were fixed by management, they would be varied by the men according to the batches they had to process. High levels of sustained effort were needed to ensure large payouts from the piecework bonus system. This also removed the need for close managerial supervision. Each gang had a strong informal hierarchy dominated by the fastest and most accomplished workers. The gang decided how to distribute tasks and people and fixed the pace of the line. The lead, most senior man worked at the first work station where the animals were killed; he dictated the pace of work. The average pace of work led to a build up at the work stations of the slower men; these men would be harassed (for example by flying entrails) into working harder and faster. Liquid excreta would be sprayed or practical jokes played on the lower status members of the gang. Very few seemed to resent the harassment and degradation to which they were subjected, believing

Culture and Gender

Organizations differ according to their gender regimes. They are both constrained by and constitute the practices that occur within them. Despite claims of gender neutrality, organizations are structured according to the symbolism of gender. Their culture is gendered (Gherardi, 1995). People weave together the symbolic order of gender in an organizational culture as they construct their understanding of a shared world or of difference. All cultures possess systems with which to signify sexual difference. Culture refers to the symbols, beliefs, and patterns of behaviour learnt, produced, and created by people in an organization. This includes something as banal as appearance and the symbolic message it transmits.

Gherardi asks, 'Have you ever met a woman manager with long hair worn loose to the waist?' She argues that a woman manager having loose long hair would be inappropriate, would be seen as having a 'sexiness' that clashes with the role of woman manager and the authority this confers; it would be 'out of tune' (1995: 13).

STOP	What would the equivalent be for a male?

Occupational segregation expresses a coherence: women do women's tasks, they occupy female jobs, they perpetuate the symbolic system of subordination and subservience. Occupational segregation protects women from male competition and men from competition from women. Sometimes the 'rules' change. There was, for example, a time when there were no full-time postwomen. (My spell check on the word processor does not recognize this word but it does recognize postman and postmen!) They were not recruited in urban areas because they were thought not to be able physically to carry the normal load. But when no man could be obtained to perform the work in rural areas, they were employed (see Grint, 1995: 198).

Jobs that Women Do?

Grave digging is normally a job that men do. A woman won the job of grave-digger at a cemetery in Italy after all ten male candidates failed the practical test—exhuming a body—by fainting (*Guardian*, 30 August 1997, p. 5). Until recently women were not allowed to work on the front line in the army. While they are still barred from combat jobs they will now be allowed in the artillery. Currently only 47 per cent of army jobs are open to women and only 7,000 of the 109,000 jobs are taken by women. Yet research from the US has shown that women can make better fighters than men and women are twice as likely as their male colleagues to fire at the enemy. Female terrorists are far more dangerous and deadly as they are more likely to kill bystanders without remorse (*The Scotsman*, 14 November 1997, p.15).

The attributes of femininity are ingrained in the subordination relationship: caring, compassion, willingness to please others, generosity, sensitivity. These are attributes that other marginalized or dependent groups of people possess. In order to be assimilated into the dominant group (male) certain groups of women in the professions and in politics have adopted the following strategies: they use deeper voices; they swear and use taboo language; they adopt a more assertive style in groups; they address themselves in public to traditionally male topics—business, politics, economics (see Coates, 1993).

Culture and Hierarchy

The BBC had a pecking order of presenters, according to a letter in a newspaper from an assistant editor of the 'Today' programme on Radio 4 between 1978 and 1983. Brian Redhead was first in the pecking order, followed by John Timpson and Libby Purves, despite the fact that Purves appeared four times a week and the other two, three times (*Daily Telegraph*, 2 October 1997).

Not all organizations are the same, nor are all female conditions the same (Alvesson and Billig, 1992). Women are likely, though, to occupy management positions in less prestigious organizations. In order to gain insight into the working of an organization look at where the power and reputation in an organization or industry are; men will be found in those areas and there will be few, if any, women.

Discussion Point

Few women make it to the top of universities. Despite the fact that nearly half of all undergraduates are women, their representation at the senior level remains low. In 1996 women represented about 27 per cent of the academic and related workforce, with just 5 per cent employed as professors. Lisa Jardine, the professor of English at London University's Queen Mary College, advises women to 'behave badly', show a tendency towards feistiness. She adds, though, that she never did (*Guardian Higher*, 1997). What would you advise women academics to do? What would be the benefits and drawbacks of your advice?

An interesting example of how culture operates in subtle ways is to be found in the unwritten rule that males dominate conversation in organizations. Men command a dominating role within conversation and gain for themselves a disproportionate amount of floor space or speaking time. Zimmerman and West (1975) found, in a study of thirty-one two-party conversations between a man and a woman, that virtually all the interruptions and overlaps in speaking were made by the male speakers. This, they say, leads to disproportionate female silence within male-female interaction which does not occur in same-sex conversation, so men deny equal status to women as conversational partners. Some have tried to suggest (e.g. O'Barr and Atkins, 1980) that this is because males, on average, hold higher status positions than women do. Woods (1993) put this idea to the test by examining gender and occupational status and their relative influence of patterns of speaking time in a work setting. She found that gender tended to exert the greater influence on speaking time. While speakers in high occupational positions spent more time holding the floor than their subordinates, nevertheless even when women held high-status occupational positions, male subordinates still dominated by, for example, interrupting more and giving less assent to women.

> **Beauty!**
>
> Our culture dictates what we regard as beautiful characteristics. Those who are disabled are not normally associated with beauty. When they are it becomes news. In 1997 it was news that a blind woman was included amongst the finalists in the Miss Italy beauty contest. She had managed to take part in several beauty contests without anyone in the audience realizing she was blind (*The Times*, 28 August 1997, p. 11).

Culture and Masculinity

Using company materials to examine corporate culture, Mills (1995) looked at the images projected by British Airways in their newsletters over time. He was struck by the centrality of men and masculinities in the images. An image of the 'heroic pilot' was first consciously constructed by the company. Around 1919–29 air travel was associated with danger and adventure. To counter that perception and to win new passengers the airlines used the image of the heroic First World War pilot. With changing times and 'normalization' of flying, the emphasis shifted from safety to service, provided by the male pilot and steward (and eventually the stewardess). The male (and white) association of the pilot's image did not change over time; this reflected recruitment practices and served to exclude and discourage female commercial pilots. BA did not recruit women flying crews until 1987, well after legislation against sex discrimination had been introduced.

Images of women did change over time. The first images, around 1945, were of hardworking wife and mother who stepped into the breach to do her part for the war effort. Later a new image of the hard-working girl-next-door appeared as female flight attendants were employed. Throughout the decade ending in the mid-1950s there was an increasing focus on female bodily attractiveness and an eroticized female form.

Mills is able to show, through his research, that corporate images can sanction and encourage certain types of male/female behaviour and implicitly prohibit others. Corporate images can encourage the exclusion of women from positions of power, authority, and prestige. Where does this come from? Boys, at a young age, feel they have to identify with men and so tend to reject any semblance of femininity and adhere instead to a rigid notion of masculinity. As men's achievements and activities are more valued in our society, the rules of membership in the masculine 'club' and even people's notions of maleness are more stereotypically framed and enforced than those relating to femaleness (Hort *et al.*, 1990).

Schools help form gendered identities, marking out 'correct' or 'appropriate' behaviour for males and females; they act as 'masculinity making devices'. Masculinity is not one-dimensional though; it has to be seen in the context of class, and sexual and ethnic relations, so for example there are white working-class gays and Asian middle-class heterosexuals. Masculinity is negotiated, rejected, and accepted. The different masculinities will have differential access to power, practices of power, and differential effects (Haywood and Mac an Ghaill, 1996). Particular styles of masculinity will become dominant in certain situations; those in power will be able to define what is normal or ordinary male behaviour. For example, Willis (1977) found that the working-class 'lads' he studied thought that doing mental work or having girls as friends was effeminate. Manual work was the province of masculinity.

Activities seen conventionally as 'underachieving' or 'dropping out' are, in fact, a prepara-tion for a life at work with few intrinsic satisfactions. Subversion at school and 'having a laff' is a preparation for a shop-floor job. In Haywood's (1993) study, a group of academic achievers were labelled as having an underdeveloped masculinity, and referred to as 'wankers'. The academic achievers in turn used terms such 'cripple', 'cabbage', and 'spanner' to describe the inadequacy of other male pupils. Masculinity is reinforced in schools through teacher behaviour too. Having power and authority as a teacher means being a 'proper man'. Good teachers were 'real men'. Incompetence was weakness or seen as being 'womanly'. Keeping a class quiet usually involved discipline and force like cuffing, shaking, and pushing.

> **A Small Practical Problem and Norms of Behaviour in a Gliding Club**
>
> Gliding clubs are organizations too. The members face a small practical problem as there are no toilets on gliders and they can be in the air for many hours (six to eight hours) at a time. They need to urinate; how do they do that? Male members can be found in the club discussing acceptable and successful ways of doing this during a flight. Some use polythene lunch bags which they discard from the glider. Others have adapted windscreen washer pumps and tubes to make useful practical contraptions. I haven't found out how women solve this problem.

Masculine culture in the police force is described very vividly in a study by Sharpe (1998; see also Brown, 1998; Fielding, 1994). Sharpe found that the 'cop culture' covered a multi-tude of sins. Much of the behaviour she could classify within specific locations. Van culture comprised largely of lavatorial humour, farting, and belching competitions. Patrol culture included making critical and judgemental assessments of individuals, invariably ordinary members of the public going about their daily business, coloured by racist and sexist re-marks. In the office culture male and female officers would be picked out for their appear-ance and their sexual appetite. Custody room culture was mostly officer dependent. Pub culture was a combination of van, patrol, and office culture but heavily dominated by talk of latest sexual conquests, sporting triumphs, and personal alcoholic consumption levels. As a researcher she reports that she was obliged to visit licensed premises with the vice squad and drink copious amounts of alcohol; failure to keep up with them was viewed with disdain and deep suspicion.

The topics of interest to the male officers were rugby, cricket, golf, horse racing, beer, cars, and women (in that order). Women were categorized and judged by their sexual proclivity and activity. Sharpe says 'To a policeman, sex was rather like a crime return—the more they could claim for, the better it looked to friends and colleagues' (1998: 15). The easiest target for gossip was the woman police officer. Official complaints about the behaviour of male of-ficers were not common; sexism was just part of the culture. Policewomen had to 'tough it out' or go under.

STOP Do you think that Sharpe's (1998) account of police culture is accurate? What image of this culture is portrayed on TV programmes? Which is likely to be the more accurate? How do you think you would feel being part of this culture?

Computing and Culture

The culture of computing is seen by many as male domain. There is no inherent gender bias in the computer itself but the computer culture is not equally neutral (Turkle, 1988). There is a legacy in the computer culture of images of competition, sport, and violence. There are still computer operating systems that use terms like 'killing' and 'aborting' programmes. Some, like Turkle (1988), would argue that women are expressing a computer reticence, wanting to stay away from computing, because it is a personal and cultural symbol of what a woman is not. Women look at computers and see more than machines; they see the culture that has grown up around computing (for example, a culture associated with dedicated and expert hackers, the heroes of the larger culture who took pride in being 'nerds' (their term), antisocial, and having no rules except mutual tolerance and respect for radical individualism, manipulation and mastery of the computer) and ask if they belong.

Early studies of this culture suggested that the adult world of computing is heavily dominated by males and transmitted to children by males (Kiesler *et al.*, 1985). The culture values technical rather than interpersonal skills, hardware over software, and engineering over business backgrounds (Turkle, 1984, 1988). Both men and women hold stereotypes about computer professionals. Computing is seen as a 'man's job' both in computer classes, in popular computer magazines, and by students. It is perceived as a job for the antisocial, those low in social ease and frequency of social interaction. (For a fuller discussion see Wilson, 1997; Wright, 1996). As a result, applications to computer science have fallen (Lightbody and Durndell, 1996). The most optimistic statistics, produced by the Higher Education Statistical Agency (Siann, 1997), show that females make up only 19 per cent of students majoring in computer science at university. As a result, the number of female computer professionals is low. The new and rapidly expanding information technology occupations should be providing opportunities for women but women are under-represented in IT jobs (Panteli *et al.*, 1997). Computer work is seen by women as a field for men and antisocial people (Newton, 1991; Shade, 1993). Females feel that taking too much interest in technology threatens their image of themselves as women (Lage, 1991).

Culture and Race

Minority groups currently comprise 5.5 per cent of the UK's population; 11 per cent of undergraduates come from minority backgrounds. Yet the culture of most organizations is not only male, it is also white. Managers involved in the recruitment process reinforce this by having a hierarchy of criteria for acceptability (Jenkins, 1985, 1988). The primary criteria involve appearance, manner, attitude, and maturity. Secondary criteria relate to 'gut feeling', employment history, experience, the ability to fit in, age, speech style, literacy, and marital status. Tertiary criteria are references and English-language competence. Minority workers are less likely to fit the stereotypical 'married with two kids and a mortgage' pattern recruiters seem to prefer; their accent may be regarded by white recruiters as inferior and they are seen as less likely to fit in (Grint, 1991).

Employers' attitudes to race discrimination have been called lazy, benignly ignorant, and complacent by the Commission for Racial Equality (*Personnel Today*, 31 January 1995). While 88 per cent of organizations have equality policies on race, fewer than half put their words into action. Racism is not difficult to demonstrate. For example, the Head of the Department of General Practice at Manchester University showed that doctors with Asian names were less likely to be interviewed for jobs than those with English names. In a controversial research project, he sent off fake curriculum vitaes, identical in terms of sex, education, and training; all the doctors had trained in Britain. Half the names were Asian and half were English. Doctors with English names were twice as likely to be called for interview as those with Asian names (*Guardian*, 3 June 1997).

Several of the UK's leading corporations, however, are beginning to recognize the need to assemble a diverse staff team and have sought to devise recruitment strategies that reach out and attract qualified ethnic minority candidates (*Independent*, 13 November 1997, p. 22). This, they realize, will help them establish credibility and expertise to help access increasingly diverse consumer markets.

Other Aspects of Culture

There are many approaches to culture. One might be to look at the moral order, the ordering of expectations and moral imperatives in a work situation. A strand of the Chicago School in sociology (see Watson, 1987) suggested we look at how an individual copes with or adapts to problems faced at work in maintaining their identity. Students were encouraged to look at the 'dirty' or deviant jobs in order to see factors of general relevance to work experience which might not be noticed in more conventional kinds of work where they might be taken for granted. We saw in Chapter 6, for example, prostitutes stress the extent to which they control their clients in order to maintain self-respect. This may also be happening when a garage mechanic insists that they tell you what is wrong with your car and may resent it if you diagnose the fault when they are the expert. The taken-for-grantedness of organizational rules is quite hard to uncover. It is often only when the rules are broken that you see what they are.

Example 1

As a student, one summer, I worked in a hotel in a small community on the west coast of Scotland. The hotel was owned and run by an ex-army colonel. He enforced strict rules which he told you about verbally. For example, you may not entertain guests in your room, may not have visitors, receive phone calls, or use the public phone in the hotel. The only ways to keep in touch with friends and family were by public phone (using a phone box in the village in the afternoon break or after 9 p.m.), by letter, or by arranging to meet them away from the hotel. This way he ensured that you defined yourself as a lowly servant and less than a guest, and noted the superiority of the guest. The culture and rules he created operated as a 'boundary device' (see Grint, 1995: 167), marking the privileged from unprivileged. But there were also some rules that you only knew about when you broke them. For example I discovered that you may not sing in the empty dining room while setting the tables. What rules have you learnt, in a work setting, only by having broken them?

Example 2

A friend of mine noticed, in a cafe, if you ordered two teas, the waiter or waitress would write down 2T (always in the singular). Intrigued by this she asked for 'two tea' and found she was always corrected by the waiter or waitress. It would appear that the waiter/waitress has a rule that they can use the singular and shorthand but you cannot. The friend was also witnessed asking for a pound of satsuma in a fruit shop. Can you think of an example of an organizational rule where there is one unwritten rule for you and another for the person enforcing the rule?

Questions for Further Work

1. Grint (1995) looks at the origins of the word 'culture' in agriculture and horticulture. Read Grint and describe how thinking about the origin of the word can help us think about culture.

2. Barley (1991) says that anything can be an expressive sign capable of signification. How is this the case with death and undertakers? Think of an occupation you have experienced and note the symbols that play an important part in creating the culture of that occupation.

3. Gherardi (1995) illustrates, through six cases of women entering all-male workplaces, how workplaces differ in how they receive a representative of the other sex. What did she find? Does what she find concur with any experience you have had?

4. Ackroyd and Crowdy (1990) give us a very graphic explanation as to how the culture of slaughterhouse men deals with the moral dimension of their job. How do they do this?

5. Brewis (1994) describes the differing cultures of two university departments and the impact the culture has on relationships. What effect did it have?

6. Does research by Woods (1993) on men dominating conversations in mixed-sex company concur with your personal experience? Read Woods's study. Try asking a mixed-sex group of friends if you can tape record a conversation and analyse the results for yourself.

7. Goffman (1961) gives us a detailed account of life in asylums. What insight can we gain from this work to help us understand the working of organizations like universities?

8. Hopfl (1995) draws the analogy between acting and customer service. Read her paper and critically assess the similarities.

9. What evidence is there to suggest that there is racism in British organizations? What research would you design to demonstrate racism and what problems might you anticipate in your research design?

10. What evidence is there to suggest that the culture within police forces is discriminatory (see Brown, 1998; Fielding, 1994; Sharpe, 1998)?

Suggestions for Further Reading

Alvesson, M., and Billing, Y. D. (1992) 'Gender, Organizational Culture and Sexuality', in *Understanding Gender and Organizations*. London: Sage.

Barley, S. R. (1991) 'Semiotics and the Study of Occupational and Organizational Culture', in P .J. Frost, L. F. Moore, M. R. Louis, C. C. Lundberg, and J. Martin (eds.), *Reframing Organizational Culture*. London: Sage.

References

Ackroyd, S., and Crowdy, P. A. (1990) 'Can Culture be Managed?', *Personnel Review*, 19/5: 3–13.

Aktouf, O. (1996) 'Competence, Symbolic Activity and Promotability', in S. Linstead, R. Grafton Small, and P. Jeffcutt (eds.), *Understanding Management*. London: Sage.

Alvesson, M., and Billing, Y. D. (1992) 'Gender and Organization: Toward a Differentiated Understanding', *Organization Studies*, 13/2: 73–106.

Barley, S. R. (1991) 'Semiotics and the Study of Occupational and Organizational Culture', in P. J. Frost, L. F. Moore, M. R. Louis, C. C. Lundberg, and J. Martin (1991) (eds.), *Reframing Organizational Culture*. London: Sage.

Bates, B. (1988) *Communication and the Sexes*. New York: Harper and Row.

Brewis, J. (1994) 'The Role of Intimacy at Work: Interactions and Relationships in the Modern Organization', in D. Adam-Smith and A. Peacock (eds.), *Cases in Organizational Behaviour*. London: Pitman Publishing, case 3.

Brown, J. M. (1998) 'Aspects of Discriminatory Treatment of Women Police Officers Serving in Forces in England and Wales', *British Journal of Criminology*, 38/2: 265–81.

Burrell, G. (1992) 'The Organization of Pleasure', in M. Alvesson and H. Wilmott (eds.), *Critical Management Studies*. London: Sage, pp. 66–89.

Coates, J. (1993) *Women, Men and Language*, 2nd edn. London: Longman.

Collinson, D. L. (1987) 'Picking Women: The Recruitment of Temporary Workers in the Mail Order Industry', *Work, Employment and Society*, 1/3: 371–87.

—— (1992) *Managing the Shopfloor: Subjectivity, Masculinity and Workplace Culture*. Berlin: De Gruyter.

—— and Collinson, M. (1997) 'Delayering Managers: Time–Space Surveillance and its Gendered Effects', *Organization*, 4/3: 357–407.

Deal, T. E. and Kennedy, A. A. (1982) *Corporate Cultures*. Reading, Mass.: Addison Wesley.

Du Gay, P. (1996) *Consumption and Identity at Work*. London: Sage.

Etzioni, A. (1961) *A Comparative Analysis of Complex Organizations*. New York: Free Press.

Fielding, N. (1994) 'Cop Canteen Culture', in E. Stanko and T. Newburn (eds.), *Just Boys Doing Business: Men, Masculinity and Crime*. London: Routledge.

Frost, P. J., Moore, L. F., Louis, M. R, Lundberg, C. C., and Martin, J. (1991) (eds.), *Reframing Organizational Culture*. London: Sage.

Gherardi, S. (1995) *Gender, Symbolism and Organizational Cultures*. London: Sage.

Goffman, E. (1961) *Asylums*. Garden City, NY: Anchor.

Grint, K. (1991) *The Sociology of Work: An Introduction*. Cambridge: Polity.

—— (1995) *Management: A Sociological Introduction*. Cambridge: Polity.

Guardian Higher (1997) 'Women Behaving Badly', (14 Oct.): p. ii.

Haywood, C. (1993) 'Using Sexuality: An Exploration into the Fixing of Sexuality to Make Male Identities in a Mixed Sex Sixth Form', unpublished MA dissertation, University of Warwick, cited in Mairtin Mac an Ghaill (ed.), *Understanding Masculinity*. Milton Keynes: Open University Press, ch. 3.

—— and Mac an Ghaill, Mairtin (1996) 'Schooling Masculinities', in Mairtin Mac an Ghaill (ed.), *Understanding Masculinities*. Milton Keynes: Open University Press.

Hofstede, G. (1991) *Cultures and Organizations: Software of the Mind*. London: McGraw Hill.

—— (1994) *Uncommon Sense about Organizations: Cases, Studies and Field Observations*. Thousand Oaks, Calif.: Sage.

—— (1998) 'Attitudes, Values and Organizational Culture: Disentangling the Concepts', *Organization Studies*, 19/3: 477–92.

Hopfl, H. (1995) 'Performance and Customer Service: The Cultivation of Contempt', *Studies in Culture, Organizations and Society*, 1: 47–62.

Hort, B. E., Fagot, B. I., and Leinback, M. D. (1990) 'Are People's Notions of Maleness More Stereotypically Framed than their Notions of Femaleness?', *Sex Roles*, 23/3–4, 197–212.

Jenkins, R. (1985) 'Black Workers in the Labour Market: The Price of Recession', in B. Roberts, R. Finnegan and D. Gallie (eds.), *New Approaches to Economic Life*. Manchester: Manchester University Press.

—— (1988) 'Discrimination and Equal Opportunity in Employment: Ethnicity and "Race" in the United Kingdom', in D. Gallie (ed.), *Employment in Britain*. Oxford: Blackwell.

Johnson, P., and Gill, J. (1993) *Management Control and Organizational Behaviour*. London: Paul Chapman.

Kiesler, S., Sproull, L., and Eccles, J. S. (1985) 'Pool Halls, Chips and War Games: Women in the Culture of Computing', *Psychology of Women Quarterly*, 9: 451–62.

Kunda, G. (1992) *Engineering Culture: Control and Commitment in a High-Tech Corporation*. Philadelphia: Temple University Press.

Lage, E. (1991) 'Boys, Girls and Microcomputing', *European Journal of Psychology of Education*, 1: 29–44.

Leidner, R. (1993) *Fast Food, Fast Talk*. Berkeley, Calif.: University of California Press.

Lightbody, P., and Durndell, A. (1996) 'The Masculine Image of Careers in Science and Technology: Fact or Fantasy?', *British Journal of Educational Psychology*, 66: 231–46.

Lupton, T. (1963) *On the Shopfloor*. Oxford: Pergamon.

McKinley, R., Sanchez, C. M. and Schick, A. G. (1995) 'Organizational Downsizing: Constraining, Cloning and Learning', *Academy of Management Executive*, 14/3: 32–44.

Marshall, J. (1995) *Women Managers Moving On*. London: Routledge.

Mills, A. J. (1988) 'Organization, Gender and Culture', *Organization Studies*, 9/3: 351–69.

—— (1995) 'Man/aging Subjectivity, Silencing Diversity: Organizational Imagery in the Airline Industry. The Case of British Airways', *Organization*, 2/2: 243–69.

Morgan, G. (1986) *Images of Organization*. London: Sage.

Newton, P. (1991) 'Computing: An Ideal Occupation for Women?', in J. Firth-Cozens and M. A. West (eds.), *Women at Work: Psychological and Organizational Perspectives*. Buckingham: Open University Press, pp. 143–53.

Newton, T. and Findlay, P. (1996) 'Playing God? The Performance of Appraisal', *Human Resource Management Journal*, 6/3: 42–58.

O'Barr, W. and Atkins, B. (1980) ' "Women's Language" or "Powerless Language"?', in S. McConnell-Ginet, R. Baker and N. Furman (eds.), *Women and Language in Literature and Society*. New York: Praeger.

Ogbonna, E., and Wilkinson, B. (1990) 'Corporate Strategy and Corporate Culture: The View from the Checkout', *Personnel Review*, 19/4: 9–15.

Ouchi, W. (1981) *Theory Z*. Reading, Mass.: Addison-Wesley.

Panteli, A., Ramsey, H., and Beirne, M. (1997) 'Engendered Systems Development: Ghettoization and Agency', Paper published in Proceedings of the 6th International IFIP Conference, 'Women, Work and Computerization: Spinning a Web from Past to Future, Bonn', 24–7 May.

Pascale, R. T. and Athos, A. G. (1982) *The Art of Japanese Management*. Harmondsworth: Penguin.

Peters, T., and Waterman, R. (1982) *In Search of Excellence*. New York: Warner Communications.

Rafaeli, A., and Sutton, R. I. (1987) 'Expression of Emotion as Part of the Work Role', *Academy of Management Review*, 12/1: 23–37.

—— —— (1989) 'The Expression of Emotion in Organizational Life', *Research in Organizational Behaviour*, 11: 1–42.

Roy, D. (1960) 'Banana Time: Job Satisfaction and Informal Interaction', *Human Organization*, 18/2: 156–68.

Shade, L. R. (1993) 'Gender Issues in Computer Networking', Paper presented at 'Community Networking: the International Fee-Net Conference', Ottawa, Aug.

Sharpe, K. (1998) *Red Light, Blue Light: Prostitutes, Punters and the Police*. Aldershot: Ashgate Publishing.

Siann, G. (1997) 'We Can, We Don't Want to: Factors Influencing Women's Participation in Computing', *Women in Computing*. Exeter: Intellect Books.

Smircich, L. (1983*a*) 'Concepts of Culture and Organizational Analysis', *Administrative Science Quarterly*, 28: 339–58.

—— (1983*b*) 'Studying Organizations as Cultures', in G. Morgan (ed.), *Beyond Method: Strategies for Social Research*. London: Sage.

—— and Calas, M. B. (1987) 'Organizational Culture: A Critical Assessment', in F. M. Jablin, L. Putnam, K. H. Roberts and L. W. Porter (eds.), *Handbook of Organizational Communication*. Newbury, Calif.: Sage.

Thompson, W. E. (1983) 'Hanging Tongues: A Sociological Encounter with the Assembly Line', *Qualitative Sociology*, 6: 215–37.

Trice, H. M. (1993) *Occupational Subcultures in the Workplace*. Ithaca, NY: ILR Press.

Turkle, S. (1984) *The Second Self: Computers and the Human Spirit*. New York: Simon and Schuster.

—— (1988) 'Computational Reticence: Why Women Fear the Intimate Machine', in C. Kramarae (ed.), *Technology and Women's Voices: Keeping in Touch*. New York: Routledge and Kegan Paul.

Watson, R. J. (1987) *Sociology, Work and Industry*, 2nd edn. London: RKP.

Willis, P. (1977) *Learning to Labour: How Working Class Kids Get Working Class Jobs*. Aldershot: Saxon House.

Wilson, F. M. (1992) 'Language, Technology, Gender and Power', *Human Relations*, 45/9: 883–904 (Sept.).

—— (1997) 'Computing, Computer Science and Computer Scientists: How they are Perceived', in R. Lander and A. Adam (eds.), *Women in Computing*. Exeter: Insight Books.

Woods, N. (1993) 'Talking Shop: Sex and Status as Determinants of Floor Apportionment in a Work Setting', in J. Coates and D. Cameron (eds.), *Women in their Speech Communities*, 4th edn. Harlow: Longman.

Wright, R. (1996) 'The Occupational Masculinity of Computing', in *Masculinities in Organizations*. London: Sage.

Zimmerman, D., and West, C. (1975) 'Sex Roles, Interruptions and Silences in Conversation', in B. Thorne and N. Henley (eds.), *Language and Sex: Difference and Dominance*. Newbury, Mass.: Rowley House.

9

Organizational Deviance? Theft,
Resistance, Struggles, Lying,
Sabotage, Romance, and Fun

ORGANIZATIONAL MISBEHAVIOUR, RESISTANCE, and crime has been relatively neglected in textbooks of management and business. It is seldom thought of as 'organizational behaviour'. Yet resistance has been acknowledged since Karl Marx as taking many forms and derived from revolutionary class consciousness. For Marx, though, class-conscious radicalism was not very likely to occur as within capitalism there was the illusion of freedom and alienation was obscured; capitalism appears normal and inevitable, like the laws of nature. 'Real resistance' was broken down (Jermier *et al.*, 1994). Acts such as sabotage, theft, or the intentional withholding of output can often be explained as reactions to frustrations (Spector, 1997).

Theft

We all know people who cheat and probably cheat ourselves. We know how to cheat and thieve, even if we don't do it. In universities plagiarism is one form of cheating much despised; theft is equally despised by most. Every now and again newspapers report a story of theft that is bound to catch the eye. Punch (1996) cites the newspaper story of nuns who had fraudulently diverted money (about $5 million) from a hospital to build an indoor swimming pool and so they could have TV sets in all the cells in their luxurious convent. He also details three highly dramatic cases of business deviance, including the case of Robert Maxwell where £300 million went missing from pension funds, BCCI who are estimated to have swindled $20 billion from depositors around the world (and run a 'black bank' within the bank), and the Savings and Loan scandal where funds were siphoned off for personal gains. These cases, he says, blow apart the rational and respectable myth of management. Top managers have manipulated their companies, regulators, and their environments for devious ends. To understand business crime and deviance we have to look at the nature of business, the realities of organizational life, and the dilemmas facing management.

It is estimated that three-quarters of all employees steal from their employers at least once (McGurn, 1988) and that many of these repeat such actions on a regular basis (Delaney, 1993). Employee theft has been blamed for 30–50 per cent of all business failures (Greenberg, 1997). In Ditton's (1977) study of British bakery workers, so extreme was the theft in one bakery, and so widely accepted the practice, that supervisors had to plan for extra loaves to be baked each day to avoid running short.

Gerald Mars, a social anthropologist, looked at ways in which ordinary people cheat at work, how they steal from their organizations (Mars, 1982). Cheating is endemic and integral to the rewards of work, he says. Fiddling is woven into the fabric of people's everyday lives. He sorts the cultures he sees in organizations into four groups: hawks, donkeys, wolves, and vultures. Each group has a distinct ideology, a set of attitudes, a set of rules, and a view of the world. Each plans to rob, cheat, fiddle, or short change subordinates, customers, employers, or the state.

Let us look at how he describes these groups he identifies. Hawks, he says, are individualists, who bend the rules to suit themselves. They are entrepreneurs, innovative professionals (including academics and journalists), and those who run small businesses. Hawkish entrepreneurs are also to be found among waiters, fairground buskers, and owner taxi drivers. The individual's freedom to transact on their own terms is highly valued. Their aim is to 'make it'. An example would be a journalist claiming good expenses for a good story or claiming first-class travel but going second class or a lawyer charging cheap time (by using trainee, unqualified, apprentice labour) but charging it at dear prices, charging full professional rates.

Donkeys are highly constrained by rules and isolated from each other. Unlike hawks who have a reasonably full choice in how they spend their time, donkeys have no such freedom. Some transport workers are donkeys, as their jobs isolate them and they feel dominated by rules (for example, those governing safety). Supermarket cashiers and machine minders are also highly constrained and isolated. These people will respond, particularly where the constraints are strongest, by breaking or sabotaging the rules which constrain them; alternatively they will fiddle. These individuals can be either powerful or powerless depending on their actions. If they passively accept the constraints they are powerless; if they are disruptive and reject the rules, they can be extremely powerful. The example given is of a supermarket cashier who was able consistently to extract five times her daily wage in fiddled cash. She might do this by ringing up less than the total charge on the till then pocket the difference or by allowing her friends and family to take goods through the checkout that had not been paid for. She hated being treated like a programmed robot and fiddled to make her job more interesting. Fiddling gave her new targets, a sense of challenge, and hurt her boss.

Wolves work and steal in packs; they have a hierarchy, order and internal controls that ensure that when they steal they do so with agreed rules and a well-defined division of labour. They have a leader and penalize their own deviants. Examples are a dockwork gang, refuse collectors, airplane crews or miners. Refuse collectors will break the rules, riding on the back of the cart or leaving it unattended. They break the 'no gratuities rule' too and will sell dustbins to those who ask. They can also sell what they collect, for example, sofas, brass, and copper. An attack on one, an exertion of management control over the fiddle, will be seen as an attack on all.

Vultures need the support of the group for the fiddle but act on their own when 'at the feast'. They depend on support and information from colleagues but are also competitive and act in isolation for much of the time. As they rely both cooperation and competition, their groups can be unstable and turbulent. Examples from this group include travelling sales people, driver-deliverers, and waiters. Waiters can overcharge for drinks from the bar; photocopy sales staff can sell paper they are supposed to give away; the delivery person can sell black economy clothing from the van. All rely on the actions of others to keep their 'scam' going.

Elsewhere Mars describes in greater depth the pilferage that takes place in a hotel in Blackpool where he worked (1989). Wages paid to waiting staff are comparatively low and labour turnover is high. Using this as justification, the waiting staff pilfer and indulge in 'the fiddle'. 'Knock-off' refers to a subtype of fiddle, the illicit acquisition of food, cutlery, and linen. Fiddles are regarded as an entitlement, as part of the wages. This could be done by, for example, fiddling on tea and coffee. A waiter would receive an order for two coffees. He goes into the kitchen and orders one coffee on an order slip. He obtains a standard coffee pot, milk jug, and one cup and saucer from the staff in the kitchen. He needs an extra cup and saucer for his customers which he will have hidden in a strategic area near the lounge. A 'bent helper' in the kitchen can make sure there is enough coffee in the pot to serve two. The waiter charges the customer for two coffees but only puts the price of one, with the order slip, into the till. Bent helpers can be paid in beer rather than cash.

Some employers in manufacturing industry have tried to combat theft by locking their workers into factories. As a result of this measure, there have been some tragic accidents. 146 workers died in a fire in a locked New York garment industry sweatshop; 84 died in a fire in a toy producing company in China, and 25 in a poultry plant in North Carolina (Nichols, 1997: 108).

Research (e.g. Greenberg and Scott, 1996) suggests that many individuals steal from their companies because they believe it is justified. They believe that the company is not providing them with a fair deal so to even the score they appropriate company property. Supporting this view is the fact that such theft is often accompanied by a total absence of guilt.

Resistance at Disneyland

We touched on the limits to organizational culture's absorption in Chapter 8 but much more could be said. Van Maanen (1991) shows the limits to which overt company propaganda in the Disney organization can be effective. Satirical banter, mischievous winking, and playful exaggeration are to be found in the classroom with the new recruits. As one notes, 'It is difficult to take seriously an organization that provides its retirees with "Golden Ears" instead of gold watches after 20 or more years of service' (1991: 67). All the newcomers are aware that the label 'Disneyland' has both an unserious and artificial connotation. A full embrace of the Disneyland role would be as deviant as its full rejection.

Sometimes a customer will overstep their role, insult an operator, challenge their authority, or disrupt the routines of the job. If a ride operator is slighted by a customer, routine practices have been developed by the operators to deal with this. Common remedies include the 'seat-belt squeeze' where the deviant customer's seat-belt is adjusted to the extent that they are doubled over at the point of departure and left gasping; the 'break-toss' where operators jump on the outside of a norm violator's car, unhitch the safety belt, then slam on the brakes, bringing the car to an almost instant stop while the driver flies over the bonnet; the 'seat-belt snap' is where an offending customer receives a sharp quick snap of the hard plastic belt across the face or other part of the body while entering or exiting a seat-belted ride; the 'break up the party' gambit is a queuing device put into officious use to separate troublesome pairs into different units, thus forcing on them the pain of strange companions for the duration of a ride; offensive guests can be drenched with water in the submarine ride. All these procedures, and more, are learnt on the job and enliven conversation time at breaks or after work. Naturally, though, operators are aware of the limits and if caught they know that restoration of corporate pride will be swift.

Resistance and Control among Nursing Auxiliaries and Care Assistants.

Women are often portrayed as a compliant workforce but this is not necessarily the case. A study of work in a nursing home for older people (Lee-Treweek, 1997) shows how female nursing auxiliary workers use resistance to get through each working day. The work is physically heavy, dirty (involving tasks such as washing soiled bodies), and low paid (wages can be as low as £1 per hour). It is assumed that this is women's work, easy and natural for women who are equipped to deal with bodily substances, are sympathetic, and that they might enjoy this type of work as 'caring people'. However, the main motivation for work was instrumental, earning a wage. Their care work had little to do with caring. Conveying this view to those outside the job was problematic for the auxiliaries.

The home's brochure advertised 'family type care' but the pressure to create the clean and orderly individual was far stronger. The main work for the nursing auxiliary was to create a sanitized 'lounge standard' patient. The product of the work was a clean, orderly, quiet patient; the work was about process and order, much the same as factory work. Knowing the people was not about knowing patients as individuals, but about knowing the type of work and how to handle the patients. This knowledge was a source of both pride and resistance to the sheer drudgery and lack of control over the nature of the work. The nurses' knowledge and role was seen by the auxiliaries as inferior—it was clean work which was neither real nor necessary. The needs of the patient were often not met as 'needy' or 'sick' patients were reconstructed into attention-seeking, pretence, or wilful childishness; they were ignored even when they were talked about in their own presence. Incidents such as being hit by a patient were referred to as 'fun', so that personal toughness was elevated to a position of importance.

> **STOP**
>
> There is a danger that the researcher is 'throwing stones at angels'. Read the article yourself and see how Lee-Treweek would handle this criticism. If you had done this research and found nothing positive to say about the care workers, how would you have handled this?

Similar disturbing descriptions of the realities of life for psychiatric nurses can be found (see Handy 1990). The issue of control over patients seems to be central in studies of nursing and care and of being tough, 'not being a bleeding, whining Minnie' (Bates, 1990). Bates (1993) also shows how 16- to 18-year-old care assistants cope with violence, incontinence, and death in their daily work. To cope they 'switched off' and kept 'busy'. A significant proportion of the work the girls regarded as 'shit shovelling' (1993: 17). The social taboo of talking about incontinence was dealt with in part through a humorous language strategy: the reversal of shit to produce 'tish'. The trainee care assistants rejected and scorned the college tutor's stress of the need for sensitivity and genuine caring in their work. What they contested was the quality of care which they were expected to offer.

Lying

Deception and lies have received little attention in the management literature yet we all know that they happen. People have ample opportunity either to lie or to tell the truth in the course of their work. Workers constantly report their behaviour or give information to others. The truck driver reports the number of hours on the road, the nurse charts vital signs, the public accountant audits, and the forester reports a tree census. Organizations generally rely on the reports to be accurate and honest but each of these individuals may have reasons to lie. We lie to avoid embarrassment or conflict, to impress others, cope with difficult situations, and to achieve personal gain. Lying jeopardizes information quality and therefore the integrity of organizations. It can have detrimental effects on how organizations function (Grover, 1997).

> **STOP** You have just read about truck drivers, nurses, accountants, and foresters. When you pictured these people, what gender were they? What does that tell you?

Grover (1993*a*) has looked at the conditions under which employees tell lies. They will lie to protect their 'turf' or when faced with conflicting demands (role conflict). For example, the truck driver may lie about speeding because there is a conflict between organizational policy (which says speed limits must be followed) and external role demands (for example, they must pick the children up by six). The nurse's time may conflict with time demands of the job assignment, leading the nurse to report vital signs not actually measured. People may also lie out of self-interest, for example to get promoted, prevent themselves from being admonished, or to make more money. Grover (1993*b*) looks at the conditions under which professionals lie about their work behaviour. Again role conflict causes lying—when, for example, the physician has a professional ethic to cure patients by diagnosing and treating them as accurately as possible but may find that the costs of the procedure are prohibitive (prescribing Viagra, the impotency drug, is the example which springs to mind here).

Role conflict and self-interest will not explain all lying. Some people may have pathological tendencies toward lying, or may lie when instructed to do so by a superior, or as revenge in response to anger. Managers employ deceptive strategies to lie to workers about the opportunities of advancement, or deceive overworked individuals about possible relief, or create fear and anxiety by selective public reprimands. They will also display indiscriminate bursts of staged anger (Jackall, 1980). Jackall (1980) also discusses how corporations lie, as was so, he says, in the case of thalidomide where, in order to continue high sales of the drug as a non-toxic tranquilliser, the managerial response to reports of children born with deformities was to 'Lie, suppress, bribe and distort' (The Insight Team, 1979).

Sabotage

Few academic studies exist on sabotage. It is often a rational and calculative act. Sabotage is deliberate action or inaction that is intended to damage, destroy, or disrupt some aspect of the workplace environment (the property, product, process, or reputation). Examples include destruction of machinery or goods, work slowdowns, passing on defective work, flattening tyres, scratching cars, intentionally misplacing important paperwork, offering a chemical company's new formula to a competitor, erasing financial records, or introducing a computer virus. Taylor and Walton (1971: 219) define sabotage as 'the conscious act of mutilation or destruction' that reduces tension and frustration, and quote the case of a frustrated salesman in a Knightsbridge store who demobilized a machine which shuttled change around the store by ramming a cream bun down its gullet.

An early study of sabotage can be found in Dubois (1979). While sabotage may be done by workers, it can also be done by management, he says. Non-productive time is sabotage—when machines are out of order, there is poor planning, shortage of raw materials, inadequate consideration of siting of machinery—all of these can be seen as management sabotage. Lock outs and strikes bring production to a halt. Sabotage by management is far more serious than sabotage from workers.

Sabotage, LaNuez and Jermier (1994) argue is a result of low levels of control. Both managers and workers can experience low levels of control due to mergers and restructuring, increased use of monitoring and other control techniques, technological changes that replace skilled labour with less skilled labour, and displacement. Sabotage can be seen as a strategic weapon that can be used by any person to revise power imbalances or seek to re-establish control of their work or workplace. Similarly they may choose to 'whistleblow', to disclose illegal, unethical, or harmful practices in the workplace to parties who might take action (see Miceli and Near, 1997; Rothschild and Miethe, 1994).

Struggles over Time

The control over working time is always a source of struggle between workers and managers. In spite of employer opposition, 'Saint Monday' was kept as a rest day in Birmingham throughout the nineteenth century. Workplace studies too have shown that time is struggled over and negotiated. The accounts show that the action with respect to time might be in an effort to relieve the monotony of work, as in Roy's (1960) study of machine operators, or as a way of creating time away from work, as in Ditton's (1979) study of a factory bakery.

Recently Heyes (1997) has shown how workers in a chemical plant created opportunities for overtime and enhanced earnings through what management termed 'illegitimate' absenteeism and the workers called 'knocking'. Knocking took two forms. In one a pair of workers from separate shifts would collaborate; a worker might deliberately go sick for a shift while his workmate would voluntarily provide cover at an overtime premium. The following week the roles would be reversed and the gains from knocking were thus shared. The second form was known as the '8 plus 4' system. A worker on an eight-hour day shift would volunteer to work the extra four hours of someone who had been unable to fulfil (had knocked off) a twelve-hour shift. Again there was an explicit, reciprocal agreement in order to enhance joint incomes. Workers also regarded occasional absences (3.5 per cent of contractual hours on average) as a necessary means of gaining relief from the pressures of a hard, physically intensive, and dangerous job.

Organizational Misdemeanour—Organizational Romance

Organizational romances are commonplace and have increased in number (Collins, 1983; Mainiero, 1993; Roy, 1974). Organizations are natural breeding grounds for romantic involvements. There is abundant evidence that individuals tend to prefer others with similar attitudes (Smith *et al.*, 1983) and similar attitudes are often found amongst people working together. The Alfred Marks Bureau (1991, 1995) found that 58 per cent of respondents in their surveys had experienced at least one relationship at work and over half the romantic relationships that start off in the office end in marriage.

Romantic relationships can, however, produce a serious practical problem because they can distort the smooth functioning of organizations (Quinn, 1977). There have been some high-level cases of romantic entanglements that have had devastating effects on careers. The Cecil Parkinson (senior politician)–Sara Keays (his secretary) affair in Britain and the Mary Cunningham (Bendix corporation)–Willam Agee case, in the US demonstrate the career risks (Harrison and Lee, 1986). Initially couples usually try to keep their relationship a secret because some organizations have explicit rules against romantic relationships and fear of gossip and disapproval fosters secrecy. Where one or both participants is married, the predominant fear is that family members find out. There can be negative impacts if favouritism or special treatment is shown to the new partner in the relationship; this causes jealousy and resentment (Lobel *et al.*, 1994). Sometimes hostility can be generated by the romance in a work group and output and productivity lowered (Mainiero, 1986). Couples can experience role conflict, conflict between personal and professional roles. For example, if the lovers attend a presentation ceremony dinner along with the company's top executives: during dinner someone at the table suggests to the male executive that it is inappropriate to bring his lover along as her corporate status is not the same as the other executive guests (Collins, 1983). A more disruptive impact can come about when the affair ends (Warfield, 1987). In office romances that cross the lines of authority in an organization there is the potential for exploitation of the relations. For example, sexual favours to the boss could be returned for promotion. Conversely a boss may manipulate a subordinate by threatening to withdraw from the relationship unless a work deadline is met (Mainiero, 1993). In the most extreme cases the affair can lead to a harassment claim. There have been a number of high-level harassment cases recently, for example Bill Clinton/Paula Jones (*American Lawyer*, 1997; Macleans, 1998; S. Taylor, 1997) and Anita Hill/Clarence Thomas (Trix and Sankar, 1998). Harassment too is misbehaviour (Wilson, 1995: ch. on sexual harassment; Wilson 1998).

It would be wrong to leave the impression that the impact of romantic relationships is only negative. Mainiero (1989) describes several cases in which couples reported that their personal and professional lives were enhanced by an office romantic involvement. For example, one couple found that when a deadline had to be met, they worked together at home to meet that deadline. In another case the couple reported they had benefited from each other's critical comment on management style and work behaviour. The sexual harassment research literature tends to show, however, that for every happy outcome, there are many more unhappy ones.

> **The Case of a University**
>
> University teachers are advised not to develop intimate relationships with students. If they do develop a consensual relationship, the university teacher is asked to declare that a relationship has developed and ask that the student's work be assessed by another member of staff.

Fun

Fun has been touched upon in other chapters, particularly where we have looked at how individuals resist organizational culture's constraints. The presence of horseplay and humour is also found in research on hospitals (Goffman, 1968), coalmines (Pitt, 1979), building sites (Riemer, 1979), schools (Willis, 1977), and shop-floors (Burawoy, 1979; Pollert, 1981; Roy, 1960). Humour serves many purposes. Roy described how the machinists avoided 'going nuts' by teasing and using mock aggression. Racial hostility was found to be diluted by humour in Burawoy's study. Linstead (1985) found that joking was closely related to resistance and sabotage. Joking helped establish an informal world outside the constraints of management control. Showing the collective elements of joking and exploring the contradictions and divisions which characterize shop-floor relations, Collinson (1988) focuses on gender identity and working-class resistance in a lorry producing factory. He shows that humour served as resistance both to the tightly controlled repetitious work tasks and to the organization of production. The men wanted to make the best of the situation and enjoy the company of others. They were concerned to show that they could laugh at themselves. The use of nicknames like 'Fat Rat', 'Bastard Jack', 'Big Lemon', and 'The Snake' created a mythical and imaginary world. 'Electric Lips' was unable to keep a secret. 'Pot Harry' had broken all the drinking pots, mugs, by dropping them. They also wanted to differentiate themselves from white-collar staff and managers. They did this by, for example, expressing how manual work was the very essence of masculinity. The joking culture was a symbol of freedom and autonomy. The uncompromising banter of the shop-floor, permeated with swearing, ridicule, displays of sexuality, and pranks, was contrasted, exaggerated, and elevated above the middle-class politeness, cleanliness, and more restrained demeanour of office staff.

Humour could also mean conformity. There were demands of group conformity, specific rules that led to social survival. Individuals had to be able to take a joke, laugh at themselves, and expected others to do the same. They needed to be aggressive, critical, and disrespectful. Apprentices had to learn to accept degrading initiation ceremonies. Humour also meant control, being used as pressure to conform to routine shop-floor values and practices, mutual control, and discipline. For example, there was a steady stream of cutting remarks to control 'deviants', lazy workers.

There are choices in how managers view the issues discussed here. They can clamp down on the activities and exercise greater control; this is likely to lead to further resistance. Or they can learn to live with these realities, as authors like Mars suggests. Fox (1973) offers us a framework to help consider potential conflict. He says there are two frames of reference, the unitary and pluralist perspective. If managers adopt a pluralist perspective they believe that within their organization there is the potential for unity, partnership, and harmony, if it does not already exist. In this organization there will be one source of authority and one focus of loyalty; the organization could, and maybe does, function much like a healthy functioning sports team. Management and workers should be striving jointly to meet company goals. Individuals should accept the authority of those who manage and managers are best qualified to manage. Managers motivate and promote an esprit de corps. Your organization is like a team, striving to achieve common goals. Any conflict is either negligible, caused by poor communication, stupidity, or the work of agitators. This view, Fox would argue, would wish to deny that theft, strikes, conflict, and sabotage exist. This view is only maintained because it suits the needs of management. Denial of conflict may be one way in which managers cope with conflict; denial of reality is one way psychologists have found individuals cope (Edwards, 1990).

A pluralist perspective would represent a more accurate description of what really happens; it would accept the existence of several different but related interest groups, each with their own leaders, loyalties, and objectives. Management and workers are two different groups who have conflicting interests. Here conflict, sabotage, and so on are seen as inevitable and a natural component of work. A certain amount of overt conflict is welcomed as a sign that aspirations are neither being drowned by hopelessness nor suppressed by power (see Armstrong and Dawson, 1989, for a fuller description of the frames of reference).

A third and radical approach would say that a pluralist ideology does not address the full extent of conflict. It does not fully appreciate the differences in power between managers and workers. This approach would focus on the power differences between various groupings and would show that management's power is greater than it appears. Employees are totally dependent on the organization and have little power or influence. Sabotage, theft, fun, and so on are some of the few ways employees have of undermining managerial power and control.

Questions for Further Research

1. Compare and contrast two of Punch's (1996) cases of organizational misdemeanour.

2. What, according to the research, are the negative impacts of romantic relationships at work? What are the positive aspects? How have organizations responded?

3. Academics have criticized the film *Disclosure* for the way in which it portrays sexual harassment in an organization. What is wrong with the film (see Brewis, 1998)?

4. Even when people are trained, paid, and told to be nice, it is hard for them to do so all of the time. Why? (See, for example, Van Maanen, 1991.)

5. Handy (1990) describes how psychiatric nurses have both to control and care for the mentally ill, which creates some highly distressing consequences. What is the problem, as described by Handy (see Handy, 1990 and 1995)?

Suggestions for Further Reading

Giacalone, R. A. and Greenberg, J. (1997) *Antisocial Behaviour in Organizations*. London: Sage.

Mars, G. (1984) *Cheats at Work: An Anthropology of Workplace Crime*. London: Unwin Paperbacks.

Noon, M., and Blyton, P. (1997) 'Time and Work', *The Realities of Work*.Basingstoke: Macmillan. ch. 4.

Punch, M. (1996) *Dirty Business: Exploring Corporate Misconduct, Analysis and Cases*. London: Sage.

Class Exercises

1. Put groups of students into the roles of hawks, vultures, donkeys, wolves, and managers. Ask them to research their potential role and be prepared the next week to play out their roles with the managers. The managers wish to stop the thieving practices. The hawks, vultures, donkeys, and wolves want to maintain the status quo.
2. Describe some of your own experiences of theft, sabotage, or fun at work to the class or use video extracts to illustrate. Divide the class into groups and ask students to share their experiences. Ask that a spokesperson from each group comes to the front and presents the stories from their group they liked best to the rest of the class.

References

Alfred Marks Bureau (1991) *Meeting Your Partner at Work: a quantitative report on the frequency and effects of relationships at work*, Dec., Borehamwood, Herts: Alfred Marks Bureau.

—— (1995) *Does Cupid Work in Your Office?*, Feb. Borehamwood, Herts: Alfred Marks Bureau.

American Lawyer, The (1997) 'Principles, Politics and Paula Jones', *The American Lawyer*, 19/1: 49.

Anderson, C. I., and Hunsaker, P. L. (1985) 'Why there's Romancing at the Office and Why it's Everybody's Problem', *Personnel*, 62/2 (Feb.): 57–63.

Armstrong, P., and Dawson, C. (1989) *People in Organizations*, 4th edn. Cambridge: ELM Publications.

Bates, I. (1990) 'No Bleeding, Whining Minnies: The Role of YTS in Class and Gender Reproduction', *British Journal of Education and Work*, 3: 91–110.

—— (1993) 'A Job which is "Right for Me"? Social Class, Gender and Individualization', in I. Bates and G. Riseborough (eds.), *Youth and Inequality*. Buckingham: Open University Press, ch. 1.

Brewis, J. (1998) 'What is Wrong with this Picture? Sex and Gender Relations in Disclosure', in J. Hassard and R. Holliday (eds.), *Organization Representation: Work and Organizations in Popular Culture*. London: Sage, ch. 4.

Burawoy, M. (1979) *Manufacturing Consent*. Chicago: Chicago University Press.

Collins, E. G. (1983) 'Managers and Lovers', *Harvard Business Review*, 16/5: 142–53.

Collinson, D. L. (1988) 'Engineering Humour: Masculinity, Joking and Conflict in Shop Floor Relations', *Organization Studies*, 9/2: 181–99.

Delaney, J. (1993) 'Handcuffing Employee Theft', *Small Business Report*, 18: 29–38.

Ditton, J. (1977) *Part-Time Crime: An Ethnography of Fiddling and Pilferage*. London: Macmillan.

—— (1979) 'Baking Time', *Sociological Review*, 27: 157–67.

Dubois, P. (1979) *Sabotage in Industry*. Harmondsworth: Penguin.

Edwards, J. R. (1990) 'The Determinants and Consequences of Coping with Stress', in C. Cooper and R. Payne (eds.), *Causes, Coping and Consequences of Stress at Work*. Chichester: John Wiley, ch. 8.

Fox, A. (1973) 'Industrial Relations: A Social Critique of Pluralist Ideology', in J. Child (ed.), *Man and Organization*. London: Allen and Unwin.

Giacalone, R. A. and Greenberg, J. (1997) *Antisocial Behaviour in Organizations*. London: Sage.

Goffman, E. (1968) *Asylums*. Harmondsworth: Penguin.

Greenberg, J. (1997) 'The Steal Motive: Managing the Social Determinants of Employee Theft', in R. A. Giacalone and J. Greenberg, *Antisocial Behaviour in Organizations*. London: Sage, ch. 5.

—— and Scott, K. S. (1996) 'Why do Workers Bite the Hands that Feed Them? Employee Theft as a Social Exchange Process', in B. M. Staw and L. L. Cummings (eds.), *Research in Organizational Behavior*, 18. Greenwich, Conn.: JAI Press, pp. 111–56.

Grover, S. L. (1993a) 'Lying, Deceit and Subterfuge: A Model of Dishonesty in the Workplace', *Organizational Science*, 4/3: 478–95.

—— (1993b) 'Why Professionals Lie: The Impact of Professional Role Conflict on Reporting Accuracy', *Organizational Behavior and Human Decision Processes*, 55: 251–72.

—— (1997) 'Lying in Organizations: Theory, Research and Future Directions', in R. A. Giacalone and J. Greenberg, *Antisocial Behaviour in Organizations*. London: Sage, ch. 4.

Harrison, R., and Lee, R. (1986) 'Love at Work', *Personnel Management* (Jan.): 20–4.

Handy, J. (1990) *Occupational Stress in a Caring Profession*. Aldershot: Avebury.

—— (1995) 'Rethinking Stress: Seeing the Collective', in T. Newton (with J. Handy and S Fineman), *Managing Stress: Emotion and Power at Work*. London: Sage, ch. 4.

Heyes, J. (1997) 'Annualized Hours and the "Knock": The Organization of Working Time in a Chemicals Plant', *Work, Employment and Society*, 11/1: 65–81.

Jackall, R. (1980) 'Structural Invitations to Deceit: Some Reflections on Bureaucracy and Morality', *Berkshire Review*, 15: 49–61.

Jermier, J. M., Knights, D., and Nord, W. R. (1994) (eds.) *Resistance and Power in Organizations*. London: Routledge.

LaNuez, D., and Jermier, J. M. (1994) 'Sabotage by Managers and Technocrats: Neglected Patterns of Resistance at Work', in J. M. Jermier, D. Knights, and W. R. Nord (eds.), *Resistance and Power in Organizations*. London: Routledge.

Lee-Treweek, G. (1997) 'Women, Resistance and Care: An Ethnographic Study of Nursing Auxiliary Work', *Work, Employment and Society*, 11/1 (Mar.): 47–63.

Linstead, S. (1985) 'Breaking the "Purity Rule": Industrial Sabotage and the Symbolic Process', *Personnel Review*, 14/3: 12–19.

Lobel, S. A., Quinn, R. E., St Clair, L., and Warfield, A. (1994) 'Love Without Sex: The Impact of Psychological Intimacy Between Men and Women at Work', *Organizational Dynamics*, 23: 5–16.

McGurn, T. (1988) 'Spotting the Thieves who Work Among Us', *Wall Street Journal* (7 Mar.): 16A.

Macleans (1998) 'Is Clinton Home Free?', *Macleans*, 111: 15, 13.

Mainiero, L. A. (1986) 'A Review and Analysis of Power Dynamics in Organizational Romances', *Academy of Management Review*, 11/4: 750–62.

—— (1989) *Office Romance: Love, Power and Sex in the Workplace*. New York: Macmillan.

—— (1993) 'Dangerous Liaisons? A Review of Current Issues Concerning Male and Female Romantic Relationships in the Workplace', in E. A. Fagenson (ed.), *Women in Management: Trends, Issues and Challenges in Managerial Diversity*. London: Sage, ch. 6.

Mars, G. (1982) *Cheats at Work*. London: Allen and Unwin.

—— (1989) 'Hotel Pilferage: A Case of Occupational Threat', in C. Littler (ed.), *The Experience of Work*. Milton Keynes: Open University Press, ch. 21.

Miceli, M. P., and Near, J. P. (1997) 'Whistle-Blowing as Antisocial Behavior', in R. A. Giacalone and J. Greenberg (eds.), *Antisocial Behaviour in Organizations*. London: Sage, ch. 7.

Nichols, T. (1997) *The Sociology of Industrial Injury*. London: Mansell.

Pitt, M. (1979) *The World on our Backs*. London: Lawrence and Wishart.

Pollert, A. (1981) *Girls, Wives, Factory Lives*. London: Macmillan.

Punch, M. (1996) *Dirty Business: Exploring Corporate Misconduct, Analysis and Cases*. London: Sage.

Quinn, R. E. (1977) 'Coping With Cupid: The Formation, Impact and Management of Romantic Relationships in Organizations', *Administrative Science Quarterly*, 22: 30–45.

Reid, D. A. (1976) 'The Decline of Saint Monday, 1766–1876', *Past and Present*, 71: 76–101.

Riemer, J. W. (1979) *Hard Hats*. London: Sage.

Rothschild, J., and Miethe, T. D. (1994) 'Whistleblowing as Resistance in Modern Work Organizations', in J. M. Jermier, D. Knights, and W. R. Nord (eds.), *Resistance and Power in Organizations*. London: Routledge, ch. 8.

Roy, D. F. (1960) 'Banana Time: Job Satisfaction and Informal Interaction', *Human Organization*, 18: 158–68.

—— (1974) 'Sex in the Factory: Informal Heterosexual Relations Between Supervisors and Work Groups', in C. Bryant (ed.), *Sexual Deviancy and Social Proscription*. New York: Human Sciences Press.

Smith, E. R., Becker, M. A., Byrne, D., and Przybyla, D. P. (1993) 'Sexual Attitudes of Males and Females as Predictors of Interpersonal Attraction and Marital Compatibility', *Journal of Applied Social Psychology*, 23/13: 1011–1034.

Spector, P. E. (1997) 'The Role of Frustration in Antisocial Behaviour at Work', in R. A. Giacolone and J. Greenberg, *Antisocial Behaviour in Organizations*. London: Sage, ch. 1.

Taylor, L., and Walton, P. (1971) 'Industrial Sabotage: Motives and Meanings', in S. Cohen (ed.), *Images of Deviance*. Harmondsworth: Penguin, pp. 219–45.

Taylor, S. (1997) 'Her Case Against Clinton', *The American Lawyer*, 18/9: 56.

The Insight Team of *The Sunday Times* of London (1979) *Suffer the Children: The Story of Thalidomide*. New York: Viking, esp. ch. 7.

Trix, F., and Sankar, A. (1998) 'Women's Voices and Experiences of the Hill-Thomas Hearings', *American Anthropologist*, 100/1: 32.

Van Maanen, J. (1991) 'The Smile Factory: Work at Disneyland', in P. J. Frost, L. F. Moore, M. R. Louis, C. C. Lundberg, and J. Martin (eds.), *Reframing Organizational Culture*. London: Sage. ch. 4.

Warfield, A. (1987) 'Co-worker Romances: Impact on the Work Group and on Career Oriented Women', *Personnel*, 64/5 (May): 22–35.

Willis, P. (1977) *Learning to Labour*. London: Saxon House.

Wilson, F. M. (1995) *Organizational Behaviour and Gender*. London: McGraw Hill.

—— (1998) 'The Subjective Experience of Sexual Harassment: Cases of Students', *Human Relations* forthcoming, 2000.

III

Changes in Work Organization

10

Beyond Bureaucracy:
Postbureaucracy Debate and New
Forms of Work Organization

B

UREAUCRACY WAS A theme which dominated organization studies throughout the 1950s and represented the most common form of organizational design. Bureaucracy is as relevant today but some would say that new forms of organization have emerged. Now there is talk of clusters, networks, and strategic alliances among organizations. Within organizations some claim that the 'new work structures' (Geary, 1995) are flatter, more flexible, places where employees can feel 'empowered'. Many writers in management talk of radical change and discontinuity. They speak of a 'revolution' (Kanter, 1989; Peters, 1987) and a 'transformation of industrial relations (Kochan *et al.*, 1986), 'new industrial relations' (Kelly and Kelly, 1991) and the 'new workplace' (Ackers *et al.*, 1996). For some writers (for example, Clegg, 1990) the new organizational forms are sufficiently different from bureaucracy to suggest they are called 'postmodern' or 'postbureaucratic' (Hecksher and Donnellon, 1994). What are these new structures and arrangements?

New Organizational Forms—External

Clusters are where usually small and medium-sized enterprises cooperate at a local level; each will have their own specialism in a part of a production cycle. For example, in the knitwear industry, one company may specialize in dyeing, another in sewing, and so on. Some clusters have developed as result of state interventions, in Northern Italy (Weiss, 1988) and Germany (Herrigel, 1993). Technology parks are also an example of a cluster, where university research laboratories and new enterprises are grouped together in the hope of creating a synergy and new collaborations.

Networks can function to exchange information, share risk, or avoid duplication of effort. Strategic alliances are mechanisms to help firms enter new markets by, for example, sharing costs of development of new technology. In order to meet the needs of these new external relations, internal arrangements may have to change.

New Organizational Forms—Internal

Postmodern organizations are decentralized and networked. Leadership has to be team based, which means that team-building, conflict-resolution, and problem-solving skills are needed. These organizations are characterized by openness, trust, empowerment, and commitment (Clegg and Hardy, 1996). Once in motion 'virtuous circles' mean collaborative, open decision-making which eliminates traditional hierarchical styles of secrecy, sycophancy, and sabotage. Decisions are sought from those with the expertise and accepted.

Clegg and Hardy's view is a very positive one. Examples of six organizations who have introduced network technology, computer networks, are found in Boddy and Gunson (1996). The networked computer systems link different organizational units, such as branches or subsidiaries. They give a vivid account of the practical difficulties, failures, and successes of the process of implementation.

Change or Continuity?

There are some writers, though, who would say that researchers and theorists have paid more attention to change than to continuity. Roy Jacques, for example, notes that many of the characteristics of 'post industrial management' proposed for the 1990s were actually ob-served and reported sixty or more years ago: 'it appears to be a condition of modernity for every generation to believe it is in the midst of revolutionary change' (Jacques, 1996: 18–19). In a different vein Blyton and Turnbull (1994), in discussing employee relations, say that we should consider both continuity and change, thinking of time as moving along a 'spiral' (Burrell, 1992). 'Nothing changes yet everything is different: as we twist around the spiral of capitalist economic development we experience progression and return, never a return to exactly the same point but always to a point that is familiar' (Blyton and Turnbull, 1994: 298). Legge (1995) would argue that all periods are characterized by both change and conti-nuity. But what about the fundamental shifts in organization and management of manufac-turing operations that have been witnessed, like teamworking, and 'flexible' and 'lean' production (Piore and Sabel, 1984; Womack *et al.*, 1990) just-in-time (JIT), quality circles, Total Quality Management (TQM), and the Japanese model of manufacturing manage-ment?

Teamworking

Teamworking can offer a benign alternative to repetitive Tayloristic work routines through the process of job enrichment and self-management (Buchanan, 1993; Carr, 1994). Workers in teams could be multi-skilled, routinely rotate tasks, organize their own work, and assume responsibility for product output and quality. It can, then, replace inflexible, dehumanizing work methods with more humanistic, involving ones. Teamwork is advocated by popular management thinkers like Drucker (1988) and Peters (1989) as well as advocates of TQM and business process re-engineering (BPR).

In the Japanese model of work organization, teamworking is central as it embodies the principle of waste elimination in labour time, important for 'lean production'. Proponents of Japanese working practices would argue that the removal of 'slack', all human and mater-ial 'waste', from the manufacturing operation is enabled by the dynamic work team (Kenney and Florida, 1993).

We must be careful though not to conflate 'teamworking' and autonomous work groups with Japanese working practices. In autonomous work groups there is a team of workers who organize their own labour and how that is deployed; they enjoy discretion over work methods and time (Buchanan, 1994: 204). In the Swedish model of autonomous group working, employees have enjoyed sufficient freedom to influence such matters as goal for-mation, performance monitoring, production methods, labour allocation, and choice of group leaders (Ramsay, 1992). This system has allowed group control over work pace through the presence of buffers and the absence of supervision (Berggren, 1993; Thompson and Sederblad, 1994). In contrast, Japanese teamworking is based on the Toyota model which is little different to classic scientific management. Here there is minimum staffing, multi-tasking, multi-machine operation, repetitive short-cycle work, powerful first-line supervision, and a conventional hierarchy (Buchanan, 1994: 219). Not all teamworking, then, will empower workers. There will be real variations in the distribution of power, resulting from how work is structured and the context in which teamworking takes place. It is possible that teamworking can lead to disempowerment and deskilling in lean production settings characterized by direct management control, repetitive task routines, and heightened labour discipline (Danford, 1998). Others have warned about the coercive and potentially totalitarian features of 'devotional' team culture and ideology (e.g. Barley and Kunda, 1992). There appears to be a small but growing number of critical in-depth studies of teamworking (see, for example, McKinlay and Taylor, 1996; Pollert, 1996).

Ezzamel and Wilmott (1998) have recently looked at the introduction of teamworking to a company they call StitchCo. While teamwork appeared to deliver universal benefits like cost effectiveness and enhanced profitability, it also concealed a variety of unsavoury features of work reorganization, including coercion masquerading as empowerment and the camouflaging of managerial expediency in the rhetoric of 'clannism' and humanization (Knights and Willmott, 1987).

Quality Circles

Quality circles or problem-solving groups normally consist of small groups of employees from the same work area who meet together regularly and voluntarily. Their chair may be a supervisor, a 'facilitator', or another employee; they may have received training in statistical analysis and group dynamics. As well as quality issues, groups can deal with work flow, productivity, safety, and other problems. The concept was originally developed in the US but quality circles were first widely adopted in Japan (Cole, 1989). Quality circles are more common in Japan than the US and more common in the US than Britain (Heller *et al.*, 1998). Quality circles can formalize the process of workplace innovation. Employees can frequently think of ways of making their job more efficient and problem-solving teams can encourage them to reveal their innovations. Most employees can see good reasons to want to improve the quality of work from a company. However in some circumstances quality circle meetings may be little more than managerial pep talks, with little opportunity for employee input. Alternatively, employees can find their ideas are ignored (Wilson, 1989). They may feel they deserve some reward for their participation. Sometimes, however, quality circles evolve into work teams or TQM.

Total Quality Management

Total Quality Management goes beyond quality circles in that it is usually an organization-wide effort involving teams of employees and managers. TQM focuses on satisfying the needs of customers who are both internal and external to the company. TQM teams typically follow a procedure whereby they start by tracking the number and timing of problems, then analyse the source of the error, generate alternative solutions and evaluate one solution, implement it, and check it. Thus it can contribute to organizational leaning and increase participation. On the other hand, in practice TQM often permits little real participation (Tuckerman, 1994).

Japan: The Post-Fordist Future?

Japanese management practices have evoked a good deal of interest in the last two decades. During the 1960s and 1970s there was a dramatic increase in Japanese manufacturing exports. In 1980 Ford Europe began an 'After Japan' programme, following a fact-finding visit to Japan, to tighten labour discipline, increase output, and enhance worker flexibility at Ford plants. In the 1980s attention shifted to the role of Japanese firms in Europe and North America as auto, auto components, and electrical manufacturing plants were set up.

It was argued that innovative and competitive Japanese car manufactures had developed a distinctive form of production organization or 'lean production' (Womack *et al.*, 1990). This was characterized by minimization of stocks and work in progress by 'just-in-time' (JIT) production (producing and delivering finished goods just in time to be sold, subassemblies just in time to be assembled, and so on) and by an emphasis on the continuous improvement of production procedures. This was the dominant form of production used by vehicle producers in Japan (particularly Toyota) and the methods were apparently transferable to locations outside Japan. The approach to the management of stocks and material flow was popularized by writers such as Schonberger (1982, 1986). The fundamental doctrine of the Toyota production system is the elimination of waste (Ohno, 1988). Under the JIT system production is driven by market requirements as information regarding demand pulls production through the processes. In contrast, the traditional mass production model pushes production scheduling as output plans are developed on the basis of historic information and production is decoupled from demand. The intention with JIT is to reduce costs through reducing stock, labour, and time. This in turn reduces the amount of 'buffering' between processes.

TQM was developed in the USA but implemented in Japan. Here the focus is on quality design and conformance to specification, using statistical processes control to monitor quality and control standards. It can also involve employees with customer responsiveness and service. Kenney and Florida (1993) too identified the leading Japanese firms as the innovators of a new model of organization of work and production they called 'innovation-mediated production', a symbiosis between research and development and continuous improvement in the production process aided by the knowledge and intelligence of all employees.

Few people have not heard of the four 'sacred treasures' of Japanese management: lifetime employment (where employees are hired fresh out of education on a lifetime basis), seniority-based wage systems and promotions (provided according to seniority as the employee accumulates skills and experience with the company), consensus decision-making, and enterprise unions (all the clerks, engineers, and labourers of a company join together, facilitating labour/management compromises). It has been argued, for example, that offering lifetime employment secures a loyal and secure workforce in Japan. The organization is viewed as a collectivity to which employees belong; there is considerable emphasis on inter-dependence, shared concerns, and mutual help. Once employees have joined an organization they are guaranteed continuing employment; in turn the employee makes a lifelong commitment to the organization which they see as an extension of their family.

How real was this Japanese dream? How easy would it be to transfer Japanese management practices into British organizations? These were the questions raised by researchers in the late 1980s. Ackroyd *et al.* (1988) believed that there were major constraints on the im-plementation of Japanese forms of work organization and employment relations in British-based organizations, as Britain and Japan had different economic and social structures with contrasting employment systems, labour markets, different organization of finance, and in-vestment policies.

Oliver and Wilkinson (1992) also emphasized how the new production methods required very specific social conditions, of the sort provided by Japanese social structures, for them to work. They found that the success of major Japanese corporations could not be readily as-signed to a specific set of practices, like manufacturing methods or personnel policies. What appeared to be crucial was the goodness of fit between a set of business strategies and a set of wider supporting conditions. They studied British companies who tried to emulate Japanese practices. They concluded that the companies faced substantial obstacles. The problems were related to the heightened dependencies of companies on their employees, suppliers, markets, and key political and economic agencies. In the case of suppliers, they must be trusted to deliver goods of the right quality, in the right quantity, and 'just in time'. Buyers have to nurture long-term relations with their suppliers and exert influence over their oper-ations. The supplier should find the buyers constantly 'on the doorstep', be dependent on the customer financially, and be under intense pressure to deliver the goods.

In terms of employees, many Japanese-style manufacturing practices require willing co-operation, not merely compliance, on the part of a workforce, for example, a willingness to perform a range of tasks, a commitment to engage in activities of continuous improvement, and a preparedness to do what is required to satisfy both internal and external customers. For the workforce this means, on the one hand, that work is likely to be more varied and higher in involvement and 'ownership'. On the other hand, accountability and responsibil-ity are increased, performance is more closely monitored, and the visibility of failings (and successes) heightened. Some Japanese companies reinforce this visibility through public displays of group or individual output and quality levels. No wonder there are mixed opin-ions on these methods. Advocates claim that the Japanese style of work organization is hu-manistic, while the critics see it as being manipulative and coercive.

There are some other interesting 'realities' about Japanese human resource strategies. The practice of lifelong employment is for an elite, favoured group of employees. It applies al-most exclusively to regular, male employees and is not as widespread as was once believed. It has been estimated that no more than 30 per cent of the Japanese labour force work for the same company throughout their career (Smith and Misumi, 1994) and rather more Ameri-cans than Japanese continue to work for their first employer. One reason that there is so lit-tle lifetime employment is that there is widespread subcontracting (for example, 70 per cent of a Nissan car is produced by subcontractors) and subcontracting workers do not enjoy job security in time of cutbacks. 'Rings of defence' are build around the core workers and their activities. Employees who find themselves in the outer rings, peripheral workers employed on temporary contract or employees of firms subcontracted to the main subcontractors, are likely to have a rather different experience of work (Oliver and Wilkinson, 1992). Close attention is given to hiring new permanent employees who will fit into the company culture. Careful screening ensures that candidates likely to endorse the company's values and philosophy are selected. Private investigators are routinely used to check a candidate's background, families, neighbours, and friends (Oliver and Wilkinson, 1992).

The adult Japanese male identifies with the immediate work group of peers and their superior; this is very intense (Dore, 1973). Comparative studies reveal that Japanese employees see work as more central to their lives than employees in ten other countries (Meaning of Working, 1987). They also spend substantial time eating and drinking with their workmates after work. Employees are also more likely to participate in company organized sports, holidays, and outings. Companies in Japan spend twice as much on social and recreational facilities for their employees than US companies (Smith and Misumi, 1994). You are obliged to develop and maintain harmonious relations with your work colleagues. National service through industry, fairness, harmony and cooperation, struggle for betterment, courtesy and humility, adjustment and assimilation, and gratitude are the values employees should adopt. New recruits share overall responsibility for their team's work; commitment to the company is fostered through extensive training programmes for new recruits.

The society is not only collective but has a hierarchical status system, the bases being education, age, gender, and the firm you work for. Authority relations are often paternalistic and highly traditional and deferential. Prospects for promotion are strongly dependent upon a senior mentor within the company. (A very detailed study of Japanese management practices can be found in Whitehill, 1991.) As Morgan (1986: 116) has noted, some of the more distasteful aspects of work experience have been ignored in many accounts of Japanese organization. The emphasis has been on how Japanese workers arrive at work early or stay late to find ways of improving efficiency through working in quality circles or how the dedicated Honda workman straightens the windshield wiper blade on all Honda cars he passes on his way home in the evening. Less attention is given to the disgruntled workers like Satoshi Kamata (1982) who describes how he lived in a camp rigidly policed by company guards. There were constant pressures to achieve demanding work targets and fulfil the requirements of company values and norms. Day-to-day life was gruelling.

Distasteful Work?

'Faced with the choice of going on the dole or working like the Japanese, the men so far would prefer the dole. It's as simple as that' (Turnbull, 1988: 44).

Williams *et al.* (1994) describe the more than intense nature of work in a car plant press shop in Japan. The shift runs for nine hours, including one hour of unpaid meal breaks. After nine hours on shift, the workers are required to work overtime as necessary; the overtime requirement is only put up on a board half-way through the shift. Two hours of overtime are routinely required so an eleven-hour day is the expected norm. The scheduled meal breaks are often taken up with company business like quality circle meetings. Workers have been obliged to work six days a week. Their one day off may not be completely free as loyal workers are expected to join in company sports and social events. Car plant managers decided the plant should work over weekends because the local electricity board charged a lower tariff at weekends; the result was that workers could not take their day off over the weekend. How would you feel about working for a Japanese company?

The apparent harmony in Japanese society may be overstated (Wagatsuma, 1982). There is clear evidence of conflict within and between organizations. The harmony of the work group may be being sustained by a sense of obligation; this obligation may be relaxed when employees are having a few drinks together. There is also evidence to suggest that Japanese workers are less satisfied than Western workers. Many Japanese workers work extremely long hours for what they regard as inadequate pay (Smith and Misumi, 1994). When viewed in the Western cultural and socio-political context, many aspects of Japanese business and management systems are socially and politically unacceptable and even illegal (Sethi *et al.*, 1984). The views of 100 British executives who had experience of working for Japanese companies is explored in depth by Jones (1991), who also is able to question many of the beliefs about Japanese companies, especially those fuelled by articles in the popular press.

Disciplined Selves?

Kondo (1990) gives a vivid account of everyday life on the shop-floor of a small family-owned sweet factory in Tokyo, where she worked for a year. At one stage in her story she is sent to an ethics school with two other employees. At this school they were organized in groups or squads. Each squad slept in the same room, ate at the same table, exercised together, and sat together in class. The position of squad leader changed daily, giving each the opportunity to be leader and share responsibility.

Here is a brief description of the activities before breakfast each day. The day started at 5 a.m. with a call to rise. Waking up late was regarded as unnatural, indulgent, selfish, slovenly. Cleaning came next and was a standard ingredient of spiritual education. Each cleaning task was to be performed with a glad heart. The counsellors would lead the group in chants of 'Fight!' as they hosed down the toilets, emptied the tins of sanitary napkins, and scrubbed the floors. After cleaning they jogged to the statue of the founder and after a rousing shout of 'Good Morning' would be briefly lectured on an inspirational theme. A tape recorder played the national anthem as the flags were raised. They then had shouting practice where they were required to scream greetings at the tops of their voices or shout 'I am the sun of x company. I will make x company number one in Japan.' Every word was rewarded by shouts of encouragement from the others and applause. The idea was to inculcate receptiveness and a willingness to greet and appreciate others and eliminate resistance toward responding positively towards authority. They ran for at least one and a half miles as a rehearsal for the 7.5 kilometre marathon scheduled for the end of the programme. Shouting and chanting was required during running. Speed was not the issue; it was important to finish and not give up. Neglect of the body was seen as lack of appreciation of the gift of life. Ritual ablution ceremonies with cold water, in order to give thanks to water, followed. The morning classes were for reciting in unison phrases like 'Hardship is the gateway to happiness' and 'Other people are our mirrors'. Students would be given instructions on how to bow at the proper angle, have a pleasant facial expression, and use the appropriate language level. Read the account yourself and answer the question: how successful was the ethics centre in crafting disciplined selves?

Graham (1994) was a participant observer for six months in a Japanese car plant in the USA. She documents both the compliance and resistance to management's technical and social control strategies. Managers had attempted to gain compliance through lengthy pre-employment and selection procedures, careful handling of training of new recruits, the team concept of working, the philosophy of continuous improvement, the shaping of shop-floor culture, and technical pacing and discipline of computerized assembly lines coupled with JIT. They used techniques like the company song, celebrations, and team meetings. But there was worker resistance, which emerged as sabotage when the workers surreptitiously stopped the assembly line. They protested and refused to participate in company rituals and confronted management in team and departmental meetings. Workers were seldom allowed to make even inconsequential decisions on their own. The company was not totally successful in instituting a spirit of cooperation and a culture of egalitarianism.

More recently Delbridge (1998) reports his finding from two periods of study as a participant observer working on the shop-floor in a European-owned automotive components supplier and a Japanese-owned consumer electronics plant. The European company was seeking to introduce cellular manufacturing, TQM, JIT inventory control, and teamworking during the time of his study while the Japanese company had many characteristics of lean production and has been cited as an exemplar of 'world class manufacturing'. He found that management at the Japanese-owned company had successfully marginalized the effects of uncertainty and shop-floor relations were clearly and explicitly founded upon a 'negotiated order' between management and labour. Workers faced very strict coercive controls and felt they had to comply. There was no heightened sense of commitment from the workforce; they remained opposed to many of management's goals and mistrustful of the rhetoric of teamworking and mutuality. At the European-owned plant the managers relied on informally negotiated solutions to problems, due to the uncertainty inherent at the plant. Workers at both plants were sceptical of management intentions and clearly favoured an oppositional stance, so needed the protection of trade unions (see also Knights and McCabe, 1998; Wilkinson et al., 1997, 1998).

An example of a company which has 'creatively' imitated the Japanese model is the car company Fiat in Italy. The production system was reorganized and initiatives launched aimed at enhancing the involvement of the workforce (Bonazzi, 1998). Traditional bureaucratic management, with its rigid division of responsibility and unwieldy linkages between various bodies, was abandoned. The new system encouraged supervisors to assume managerial responsibilities in order to ensure maximum reactivity as and when process and product anomalies arose. Fiat appears to have taken some elements of the Japanese methods and used them for their own benefit.

There are then some clear lessons to draw from the research on Japanese manufacturing methods. The main conclusion is that we need to be sceptical about claims of the unitarist management writers who present Japanese management practices only in a positive light and paint organizations as unitarist, where workers and managers simply work happily together to fulfil mutual goals. There need to be serious questions asked about the ease with which Japanese management practices can be appropriated and used in both Japanese and other organizations.

Questions for Further Research

1. Taking the sources cited here, weigh and balance the pros and cons, from the workforce point of view, of working under Japanese methods.

2. Japanese managers transfer as little or as much as they wish of their management practices to the new environment (Dedoussis and Littler, 1994). How much evidence is there to suggest this is the case (see Delbridge, 1998: ch. 10, for sources)?

3. Much has been written about Volvo and their experimentation with work organization and teams. What can you find out about the history of the experiment from Berggren (1993) and other sources?

4. Why was there resistance to teamworking at StitchCo (see Ezzamel and Wilmott, 1998)? Teamworking can have the unintended effect of fermenting hostility towards management, Ezzamel and Wilmott (1998) argue. How?

5. To its advocates, TQM is unequivocally good. To some management researchers, it produces some bad outcomes. What are the realities? See Wilkinson *et al.*, 1997, 1998; Knights and McCabe, 1998; and related sources.

Suggestions for Further Reading

Elger, T., and Smith, C. (1994) *Global Japanization? The Transnational Transformation of the Labour Process*. London: Routledge.

Jones, S. (1991) *Working for the Japanese: Myths and Realities, British Perceptions*. London: Macmillan.

References

Ackers, P., Smith, C., and Smith, P. (1996) (eds.) T*he New Workplace and Trade Unionism*. London: Routledge.

Ackroyd, S., Burrell, G., Hughes, M., and Whitacker, A. (1988) 'The Japanization of British Industry?', *Industrial Relations Journal*, 19/1: 11–23.

Barley, S., and Kunda, G. (1992) 'Design and Devotion: Surges of Rational and Normative Ideologies of Control in Managerial Discourse', *Administrative Science Quarterly*, 37: 363–99.

Berggren, C. (1993) *The Volvo Experience: Alternatives to Lean Production in the Swedish Auto Industry*. London: Macmillan.

Blyton, P., and Turnbull, P. (1994) *The Dynamics of Employee Relations*. London: Macmillan.

Boddy, D., and Gunson, N. (1996) *Organizations in the Network Age*. London: Routledge.

Bonazzi, G. (1998) 'Between Shock Absorption and Continuous Improvement: Supervisors and Technicians in a Fiat "Integrated Factory" ', *Work, Employment and Society*, 12/2: 219–43.

Buchanan, D. (1993) 'Principles and Practice in Work Design', in K. Sisson (ed.), *Personnel Management in Britain*. Oxford: Blackwell.

—— (1994) 'Cellular Manufacture and the Role of Teams', in J. Storey (ed.), *New Wave Manufacturing Strategies*. Liverpool: Paul Chapman.

Burrell, G. (1992) 'Back to the Future: Time and Organization', in M. Reed and M. Hughes (eds.), *Rethinking Organization*. London: Sage, pp. 165–83.

Carr, F. (1994) 'Introducing Teamworking: A Motor Industry Case Study', *Industrial Relations Journal*, 25/3: 199–209.

Clegg, S. R. (1990) *Modern Organizations: Organizational Studies in the Post-modern World*. London: Sage.

—— and Hardy, C. (1996) 'Organizations, Organization and Organizing', Introduction to S. R. Clegg, C. Hardy, and W. R. Nord (eds.), *Handbook of Organization Studies*. London: Sage.

Cole, R. (1989) *Strategies for Learning. Small Group Activities: America, Japan and Sweden*. Berkeley, Calif.: University of California Press.

Danford, A. (1998) 'Teamworking and Labour Relations in the Autocomponents Industry', *Work, Employment and Society*, 12/3: 409–31.

Dedoussis, V., and Littler, C. (1994) 'Understanding the Transfer of Japanese Management Practices: The Australian Case', in T. Elger and C. Smith (eds.), *Global Japanization? The Transnational Transformation of the Labour Process*. London: Routledge, pp. 175–95.

Delbridge, R. (1998) *Life on the Line in Contemporary Manufacturing: The Workplace Experience of Lean Production and the 'Japanese' Model*. Oxford: Oxford University Press.

Dore, R. P. (1973) *British Factory, Japanese Factory*. London: Allen and Unwin.

Drucker, P. (1988) 'The Coming of the New Organization', *Harvard Business Review* (Jan.–Feb.): 45–53.

Ezzamel, M., and Wilmott, H. (1998) 'Accounting for Teamwork: A Critical Study of Group-Based Systems of Organizational Control', *Administrative Science Quarterly*, 43: 358–96.

Geary, J. (1995) 'Work Practices: The Structure of Work', in P. Edwards (ed.), *Industrial Relations: Theory and Practice in Britain*. Oxford: Blackwell, pp. 368–96.

Graham, L. (1994) 'How Does the Japanese Model Transfer to the United States: A View from the Line', in T. Elger and C. Smith (eds.), *Global Japanization? The Transnational Transformation of the Labour Process*. London: Routledge, ch. 4.

Hecksher, C., and Donnellon, A. (1994) *The Post Bureaucratic Organization: New Perspectives on Organizational Change*. Thousand Oaks: Sage.

Heller, F., Pusic, E., Strauss, G., and Wilpert, B. (1998) *Organizational Participation: Myth and Reality*. Oxford: Oxford University Press.

Herrigel, G. B. (1993) 'Power and the Redefinition of Industrial Districts: The Case of Baden-Wurttemberg', in G. Graber (ed.), *The Embedded Firm: On the Socioeconomics of Industrial Networks*. London: Routledge, pp. 227–51.

Jacques, R. (1996) *Manufacturing the Employee: Management Knowledge from the Nineteenth to Twenty-First Centuries*. London: Sage.

Jones, S. (1991) *Working for the Japanese: Myths and Realities, British Perceptions*. Basingstoke: Macmillan.

Kamata, S. (1982) *Japan in the Passing Lane*. New York: Pantheon.

Kanter, R. (1989) 'The New Managerial Work', *Harvard Business Review*, 67/6: 85–92.

Kelly, J., and Kelly, C. (1991) ' "Them and Us": Social Psychology and "The New Industrial Relations" ', *British Journal of Industrial Relations*, 29/1: 25–48.

Kenney, M., and Florida, R. (1993) *Beyond Mass Production: The Japanese System and its Transfer to the US*. Oxford: Oxford University Press.

Knights, D., and McCabe, D. (1998) 'Dreams and Designs on Strategy : A Critical Analysis of TQM and Management Control', *Work, Employment and Society*, 12/3: 433–56.

Knights, D., and Willmott, H. (1987) 'Organizational Culture as Corporate Strategy', *International Studies of Management and Organization*, 17/3: 40–63.

Kochan, T., Katz, H., and McKersie, R. (1986) *The Transformation of American Industrial Relations*. New York: Basic Books.

Kondo, D. K. (1990) *Crafting Selves: Power, Gender and Discourses of Identity in a Japanese Workplace*. Chicago: University of Chicago Press.

Legge, K. (1995) *Human Resource Management: Rhetorics and Realities*. London: Macmillan.

McKinlay, A., and Taylor, P. (1996) 'Power, Surveillance and Resistance', in P. Ackers, C. Smith, and P. Smith (eds.), *The New Workplace and Trade Unionism*. London: Routledge, pp. 279–300.

Meaning of Working, International Research Team (1987) *The Meaning of Working*. London: Academic Press.

Morgan, G. (1986) *Images of Organization*. London: Sage.

Ohno, T. (1988) *Just-In-Time: For Today and Tomorrow*. Cambridge, Mass.: Productivity Press.

Oliver, N., and Wilkinson, B. (1992) *The Japanization of British Industry*. Oxford: Basil Blackwell (originally published in 1988).

Peters, T. (1989) *Thriving on Chaos: Handbook for a Management Revolution*. New York and London: Harper and Row.

Piore, M., and Sabel, C. (1984) *The Second Industrial Divide*. New York: Basic Books.

Pollert, A. (1996) ' "Teamwork" on the Assembly Line', in P. Ackers, C. Smith, and P. Smith (eds.), *The New Workplace and Trade Unionism*. London: Routledge, pp. 178–209.

Ramsay, H. (1992) 'Swedish and Japanese Work Methods: Comparisons and Contrasts', *European Participation Monitor*, 3: 37–40.

Schonberger, R. (1982) *Japanese Manufacturing Techniques: Nine Hidden Lessons in Simplicity*. New York: Free Press.

—— (1986) *World Class Manufacturing: The Lesson of Simplicity Applied*. New York: Free Press.

Sethi, S. P., Namiki, N., and Swanson, C. L. (1984) *The False Promise of the Japanese Miracle: Illusions and Realities of the Japanese Management System*. London: Pitman.

Smith, P. B., and Misumi, J. (1994) 'Japanese Management: A Sun Rising in the West?', in C. L. Cooper and I. T. Robertson (eds.), *Key Reviews in Managerial Psychology, Concepts and Research for Practice*. Chichester: John Wiley, ch. 4.

Thompson, P., and Sederblad, P. (1994) 'The Swedish Model of Work Organization in Transition', in T. Elger and C. Smith (eds.), *Global Japanization? The Transformation of the Labor Process*. London: Routledge.

Tuckerman, A. (1994) 'The Yellow Brick Road: TQM and the Restructuring of Organizational Culture', *Organization Studies*, 15: 727–51.

Turnbull, P. (1988) 'The Limits to Japanization: Just-in-Time, Labour Relations and the UK Automotive Industry', *New Technology, Work and Employment*, 3/1: 7–20.

Wagatsuma, H. (1982) 'Internationalization of the Japanese: Group Model Reconsidered', in H. Mannari and H. Befu (eds.), *The Challenge of Japan's Internationalization: Organizations and Culture*. Tokyo: Kodansha, pp. 298–308.

Weiss, L. (1988) *Creating Capitalism: The State and Small Business since 1945*. Oxford: Blackwell.

Whitehill, A. M. (1991) *Japanese Management: Tradition and Transition*. London: Routledge.

Wilkinson, A., Godfrey, G., and Marchington, M. (1997) 'Bouquets, Brickbats and Blinkers: Total Quality Management and Employee Involvement in Practice', *Organization Studies*, 18/5: 799–819.

Wilkinson. A., Redman, T., Snape, E., and Marchington, M. (1998) *Managing with Total Quality Management: Theory and Practice*. London: Macmillan Business.

Williams, K., Mitsui, I., and Haslam, C. (1994) 'How Far From Japan? A Case Study of Japanese Press Shop Practice and Management Calculation', in T. Elger and C. Smith (eds.), *Global Japanization? The Transnational Transformation of the Labour Process*. London: Routledge, ch. 2.

Wilson, F. M. (1989) 'Productive Efficiency and the Employment Relationship', *Employee Relations*, 11/1: 27–32.

Womack, J., Jones, D., and Roos, D. (1990) *The Machine that Changed the World*. New York: Rawson Associates.

11

Unemployment and the Changing Meaning and Time of Work

THE DAYS OF low unemployment in the UK, particularly in the years between 1946 and 1970 when there was an average of only 2 per cent unemployment, seem like a distant aberration. It is hard now to believe that in 1948 the Labour Cabinet seriously discussed banning the football pools in order to take women away from checking coupons and into the labour-starved textile industry (Fineman, 1987). Since the mid-1970s the number registered as unemployed has never dropped below a million and has been well over double that or more, despite numerous changes in the ways in which the unemployed were counted (Brown, 1997).

The burden of unemployment is not evenly spread throughout the social classes but lies heavily with the semi and unskilled group. Those who have become even more vulnerable to unemployment are also likely to have fewer resources with which to protect themselves and their families from their loss of earning power. It has become harder to move from unemployment to employment; the proportion of people from worker-less households who made the transition from non-employment into work more than halved between 1979 and 1993 (Gregg and Wadsworth, 1994).

An integral part of the experience of unemployment is the task of actively seeking paid work. There is, for many, particularly those in employment, a moral imperative on the unemployed to seek work actively or be labelled a scrounger or undeserving. The logical corollary of this attitude is that the unemployed only have themselves to blame if they fail. This attitude ignores facts like there are far more registered unemployed than there are job vacancies. *Regional Trends* (1997) notes that there were 226,000 vacancies at Jobcentres but 1,907,800 unemployed claimants.

The media are inclined to present unemployment as social disintegration occasioned by male job loss. Pit closures, for example, focused on male job loss, the loss of community pride in the wake of male redundancy, and the loss of the community's 'heart' with the closure of the colliery. Yet women in these communities suffered in parallel ways to men. What emerges from Dicks's (1996) study of pit closures in two communities was that women's ability to cope with the aftermath of pit closure was not decided so much by their spouses' employment fate as by the material, social, and emotional resources that they could draw on. Since the women remained largely responsible for household management and childcare, the tasks of budgeting and catering on a reduced income as well as the provision of emotional support to distressed partners, largely fell on their shoulders.

In Europe unemployment is no longer seen as cyclical but structural (Bhavnani, 1994). Unemployment has nearly always been a significant feature in the lives of black men and women in Britain. Black women may not register as unemployed for fear of being questioned about immigration status and racist and discriminatory practices in bureaucracy. Despite this, unemployment rates for black people are higher than those for whites. Within this group unemployment is higher for Pakistani, Bangladeshi, African, and Afro-Caribbean women and men (Sly, 1996); the lowest rates are for Chinese men and women (Bhavnani, 1994). Even when black and ethnic minority women are skilled and experienced, they are twice as likely to be unemployed or work longer hours, in poorer conditions, for lower pay than white women (Roberts, 1994). Pakistani and Bangladeshi women are five times more likely to be unemployed than white women, the gap being greatest in recessionary periods. Ethnic women work through financial necessity, due to higher rates of black male unemployment, larger family size, lower household incomes, and the necessity of working longer hours to bring home a living wage (Phizacklea and Wolkowitz, 1995). The rate of unemployment among young black men stands at three times that of young white men (Sly, 1995).

Effects of Unemployment

Research since the 1930s has very clearly shown the negative effects of unemployment on well-being (Fryer, 1992; Warr, 1987; Warr *et al.*, 1988). For most individuals unemployment manifests itself in ill health, despair, and chronic lethargy (symptoms remarkably like those to be found in bereaved individuals: see Archer and Rhodes, 1987). The effect may not be universal as a small minority will show gains in mental health after job loss. These people will have been in stressful jobs or will be happy to tolerate unemployment, taking jobs as they come along; a small minority will see it as a challenge and an opportunity to develop skills or interests. But for the majority, unemployment impairs mental health. The impairment can involve increased psychological distress, including anxiety and depression, lowered self-esteem, resigned apathy, helplessness, powerlessness, social isolation, and disintegration. These disorders have been confirmed in many countries (Fryer, 1992).

Classic studies in the 1930s began to detail what it meant to people to be unemployed. In the 1930s a group of researchers lived for some months in an Austrian village which had suffered from the demise of the textile industry. The research reported that, although the unemployed inhabitants of the village spent more time in bed to shorten the length of the day, they were unable to account for other ways in which their days had been spent. They reported that they were slower moving about and were unpunctual for fixed arrangements like meals. Weekends blended into weekdays and they lost 'structured meaning', their sense of time disintegrated (Jahoda, 1982). Women's sense of time was less disrupted because they still had a domestic routine to follow but many wanted to return to work because they missed the social contact of the factory. Despite the economic stringencies caused by unemployment, the researchers reported that people chose to do 'irrational' acts, for example spending money on a cream cake or growing flowers instead of vegetables when there was a food shortage.

Jahoda (1982, 1987) provides five categories of psychological experience which she says are not only conducive to feelings of well-being but vital. As unemployed people are deprived of these experiences, so their well-being declines. These experiences are:

time structure—work imposes a time structure on the waking day
social contact—work compels contact and shared experiences with others outside the
    family
collective effort or purpose—work demonstrates that there are goals and purposes
    which are beyond the purpose of the individual but require collectivity
social identity or status—work imposes status or social identity through the division of
    labour
regular activity—work enforces activity. (For a more detailed discussion of the
    categories see Haworth, 1997: 25.)

> **STOP**   To what extent are these psychological experiences an integral feature of student life?

The employed take these categories of experience for granted but the unemployed have to find experiences within these categories if they can or suffer if they cannot. 'What preoccupies them is not the category but the quality of experience within it' (Jahoda, 1982: 39). She recognizes that the quality of experience in some jobs can be very poor and stresses the importance of improving and humanizing employment.

Jahoda has been criticized for missing the fact that lack of money and contending with bureaucracy are two of the features of unemployment which contribute to feelings of lack of well-being. Also, the unemployed can gain access to the five categories of experience. Those unemployed with better access will have better well-being. But she concludes that the employed have better access to the categories of experience than the unemployed. Unemployment destroys the very structures that the employed take for granted—structures of time, routine, status, social networks—as Bostyn and Wright (1987) also concur. Given the excessive amount of time the unemployed have on their hands, they ought not to be late for interviews, but they are (Miles, 1983); they ought to have more time for leisure activities but retreat from such social interaction (Grint, 1991).

Warr (1987) has built on the categories of experience by proposing a model of mental health. This model incorporates the five categories of experience advocated by Jahoda. He emphasizes nine principal environmental influences:

- opportunity for control—the opportunity for a person to control activities and events
- environmental clarity—feedback about the consequences of your actions, certainty about the future, and clarity of understanding about what is expected of you in the job
- opportunity for skill use
- externally generated goals
- variety
- opportunity for interpersonal contact
- valued social position
- availability of money
- physical security

These nine principal environmental influences or environmental categories of experience are seen as acting together in conjunction with personal factors to help or hinder psychological well-being or mental health. Warr likens these influences to vitamins; some will improve mental health up to a certain point and have no further effect, others producing benefits up to a certain level beyond which increases would be detrimental. He argues that there can be good and bad jobs and good and bad unemployment depending on how much of these influences are present in the individual's experience.

The nine-factor framework tells us a good deal of what work means to people in a psychological sense. There is also a widespread view amongst the unemployed that they should not be seen as lazy, even if this means taking a job which pays only marginally more than unemployment benefit (Turner *et al.*, 1985). Being a breadwinner is also important to men for a sense of masculine identity (McKee and Bell, 1986; Yankelovich, 1973).

One of the responses to massive rises in unemployment has been the growth of agencies, schemes, and initiatives designed to spread the gospel of enterprise and encourage new businesses (MacDonald and Coffield, 1991). The new jobs tend to be in the service sector—clothes retailers, beauticians, car valets, sandwich deliverers, sign writers, car mechanics, private detectives. Yet we do not seem to be witnessing the birth of local enterprise culture. New small firms, even those which seem to do well initially, are unable to continue in the long term (MacDonald and Coffield, 1991). The smallest and youngest firms are the least likely to survive and grow (Chittenden and Caley, 1992). This is 'survival self employment' (MacDonald, 1997) as individuals trade with skills informally learnt and experience from hobbies and pastimes. But competition is too fierce and the market place is saturated with similar businesses so the local economy cannot support all these new businesses.

Callender (1987) argues that women's experience of job search and job acquisition can be different from that of men. The demand and supply side of men's and women's labour are not the same. Her study of a group of married women who had experienced redundancy through the partial closure of a clothing factory showed that all the redundant women wanted to work again and were very flexible about the conditions and type of paid work they were prepared to accept. Many were willing to take a reduction in pay. The women had an astute view of the state of the labour market and of the way in which demand structured their choices and opportunities; they had little choice so were prepared to accept any job. They organized and marshalled resources, like assistance with childcare and dependent relatives, for coping with their paid and unpaid work, but paid work was not a moral imperative for them, unlike men. The most effective strategy for finding work was through informal social networks, such as family and friends, by word of mouth. Those women who succeeded in finding work were highly reliant upon other people in their social network for information about jobs and recommendations. These networks were closed, restricted, home and female centred; this then determined the type of jobs the women obtained and their opportunities. If the women got jobs, they were similar jobs to those their female contacts had, typical 'women's work'.

Those of us in work are in fear of becoming unemployed. Unemployment is not restricted to those at the bottom of the socio-economic hierarchy; the managerial and professional middle class also feel anxious and insecure about their jobs (Pahl, 1996). Increases in managerial redundancy have followed in the wake of recession and fiercer competition. Managers may believe they are less vulnerable when it comes to redundancies, having invested a lifetime of service in return for job security (Hallier and Lyon, 1996), so when job loss comes, it can be a fundamental shock to their personal identity and financial security (Kozlowski *et al.*, 1993). Those with qualifications and job experience can, though, usually face redundancy with greater confidence that those without, as they have skills, competencies, and networks that others may lack. The highest rates of unemployment tend to be amongst those with no qualifications, from the working class, amongst the chronically sick and disabled, and whose ethnic background is Pakistani or Bangladeshi (Grint, 1991).

Working Time

As those of us in jobs in the UK work longer hours, the numbers without jobs increase. Those who work have a decrease in their available free time. Research (Tyrell, 1995) shows that available free time for full-time male workers declined by 4 per cent between 1985 and 1993 and for females the decline has been just over 10 per cent. In the USA the average American works the equivalent of an extra month each year compared to 1969 (Schor, 1995). Yet many people do not want to work as long hours as they do. Survey research in Britain has shown, for example, that over 70 per cent of people working over forty hours a week wanted to work less (Mulgan and Wilkinson, 1995). Schor (1995) shows how one-third of respondents wanted to work fewer hours even if this meant a 20 per cent reduction in household income. With this comes the admission that much of our spending is habitual, though; we are used to having our spending creep up with income.

STOP	Why do you think the proportion of free time for females has been less?

The other change in working time that has come about is a change in the number of part-time jobs. As employment levels have recovered following recessions, most job growth is in part-time work and the bulk of the new jobs have been taken by women, though some part-time work has gone to men. Although the employed labour force grew by nearly two and a half million between 1984 and 1986, for example, male full-time work fell by 2 per cent while male part-time work grew fivefold (Convery, 1997). You might ask what is wrong with part-time work and more women working? While the majority of part-timers choose to work fewer hours than full timers, a significant minority do not. In 1984 about 420,000 people were doing part-time work because they could not get a full-time job. By 1996 this had risen to 800,000 'involuntary' part-time workers (Convery, 1997). Part-time jobs are worse than full-time jobs in skill levels, wage rate, and promotion prospects. While part-time work is not associated with job insecurity and unemployment, it constitutes a trap which lowers women's lifetime employment prospects and earnings (Tam, 1997).

Voluntary Work

Voluntary work has received little attention in the UK (Harris, 1990; MacDonald, 1997) but levels of voluntary work have been high and rising (Joseph Rowntree Foundation, 1991) and can help give insight into the changing nature of what work and unemployment mean to people. In economically depressed areas volunteering has been taken up increasingly by people not in employment. MacDonald's (1997) research on volunteer workers gives us some useful information. Volunteers are predominantly engaged in looking after the disadvantaged as carers or as fund-raisers. A minority work for only a few hours a week; most work virtually full-time. All are motivated by a moral concern for the disadvantaged in their communities. Some, particularly middle-aged and older women, rebuild their lives left empty through redundancy or bereavement (as husbands have died, children left home, or employment ceased) by volunteering. Volunteering gives them the opportunity to maintain self-identity in their socially ascribed roles as carers at home. Volunteering replaced many of the positive social psychological categories of experience (Jahoda, 1982).

Voluntary work was also a semi-permanent response to being excluded from employment, particularly for the middle-aged men. They had realized that unemployment could be the norm for them. Volunteering provided new opportunities and challenges and the chance to give up images of worker and breadwinner. The new work had the potential to broaden their work aspirations and expectations. Volunteering could be a strategy for finding 'proper jobs' in the case of teenage and young adults. They were gaining work experience, skills, contacts, and references. It must be noted, however, that not all the responses were positive. The work could be hard, physically and emotionally, and they could be treated like 'skivvies'; their treatment could come close to exploitation as it is unpaid and often difficult and demanding.

Being 'on the Fiddle' or Working 'on the Side'

This is work carried out for pay by those who are also claiming social security or unemployment benefits to which they would not be wholly entitled if they declared this work to the benefit authorities. Some research (e.g. Bradshaw and Holmes, 1989; Pahl, 1984) shows that the unemployed are far less likely than the employed to engage in illicit work. Other work (e.g. Jordan *et al.*, 1992) has found that around two-thirds of poor households benefit from undeclared work.

In MacDonald's (1997) sample of non-standard employed (self-employed in very small businesses, those in voluntary work, 'on the fiddle', or in community enterprise and cooperatives) one-third had been 'on the fiddle'. These jobs were not preferred to 'proper' jobs; combining 'fiddly' work with unemployment benefits was a survival strategy initiated in the face of mass, structural unemployment and a system of benefits which failed to meet material needs. For the poor and long-term unemployed the fiddle is described by MacDonald as a necessary way of maintaining individual self-respect and household income. Fiddly work is better understood as representing a culture of enterprise rather than one of dependency. Those engaged in it fitted the model of entrepreneur showing high degrees of personal motivation, initiative, local knowledge, and risk taking.

Fiddly jobs tended to be short-lived, irregular, infrequent, and poorly rewarded. One young woman in the sample had just worked thirty hours in the week as a care assistant in a residential home on the 'fiddle'. Together with her Income Support she had netted the grand sum of £75. The jobs were most common in subcontracted labour at steel works, in construction, as car mechanics, taxi driving, cleaning, and bar work. Some contractors cut their costs and won tenders by offering low pay to people they knew to be in receipt of benefit and therefore able to 'afford' to work cheaply. For those involved in fiddly work the material experience of unemployment was ameliorated. The social psychological impact of unemployment was softened and it helped tie the individuals back into work culture. The majority of those on the fiddle were white working-class males in their twenties and thirties in neighbourhoods of high and long term unemployment with tradable skills and/or reliable record of manual work experience. The work was distributed through local, pub-centred social networks.

The picture painted by MacDonald's (1997) work is not one of a dangerous parasitical underclass. There was an incipient culture of survival, resilience, and getting by. Reorganization of work in the late twentieth century is forcing an increasingly large proportion of people to seek the means for their economic and social survival through various types of disorganized, insecure, risky, and casualized work.

Non-Work?

It can be interesting to look at the work of anthropologists and studies of identity and labour. Gypsies have consciously rejected wage labour. Judith Okley (1983) lived alongside a group of gypsies, in a trailer caravan, for about two years. She went out to work with them, calling for scrap metal, and joined a potato picking gang. She found that the identity of gypsies served as a political weapon for non-gypsies. Gypsies could be rejected as 'counterfeit' in contrast to a mythically 'real Romany'; through this discrimination, harassment, and oppression could be legitimated. They had a huge variety of occupations but spoke of wage labour with contempt. They could not be 'trained' for 'ordinary' employment.

Questions for Further Research

1. What are the personal and social consequences of unemployment? Are the consequences different for different groups of individuals? How?

2. Unemployment is associated with a psychologically distressing experience of time. Discuss. (see Fryer and McKenna, 1987).

3. How is managers' reaction to lay-off the same as or different from other workers (see Hallier and Lyon, 1996)?

4. Hakim (1991) argued that women choose to reduce their number of working hours out of personal preference. She created a bigger storm with her 1995 paper (see, for example, *Guardian*, 2 April 1996, pp. 6–7). What evidence can you find in the research about part-time employment to support or refute that argument (see Convery, 1997; Hakim, 1991, 1995 and Hakim's critics who follow her in the 1995 paper; Tam, 1997)?

Suggestions for Further Reading

Brown, R. (1997) (ed.) *The Changing Shape of Work*. Basingstoke: Macmillan.

Fineman, S. (1987) *Unemployment: Personal and Social Consequences*. London: Tavistock Publications.

Haworth, J. (1997) *Work, Leisure and Well-Being*. London: Routledge.

Noon, M., and Blyton, P. (1997) 'The Meaning of Work', *The Realities of Work*. Basingstoke: Macmillan, ch. 3.

Watson, T. (1997) 'Work: Meaning, Opportunity and Experience', *Sociology, Work and Industry*, 3rd edn. London: Routledge.

References

Archer, J., and Rhodes, V. (1987) 'Bereavement and Reactions to Job Loss: A Comparative Review', *British Journal of Social Psychology*, 26/3: 211–24.

Bhavnani, R. (1994) *Black Women in the Labour Market: A Research Review*. Manchester: Equal Opportunities Commission.

Bostyn, A., and Wright, D. (1987) 'Inside a Community: Values Associated with Money and Time', in Fineman, S. (ed.), *Unemployment: Personal and Social Consequences*. London: Tavistock.

Bradshaw, A. and Holmes, H. (1989) *Living on the Edge*. Tyneside: Tyneside Child Poverty Action Group.

Brown, R. (1997) (ed.)*The Changing Shape of Work*. Basingstoke: Macmillan.

Callender, C. (1987) 'Women Seeking Work', in S. Fineman (ed.), *Unemployment: Personal and Social Consequences*. London: Tavistock, ch. 3.

Chittenden, F., and Caley, K. (1992) 'Current Policy Issues and Recommendations', in K. Caley *et al.* (eds.), *Small Enterprise Development*. London: Paul Chapman Publishing.

Convery, P. (1997) 'Unemployment', in A. Walker and C. Walker (eds.), *Britain Divided: The Growth of Social Exclusion in the 1980s and 1990s*. London: Child Poverty Action Group.

Dicks, B. (1996) 'Coping with Pit Closure in the 1990s: Women's Perspectives', in *Gender and Qualitative Research*. Aldershot: Avebury, ch. 2.

Fineman, S. (1987) *Unemployment: Personal and Social Consequences*. London: Tavistock.

Fryer, D. (1992) 'Psychological or Material Deprivation: Why Does Unemployment have Mental Health Consequences?', in E. McLaughlin (ed.), *Understanding Unemployment*. London: Routledge.

—— and McKenna, S. (1987) 'The Laying off of Hands: Unemployment and the Experience of Time', in S. Fineman, *Unemployment: Personal and Social Consequences*. London: Tavistock, ch. 4.

Gregg, P., and Wadsworth, J. (1994) 'More Work in Fewer Households', in J. Hills (ed.), *New Inequalities: The Changing Distribution of Income and Wealth*. Cambridge: Cambridge University Press.

Grint, K. (1991) *The Sociology of Work: An Introduction*. Cambridge: Polity.

Hakim, C. (1991) 'Grateful Slaves and Self-Made Women: Fact and Fantasy in Women's Work Orientations', *European Sociological Review*, 7: 101–21.

—— (1995) 'Five Feminist Myths about Women's Employment', *British Journal of Sociology*, 46/3: 429–55 (see also replies from eleven academics which follow).

Hallier, J., and Lyon, P. (1996) 'Job Insecurity and Employee Commitment: Managers' Reactions to Threat and Outcomes of Redundancy Selection', *British Journal of Management*, 7/1: 107–23.

Harris, M. (1990) 'Working the UK Voluntary Sector', *Work Employment and Society*, 4/1: 125–40.

Haworth, J. (1997) *Work, Leisure and Well-Being*. London: Routledge.

Jahoda, M. (1982) *Employment and Unemployment: A Social Psychological Analysis*. Cambridge: Cambridge University Press.

—— (1987) 'Unemployed Men at Work', in D. M. Fryer and P. Ullah (eds., *Unemployed People: Social and Psychological Perspectives*. Milton Keynes: Open University Press.

Jordan, B., *et al.* (1992) *Trapped in Poverty? Labour-Market Decisions in Low-Income Households*. London: Routledge.

Joseph Rowntree Foundation (1991) *National Survey of Volunteering*, Social Policy Research Findings, 22. York: JRF, Dec.

Kozlowski, S. W., Chao, G. T., Smith, E. M., and Dedlund, J. (1993) 'Organizational Downsizing: Strategies, Interventions and Research Implications', in C. L. Cooper and I. T. Robertson (eds.), *International Review of Industrial and Organizational Psychology*. London: John Wiley, pp. 263–332.

MacDonald, R. (1997) 'Informal Working, Survival Strategies and the Idea of an "Underclass" ', in R. Brown (ed.), *The Changing Shape of Work*. Basingstoke: Macmillan, ch. 6.

—— and Coffield, F. (1991) *Risky Business? Youth and the Enterprise Culture*. Basingstoke: Falmer Press.

McKee, L., and Bell, C. (1986) 'His Unemployment, her Problem: The Domestic and Marital Consequences of Male Unemployment', in S. Allen, A. Waton, K. Purcell, and S. Wood (eds.), *The Experience of Unemployment*. Basingstoke: Macmillan.

Miles, I. (1983) *Adaptation to Unemployment?* Occasional Paper no. 20. Brighton: Science Policy Review Unit.

Mulgan, G., and Wilkinson, H. (1995) 'Well-Being and Time', *Demos*, 5: 2–11.

Okley, J. (1983) *The Traveller-Gypsies*. Cambridge: Cambridge University Press.

Pahl, R. (1984) *Divisions of Labour*. Oxford: Blackwell.

—— (1996) 'Reflections and Perspectives', in C. H. A. Verhaar *et al.* (eds.), *On Challenges of Unemployment in Regional Europe*. Aldershot: Avebury Press.

Phizacklea, A., and Wolkowitz, C. (1995) *Homeworking Women: Gender, Racism and Class at Work*. London: London.

Regional Trends (1997) No. 32, compiled by the Office of National Statistics. London: HMSO, 'Unemployment Claimants' (p. 78) and 'Vacancies at Jobcentres' (p. 76).

Roberts, B. (1994) *Minority Ethnic Women: Work, Unemployment and Education*. Manchester: Commission for Racial Equality.

Schor, J. (1995) 'The New American Dream', *Demos*, 5: 30.

Sly, F. (1995) 'Ethnic Groups and the Labour Market: Analyses from the Spring 1994 Labour Force Survey', *Employment Gazette*, June (Dept. of Employment, HMSO): 251–62.

—— (1996) 'Ethnic Minority Participation in the Labour Market: Trends for the Labour Force Survey 1984–1995', *Labour Market Trends* (HMSO), 104/6: 259–70.

Tam, M. (1997) *Part-Time Employment: A Bridge or a Trap?* Aldershot: Avebury.

Turner, R., Bostyn, A. M., and Wight, D. (1985) 'The Work Ethic in a Scottish Town with Declining Employment', in B. Roberts, R. Finnegan, and D. Gallie (eds.), *New Approaches to Economic Life*. Manchester: Manchester University Press, pp. 476–89.

Tyrell, B. (1995) 'Time of Our Lives: Facts and Analysis on the 1990s', *Demos*, 5: 23–5.

Warr, P. (1987) *Work, Unemployment and Mental Health*. Oxford: Clarendon Press.

Warr, P., Jackson, P., and Banks, M. (1988) 'Unemployment and Mental Health: Some British Studies', *Journal of Social Issues*, 44: 37–68.

Yankelovich, D. (1973) 'The Meaning of Work', in R. Rosnow (ed.), *The Worker and the Job*. New York: Columbia University Press/Prentice Hall, pp. 19–47.

12

Stress

BORING REPETITIVE JOBS can lead to mental strain. As early as 1965 Kornhauser's research with Detroit car workers was showing that the higher the occupation level, the better the mental health of the worker; better jobs with greater work skill, variety, responsibility and pay lead to better mental health. The lower the occupational level the more likely workers are to have little support or discretion in their jobs. Recent research too shows how low job control and high demand makes for stress (Bosma *et al.*, 1997; Schnall and Landbergis, 1994). Yet the higher the status of the worker the more likely they are to admit or believe they have stress problems (see Fletcher, 1990). This may be explained by the fact that many of those in white-collar jobs, not least in the public sector (e.g. university lecturers, schoolteachers, and social workers), have experienced a deterioration in their work conditions and that these people are more articulate than most (Nichols, 1998). Perhaps this is why most courses on stress management are aimed at professional employees.

You do not need to be employed to experience stress, though. Stressful events include moving house, getting married, having fights and conflicts, or the death of a loved one. When people are under high stress they tend to fail to sleep a full eight hours, fail to eat full meals, and tend to stay up late at night. Stressful events affect health by decreasing health-sustaining behaviours which in turn play a role in physical and psychological illnesses.

Stress has been a topic of interest to researchers since the Second World War. Newton (1995) notes how an interest in stress arose out of ideas within Social Darwinism eugenics and a concern for maintaining a healthy race, with writers like Walter Cannon and Graham Wallas. Cannon studied the effects of stress on animals and people, focusing on the 'fight or flight' reaction, whether they choose to stay and fight or try to escape when confronting extreme danger. Post-war laboratory research later reflected military concerns as stress was assumed to affect the performance of pilots, gunners, and others. In the 1970s, though, role stress gathered interest, with 200 articles being written on the topic between 1970 and 1983 (Jackson and Schuler, 1985).

Hans Seyle, researching in 1946, described three stages to a person's response to stress: alarm, resistance, and exhaustion (see Seyle, 1976). In the first stage the muscles tense, and the respiration, heart, and blood-pressure rates increase. Next the person experiences anxiety, anger, and fatigue as they resist stress; they may make poor decisions or experience illness at this stage. The person will not be able to sustain this resistance and, if the level of stress continues, they will experience exhaustion and stress-induced illness (like headaches and ulcers). Seyle claims that all individuals go through the same pattern of response and we can only tolerate so much stress before a serious debilitating condition is brought about. Critics of Seyle's work say it ignores both the psychological impact of stress upon an individual and the individual's ability to recognize stress and act in various ways to change his or her situation (Cooper *et al.*, 1988). Later theories of stress emphasized the interaction between a person and their environment. Others have added to this by discussing the individual's reaction. For example, Lazarus (1976) has suggested that an individual's stress reaction 'depends on how the person interprets or appraises (consciously or unconsciously) the significance of a harmful, threatening or challenging event'. All is dependent then on whether the person feels they can cope with a threat.

Cooper and Cummings (see Cooper *et al.*, 1988) believe that stress results from a misfit between an individual and their environment. This helps explain why one person seems to flourish in a setting while another suffers. Individuals, they say, for the most part, try to keep their thoughts, emotions, and relationships in a 'steady state'. They have a range of stability with which they feel comfortable. When forces disrupt the emotional and physical state, the individual must act or cope to restore a feeling of comfort. If they fail to cope, the stress will continue. Symptoms of stress can be manifested physically in, for example, lack of appetite or craving for food, headaches, skin problems, insomnia, fainting spells, and high blood pressure. Mental symptoms may include irritability, feeling unable to cope, difficulty in concentrating, and a lack of interest in life.

The latest Health and Safety Executive survey of self-reported work-related illnesses in Great Britain found stress, depression, and anxiety to be the second most prevalent condition claimed to be caused or made worse by work (HSC, 1997: 129–30). It has been suggested that 60 per cent of absence from work is caused by stress-related disorders (Kearns, 1986) and that in the UK 100 million days are lost each year because people cannot face going to work. Here stress-related absences from work were ten times more costly than industrial disputes. In terms of sickness, absence, and premature death or retirement due to alcoholism, stress costs the UK economy £2 billion per year (Cartwright and Cooper, 1997: 2).

What are the causes of stress? The following is a list of some of the factors which have been shown to contribute towards stress and strain:

1. The physical environment, for example being exposed to hazardous and noxious substances, density and crowding, lack of privacy, high noise levels, high or low temperature, poor quality lighting
2. Role conflict, when the individual is torn by conflict in job demands or doing things they do not want to do or believe are not part of the job, or role ambiguity, when an individual does not have a clear picture about work objectives, co-workers' expectations, the scope and responsibilities of the job
3. Characteristics of the job, for example, work overload, lack of career progression, lack of autonomy, under-utilization, too many meetings, shift work, or long hours
4. Relationships with others, e.g. poor relationships with supervisors, work/family conflict. (For a fuller list see Cartwright and Cooper, 1987: ch. 1; Cooper *et al.*, 1988, ch. 4.)

The Latest Phenomenon: Job Rage

Some have suggested that job rage is rapidly becoming a phenomenon to rival road rage. A receptionist was dismissed, having run foul of the temper of her superior, for not being able to make coffee as he liked it (*The Scotsman*, 4 April 1998, p. 11).

Shift work is a common stress factor affecting blood (temperature and sugar levels), metabolic rate, mental efficiency, work motivation, sleep patterns, family, and social life (Arnold *et al.*, 1995). A study of offshore oil-rig workers showed work patterns, including shift work, physical conditions, and travel, to be the third most important source of stress (Sutherland and Cooper, 1987). The longer the work shift (for example, twenty-eight days on, twenty-eight days off versus fourteen days on, fourteen days off) the greater the stress.

The shift patterns were a predicator of mental and physical ill health, particularly when the oil-rig workers were married and had children.

Research on balancing the needs of work and family and stress shows that mothers who work outside the home have better mental and physical health than those who do not. However, if partners contribute little to domestic tasks, they will have poorer mental health. The vast majority of mothers had partners who contributed less than 20 per cent to the domestic tasks (Khan and Cuthbertson, 1994).

The home is a source of stress for women as they try to balance the dual needs of work and domestic responsibilities (Ginn and Sandell, 1997; Wheeler and Lyon, 1992) but it would appear that work probably impacts on family more than family impacts on work. Interestingly, husbands' attitudes towards wives working has been studied extensively but wives' attitudes towards husbands' employment has not been so extensively researched. Also, research on impact of children on job stress has focused more on women than on men. While mothers might experience stress due to role overload, fathers might experience some stress as they attempt to fulfil the role of good provider (Gutek *et al.*, 1990).

Stress in the City

Nicola Horlick recently hit the headlines by losing a top city job. She had a very large salary, a high-pressured job, and five children. The costs of holding highly paid but high-pressured jobs can be large. For example an increasing number of senior women are likely to be found in second or third marriages. Women in top jobs are more likely to suffer from stomach problems, reflecting their struggle with stress. Few women will have been mentored for top jobs. Some are beginning to wonder if they can 'have it all'—a high-powered job and a family. 'Miranda Lawson' (not her real name) says 'I know that I could not do this job and have a family. I can't have it all, it would be completely impossible. But it would be possible for a man to do my job and have a family. Is that really equality?' (Interview with Lisa Buckingham, 'Room at the Top for Hard Choices', *Guardian*, 18 October 1997, p. 25).

Individual differences are involved in the stress process. There may be collections of traits which protect people from stress, for example 'hardiness'(Maddi and Kobasa, 1984), positive self-image or self-esteem, flexibility. The individual's vulnerability to stress may be affected by their personality, coping strategies, personal history, and social support. Some jobs are more stressful than others. The uniformed professions (prison service, police force, or civil aviation) have the highest average stress ratings (Cooper *et al.*, 1988). There is also concern about the psychological health of doctors; rates of suicide for doctors are approximately two to three times that of populations of comparable social class. In 1996 doctors hit headline news when the British Medical Association published a report showing how doctors were turning to drink and drugs to cope with increased stress and one in five doctors had thought about killing themselves (e.g. *Daily Mail*, 10 April, p. 21; *The Scotsman*, 13 April, p. 10). Substance abuse may be up to thirty times more common among doctors than the general population (King *et al.*, 1992). There is also a relatively high suicide rate among nurses (*Observer*, 19 March 1995, p. 1) and other health service workers (Rees, 1995).

It may be that some individuals have personalities which predispose them to the effects of stress. One such difference that has been examined is Type A coronary-prone behaviour. Type A behaviour is characterized by sustained drive towards poorly defined goals, preoccupation with deadlines, competitiveness and a desire for advancement and achievement. It is also characterized by mental and behavioural alertness or aggressiveness, chronic haste, and impatience. Typically more than 50 per cent of the workforce would be classified as Type As. (You can gain a rough idea of the degree to which you might be a Type A personality by completing the questionnaire in Cooper *et al.*, 1988: 51 or Arnold *et al.*, 1995: 376.) This type of behaviour has been shown to be an important risk factor in the development of coronary heart disease, a leading cause of death in Britain and North America. It kills more than 150,000 people a year, one person every three or four minutes (Arnold *et al.*, 1995). Type B personality types, a more relaxed type, in contrast have a low risk of coronary heart disease. There are some studies, though, which show contradictory results (see Cooper *et al.*, 1988: 48).

The Dilemma

Type A behaviour can lead to heart disease yet is consistently found to predict career success (Steffy *et al.*, 1989). The individual thus faces a conflict: should they work hard (going beyond what is expected is a virtue) or should they take care not to suffer the psychological and physiological effects of overwork? The individual faces the dilemma, not the organization. The individual has to adjust to work.

We have, through the measure of Type A behaviour and other measures of stress, like the General Health Questionnaire, a view of normality which is operationally defined through reference to abnormality (see Newton, 1995: 65). There are other ways of looking at stress, for example taking a sociological approach and looking at the subjective experience of the distress of dealing with the impending closure of a factory, as Anna Pollert did (see Handy, 1995; Pollert, 1981). Most current models of work stress fit firmly within a functionalist paradigm but this is not the only way the subject-matter could have been treated.

If you find that you are suffering from stress, there are a number of ways of coping, to 'transform maladaptive behaviour' (Cooper *et al.*, 1988). The techniques Cooper *et al.* (1988) would recommend include becoming assertive, identifying the incidents that cause distress by keeping a stress diary, and noting what action you took and how effective it proved. You need to attempt to eliminate or change the problem or stressor. If the problem or stressor cannot be changed, find ways of coping with the problem, then monitor and review the outcome (Arnold *et al.*, 1995).

A Blind Spot on Stress

An example of an employer who did nothing to eliminate or change the problem or the stressor, and was punished for doing nothing, was Northumberland Social Work Department. John Walker, a social worker in Northumberland, was awarded £200,000 after his employer put him back into a position in which stress from his job had already caused him health problems (*Independent on Sunday*, 3 March 1996, p. 21; see also Bond, 1996).

Using highly individualized methods, some organizations have tried to answer to the negative effects of stress by pre-empting it. Companies such as Federal Express, Hewlett Packard, and Conoco have adopted Stephen Covey's program 'The Seven Habits of Highly Effective People' (Vecchio, 1995). Stress can be managed in a number of different ways: employment assistance programmes (EAPs), stress management training, and stress reduction or intervention (Murphy, 1988; Newton, 1995). EAPs generally refer to the provision of employee counselling for problems like alcoholism, drug abuse, and mental health. Stress management training is designed to provide employees with improved coping skills and so includes techniques like meditation, biofeedback, and muscle relaxation to help the individual. Stress reduction or intervention would usually change a job to reduce job stressors. Most workplace initiatives focus on stress management training or counselling and health promotion, not changing jobs. Companies like the Post Office, Whitbread Brewers, and the TSB bank are amongst those in Britain who have been using techniques like EAPs and stress management training (see King, 1994, for more UK examples). The US Department of Health and Human Services found that more than 60 per cent of work-sites there offered some form of stress management or health promotion activity (Cooper and Cartwright, 1994). For example, the New York Telephone Company introduced a wellness programme for cardiovascular fitness, while PepsiCo created a physical fitness programme (see Cooper *et al.*, 1988: 179–85, for more examples). Evidence of the success of such schemes is generally confusing and imprecise, possibly reflecting the idiosyncratic nature of the form and content of courses (Arnold *et al.*, 1995: 383). The growing evidence that individual and company performance is adversely affected by stress has had little effect on companies in Britain (Wheeler and Lyon, 1992).

> ### Cheap and Cheerful
>
> Sheffield's Weston Park Hospital trust decided to improve the health and welfare of the 460 staff who worked in this specialist oncology and cancer hospital. Staff identified a need for stress management, back-care, and exercise. A ten-week, two hour a week course of relaxation, exercise, and back-strengthening was developed by a master's degree student in sport and exercise science. The main improvement was in people's ability to cope. Everyone said they felt better and that morale had improved (*Health Service Journal* (16 Dec. 1993): 15: other examples from the Health Service can be found in *Health Service Journal* (Jan. 1994): 10–11).

While programmes like EAP programmes may have genuine benefits for employees, they may also represent an extension of corporate control over staff who are now expected not only to sell their skills and time but to ensure that their total lifestyle ensures maximum corporate gain (Handy, 1988). Newton (1995) argues that stress management techniques are not impartial and are not applied by caring progressive management; in fact they may be 'nakedly coercive', a tool of a cunning management intent upon domination and control of their workforce. Fineman (1995) shows how managers at a nuclear research establishment treated the results of a study on employee role stress. The managers were so alarmed by the results that they immediately suppressed the findings and tried to discredit the analysis.

> ### Counterpoint?
>
> Marks and Spencer has an occupational health service. The focus is on health promotion but the cost benefits are very difficult to assess. One of Marks and Spencer's line managers in a London store is quoted as saying 'The headway that's been made on the health care front is being counterbalanced by cutting staff levels to leave remaining staff under greater pressure and therefore greater stress'. (*Financial Decisions* (Aug. 1988): 46–8).

Stress, Fineman (1995) would argue, has much to do with the organization and social context of the job. Stress is an emotional product of the social and political features of work and organizational life. The individual is actively involved in reproducing the social structures and there may be little they can do to affect them, either because they are tacit, taken-for-granted features of organizational life, operating at a more or less preconscious level, or because the individual is relatively powerless to affect them. We learn feeling rules; we have learnt how much emotion to display, about how to appear, and appropriate demeanour for the workplace. Some of the rules will reflect our gender, age, or class. Others will reflect the nature of the business we work in. Crucially we privately labour with, and work in, our feelings in order to create the socially desired emotional expression and impression. Stress feelings, like anxiety, fear, and dread will have to be dressed up for managers, customers, clients, and colleagues. In doing the 'face work' (Goffman, 1961) camouflaging our feelings, we create new tensions. The polite automatic smile from the waitress may be relatively stress free but the emotional labour cost rises when the waitress starts to hate her work and the people she serves. We have discussed the explicit feeling rules in the chapter on routinization and, when looking at Hochschild's (1983) work, on emotions and the view from outside. There are also implicit feeling rules. These would include, for example, the rules on what should remain a private doubt and worry and what can be openly expressed. Fineman (1995) shows how social workers provide much illustration of this. The social workers did not share their concerns with their colleagues and 'played a charade' with each other's stresses. They did not admit to their own stresses and would fail to care for colleagues. What they did to cope was go sick or absent, as this was organizationally acceptable. These tacit assumptions and rules about emotion and stress are not going to fall out neatly from the questions and answers in interviews or questionnaires but can be the unintended product of a lengthy process of establishing a relationship with individuals in a study.

We have touched on the subject of managing emotions in an earlier chapter. A discussion of emotion management can also be found in a study of The Body Shop (Martin *et al.*, 1998). Here the constrained expression of emotions at work was encouraged as it facilitated a sense of community and personal well-being. Employees of The Body Shop frequently discuss intimate personal issues with co-workers; employees felt they could 'be themselves at work' (1998: 460). Most employees shared a strong sense of being part of The Body Shop community. Anita Roddick herself repeatedly and persuasively articulated values such as caring, sharing, and love. These values were enacted by employees in practices such as one intimate self-disclosure encouraging another, hugs and kisses as common ways of saying hello, thank you, and goodbye. These expressions of emotion were, however, constrained.

Questions for Further Research

1. If you were an employer, what steps would you take to (*a*) research stress, (*b*) act to reduce stress levels?

2. Take one occupational group, like doctors, and try to assess, through research and reading, how vulnerable they are to stress compared to another group, like nurses.

3. Newton (1995) asks us to challenge the way we look at stress. How does he recommend we do this?

4. According to some (see *The Times*, 21 December 1994, p. 4) women cope better with stress in demanding jobs than men. What evidence can you find to support or refute this statement?

5. Some believe that stress can be measured (e.g. Cohen *et al.*, 1995). What would be the strengths and limitations of such an approach?

6. Anna Pollert's study of women workers' responses to the impending closure of the tobacco factory where they were employed provides a sociological study of distress. Describe the stresses created by this work environment and the dual burden of work and family responsibilities that she uncovered.

7. How would Handy (1988) and others, like Newton, argue that while employees benefit from EAP programmes and other stress management programmes, it is the employers who mainly benefit?

Further Reading

Arnold, J., Cooper, C. L., and Robertson, I. T. (1995) *Work Psychology: Understanding Human Behaviour in the Workplace*, 2nd edn. London: Pitman Publishing, chs. 17 and 18.

Cartwright, S., and Cooper, C. L. (1997) *Managing Workplace Stress*. London: Sage Publications.

Cooper, C. L., and Payne, R. (1990) *Causes, Coping and Consequences of Stress at Work*. Chichester: Wiley.

Newton, T. (1995), with J. Handy and S. Fineman, *Managing Stress: Emotions and Power at Work*. London: Sage.

Vecchio, R. P. (1995) *Organizational Behaviour*, 3rd edn. London: Dryden Press, ch. 15.

References

Arnold, J., Cooper, C. L., and Robertson, I. T. (1995) *Work Psychology: Understanding Human Behaviour in the Workplace*, chs. 17 and 18.

Bosma, H., Marmot, M. G., Hemingway, H., Nicholson, A. C., Brunner, E., and Stansfield, S. A. (1997) 'Low Job Control and Risk of Coronary Heart Disease in Whitehall II (Prospective Cohort) Study', *British Medical Journal* (22 Feb.): 558–65.

Bond, H. (1996) 'Stress Fractures', *Community Care* (4 July): 14–15.

Cartwright, S., and Cooper, C. L. (1997) *Managing Workplace Stress*. London: Sage.

Cohen, S., Kessler, R. C., and Gordon, L. U. (1995) (eds.) *Measuring Stress: A Guide for Health and Social Scientists*. Oxford: Oxford University Press.

Cooper, C. L. and Cartwright, S. (1994) 'Healthy Mind; Healthy Organization: A Proactive Approach to Occupational Stress', *Human Relations*, 47/4: 455–71.

Cooper, C. L. and Payne, R. (1990) *Causes, Coping and Consequences of Stress at Work*. Chichester: Wiley.

Cooper, C. L., Cooper, R. D., and Eaker, L. H. (1988) *Living with Stress*. Harmondsworth: Penguin.

Fineman, S. (1995) 'Stress, Emotion and Intervention', in T. Newton, *Managing Stress: Emotion and Power at Work*. London: Sage.

Fletcher, B. (1990) 'The Epidemiology of Occupational Stress', in C. L. Cooper and R. Payne (eds.), *Causes, Coping and Consequences of Stress at Work*. Chichester: Wiley, ch. 1.

Ginn, J., and Sandell, J. (1997) 'Balancing Home and Employment: Stress Reported by Social Services Staff', *Work, Employment and Society*, 11/3: 413–34.

Goffman, E. (1961) *Asylums*. Harmondsworth: Penguin.

Gutek, B. A., Repetti, R. L., and Silver, D. L. (1990) 'Non-Work Roles and Stress at Work', in C. L. Cooper and R. Payne (eds.), *Causes, Coping and Consequences of Stress at Work*. Chichester: Wiley, ch. 5.

Handy, J. A. (1988) 'Theoretical and Methodological Problems with Occupational Stress and Burnout Research', *Human Relations*, 41/5: 351–69.

Handy, J. (1995) 'Rethinking Stress: Seeing the Collective', in T. Newton, *Managing Stress: Emotion and Power at Work*. London: Sage, ch. 4.

Hochschild, A. R. (1983) *The Managed Heart: Commercialization of Human Feeling*. Berkeley, Calif.: University of California Press.

HSC (1997) *Health and Safety Commission Annual Report and Accounts 1996/1997*. London: HSE Books.

Jackson, S. E., and Schuler, R. S. (1985) 'A Meta-analysis and Conceptual Critique of Research on Role Ambiguity and Role Conflict in Work Settings', *Organizational Behaviour and Human Decision Processes*, 36: 16–78.

Kearns, J. (1986) 'Stress at Work: The Challenge of Change', BUPA series *The Management of Health*, cited in C. L. Cooper and R. Payne (eds.), *Causes, Coping and Consequences of Stress at Work*. Chichester: Wiley.

Khan, H., and Cuthbertson, J. (1994) 'Mothers who Work and Mothers who "Only" Stay at Home: Are the Stressors Different?', Paper presented to the annual conference of the Scottish Branch of the British Psychological Society, Crieff Hydro, 25–7 Nov. 1994.

King, M. B., Cockcroft, A., and Gooch, C. (1992) 'Emotional Distress in Doctors: Sources, Effects and Help Sought', *Journal of the Royal Society of Medicine*, 85: 605–8.

King, S. (1994) 'Counselling through Employee Assistance Programmes', *Management Development Review*, 7/2: 38–40.

Lazarus, R. S. (1976) *Patterns of Adjustment*. New York: McGraw Hill.

Maddi, S. R., and Kobasa, S. C. (1984) *The Hardy Executive: Health under Stress*. Homewood, Ill.: Dow Jones-Irwin.

Martin, J., Knopoff, K., and Beckman, C. (1998) 'An Alternative to Bureaucratic Impersonality and Emotional Labor: Bounded Rationality at The Body Shop', *Administrative Science Quarterly*, 429–69.

Murphy, L. R. (1988) 'Workplace Interventions for Stress Reduction and Prevention', in C. L. Cooper and R. Payne (eds.), *Causes and Coping and Consequences of Stress at Work*. Chichester: Wiley.

Newton, T. (1995), with J. Handy and S. Fineman, *Managing Stress: Emotions and Power at Work*. London: Sage.

Nichols, T. (1998) 'Health and Safety at Work', Review article in *Work, Employment and Society*, 12/2 (June): 367–74.

Pollert, A. (1981) *Girls, Wives, Factory Lives*. London: Macmillan.

Rees, D. W. (1995) 'Work-Related Stress in Health Service Employees', *Journal of Managerial Psychology*, 10/3: 4–11.

Schnall, P. L., and Landsbergis, P. A. (1994) 'Job Strain and Cardiovascular Disease', *Annual Review of Public Health*, 15: 381–411.

Seyle, H. (1976) *The Stress of Life*. New York: McGraw Hill.

Steffy, B. D., Shaw, K., and Noe, A. W. (1989) 'Antecedents and Consequences of Job Search Behaviours', *Journal of Vocational Behavior*, 3: 254–69.

Sutherland, V., and Cooper, C. L. (1987) *Man and Accidents Offshore*. London: Lloyds.

Vecchio, R. P. (1995) *Organizational Behaviour*, 3rd edn. London: Dryden Press.

Wheeler, S., and Lyon, D. (1992) 'Employee Benefits for the Employer's Benefit: How Companies Respond to Employee Stress', *Personnel Review*, 21/7: 47–63.

13

Alternative Organizational Ownership Forms: Their Effect on Organizational Behaviour

COOPERATIVES could help solve a lot of the organizational ills discussed so far. They can potentially reduce levels of industrial conflict and enhance productivity by aligning the interests of workers with those of their firm. In principle cooperatives offer a model of a more humane and productive alternative to bureaucratic organization (Rothschild-Whitt, 1982). Some may claim (e.g. Mellor *et al.*, 1988) that, in cooperatives, the dispossessed seek to control the very existence of work itself. Ultimately it is a desire to change the whole basis of control and radically shift it towards those who have so little.

Cooperatives

A cooperative is a business that is wholly or substantially owned and controlled by those who work in it; it is run for their mutual benefit. Control is exercised on the basis of one person, one vote; membership is open as far as possible to all workers. Italy has the largest cooperative sector of any European country. Earle (1986) records that, following Mussolini's fall, 9,000 cooperatives were set up between 1944 and 1946, and the total reached 23,000 in 1949. Cooperation was also well established in France. Government legislative and financial support for cooperatives has continued in both France and Italy, in marked contrast to the experience of Britain. In West Germany a network of business projects was initiated in the alternative sector. These businesses did not necessarily adopt formal cooperative status but share many of their characteristics, such as collective ownership and democratic management. They also have a strong commitment to providing a socially useful product or service and aim to pay an income equivalent to the general level of wages. In the USA, as in Europe, the new wave of cooperative development was associated with the alternative movement (see Ehrenreich and Edelstein, 1983; Lichtenstein, 1986). An estimated 500,000 people are employed by producer cooperatives in Western Europe (Heller *et al.*, 1998).

Interest in cooperatives has waxed and waned in Britain over the years. In 1945 there were just forty-four cooperatives (Mellor *et al.*, 1988). Their numbers reached a low point in the early 1970s when there were about thirty-five registered in Britain. However, an alternative movement in the 1970s brought about a number of idealistic cooperatives. With growing unemployment in the late 1970s and early 1980s interest in cooperatives increased; by 1985 there were over 1,000 cooperatives in Britain. Local authorities and government agencies, like the Highlands and Islands Development Board in Scotland, promoted cooperatives as a means of job creation. The average size of cooperatives in Britain is, though, not large. The mean size is about seven workers and the median only four. They are concentrated in particular sectors like clothing, printing, catering, wholefoods, and bookshops (Cornforth *et al.*, 1988).

What is the experience of cooperative working? In a study of sixteen British case studies Cornforth *et al.* (1988) found that cooperative working was intense and involving, whether for better or worse. The individuals felt a heightened emotional involvement with their work. The worries could be severe but when cooperative working was going well, it gave rise to feeling of great excitement and satisfaction that was far more stimulating than conventional employment had ever been. While instrumental benefits, like job security, were important and a powerful spur to founding or working in a cooperative, social benefits were also an advantage. It was a welcome luxury to work with people who were congenial, both politically and personally. Working in a cooperative is a way in which self-esteem and self-identity needs can be met within a work environment. Many of the members of the cooperatives had joined because they felt attracted to the radical products or services and egalitarian working practices. Many found it difficult to think of the things they liked least about their work but there were costs like low pay (especially at the start of the cooperative) and tiredness due to long hours. Workers in cooperatives were able to secure more control over organization and management of work on the shop-floor than is usually the case, although there were limits imposed by the need for efficiency, the nature of technology, the workers themselves, knowledge, and experience. The cooperatives' achievements included less supervision, more flexible working arrangements, more variety of work, lower wage differentials, and more direct control over how workers carry out their jobs. Over time, however, the increasing complexity of some businesses and pressures for specialization and continuity have led to limits being placed on job rotation and the introduction of small differentials.

Cooperatives and the Labour Process

It cannot be assumed that ownership of a job bestows control over that job. The nature of the labour process in the particular industry or service will affect the control an individual has. The labour process can be defined as 'The means by which raw materials are transformed by human labour, acting on the objets with tools and machinery: first into products for use and, under capitalism, into commodities to be exchanged on the market' (Thompson, 1983: p. xv). When it comes to technology in cooperatives there is often little choice about the technology that is purchased or hired. Inappropriate or outdated equipment might actually contribute to the demise of a cooperative (Wajcman, 1983). A fledgling cooperative might be tied to previous production methods and even to previous suppliers or customers. Others will be constrained by the amount of money available. Machinery itself will impose its own limits. The workforce, will, though, within certain parameters have some choice about specific equipment and work design. They might choose less efficient machinery that is more safe; they may choose to situate workers facing each other in pairs to allow them to talk, allow workers discretion in unscheduled breaks, or flexibility in hours of work.

As cooperatives are unlikely to find themselves in a monopoly selling position or as a market leader, they are unlikely to be able to determine the type, quantity, or price of the product, particularly if linked to a single buyer. The speed and skill required to produce competitively conflicts with the ability of cooperatives to practice preferred forms of work organization such as job rotation. Worker cooperatives can, then, face stark choices in often very unfavourable circumstances and poor economic climates. A different set of problems based on ideological differences arose within the Israeli experience of worker cooperatives (see Russell, 1995). Before a real note of pessimism sets in, let us look at an example of how cooperatives can succeed.

Mondragon

In 1956 Father Jose Maria Arizmendi-Arieta inspired workers in the Basque region of Spain to take over a redundant factory. (The ideas of egalitarianism and industrial democracy are an important constituent of Basque identity: Kasmir, 1996.) By 1982 over 18,000 people were employed by the Mondragon group of cooperatives and they had created their own network of financial and welfare services; in 1986 the numbers employed were 19,500. In the 1980s the Spanish economy was more severely affected by recession than other Western industrialized nations yet the Mondragon cooperatives coped with the extreme economic adversity.

In Mondragon there are primary cooperatives that produce a variety of manufactured products including electrical goods, refrigerators, and machine tools. The difficulty of obtaining funding and the need to provide social and welfare services led to the establishment of secondary cooperatives of which the most important is the Caja Laboral Popular, a savings bank. The Caja lays down a democratic governing structure and a code of practice for each cooperative (Mellor *et al.*, 1988) and provides about 60 per cent of the funding for new cooperatives. Workers, though, must make an investment; this provides incentive to workers' commitment to the cooperative's success. Successful cooperatives like Mondragon provide jobs, security, reduced labour-management strife, flexibility in hours, and work location. All profits return to workers or to community welfare (Hacker, 1987).

Participation by workers is mediated though a committee system. Directors are elected on the basis of one person, one vote; directors are accountable to a general assembly. The general assembly meets at least annually and members of the firm have an obligation to vote there. The governing council is the top policy-making body which may call meetings. This governing council is elected by the members, who are all workers; non-members may attend but are not members. A works or social council effectively replicates the role of trade unions and could, for example, question abuses committed by management, make suggestions on safety and health, social security, systems of compensation, and social work activities or projects. Many of the cooperatives employ no non-members and by their own constitution and by-laws, no cooperative may employ more than 10 per cent of non-members.

Until the early 1970s worker participation was limited to governance. In the late 1970s this was extended to the organization and management of work. A manager was asked to look at personnel and human relations and concluded that:

- The personnel department should play a leading role in linking the economic and technological objectives of the firm with the social concerns of the members.
- The growing tensions in the workplace revealed the inherent contradiction between the democratic system of cooperative governance and the rigid authoritarian system for organizing work according to the scientific management principles of Taylor.
- Management should explore the possibility of creating new forms of work organization that would be economically efficient yet more in harmony with the social values on which the cooperative movement was based. Personnel should work with line managers to do this (see Whyte and Whyte, 1988: 113–14).

Changes were made to work organization, for example an assembly line for the manufacture of thermostats was removed and work tables substituted. Workers could now set their own work rhythm and freely exchange information and ideas. All workers were expected to perform all the tasks and could rotate tasks as they themselves decided. As they gained skill and confidence they began to take over supervisory and staff functions, such as requisitioning tools and materials and recording their output. As a result of reorganization the workers could more readily visualize their contribution to the total product; they were better able to respond to customer needs and improve the planning process; the inventory of work in progress was reduced and the research and development process strengthened. Both managers and workers were in favour of the new ways of working. The monotony of work was relieved. The work groups increased workers' self-esteem and made individuals feel responsible to the group for their performance and workers welcomed the opportunity to learn new skills and improved relationships with supervisors. Improved productivity and quality reduced scrap and stock levels.

Mondragon is not without its critics. For example, Kasmir (1996) is disappointed that the more or less democratic entrepreneurial decisions are implemented through a hierarchy of managers, experts and skilled workers. Hacker claims that empirical research on work democracy has tended to ignore issues of gender, with studies of Mondragon failing to note the situation of women or ask questions about gender before she arrived (1987). Yet Whyte and Whyte do look briefly at the situation of women and find that at the outset single women had been required to leave the firm when they married but by the mid-1960s this policy had been abandoned. They also note the efforts made to establish a woman's cooperative within Mondragon.

Sally Hacker's (1987) study (which was aided by Clara Elcorobairutia) suggests that women fare somewhat better in Mondragon cooperatives than in private firms in the region, in employment, earnings, and job security. But the concentration of technical and scientific skill lay with the men in the cooperatives. Women workers are found clustered at the bottom of the pay and occupational hierarchies.

The Israeli Kibbutz

The kibbutz movement in Israel remains a viable attempt to provide an alternative to capitalism without managerial authority and worker subordination and exploitation (Warhurst, 1998). The kibbutz movement was founded at the beginning of the twentieth century and grew rapidly in the two decades after 1931. The pioneers wished to create an economy and society that was free, working, and classless. The organizational design uses socialist principles where the means of production are owned by the community and all work is shared equally and rotated to give every member experience of every activity, including the most routine and demeaning work. In the kibbutz members live and work communally. This is a logical extension of cooperative working. A common 'household' and treasury exists. Nobody receives payment but all basic needs are met on an agreed basis with equality; all members receive a small, personal, and equitable allowance regardless of contribution. A general assembly is the source of power and every member has equal access to it. This assembly is supplemented by committees of work branches, work allocation, culture, services, economic planning and others. The typical kibbutz will have as many as thirty different committees and between 30 and 50 per cent of members annually participate in them. General managers are elected and open to regular rotation approximately every five to seven years. In recent years the situation has become less favourable as support for socialist solutions has dwindled (Heller *et al.*, 1998). Today there are 269 kibbutzim with a total population of 123,900 members (Yad Tabenkin, 1997). The average size is just less than 500 members. Membership is voluntary but subject to the approval of the community.

Warhurst (1998) has recently produced a case study of a kibbutz through open participant observation, living and working there. In this kibbutz he found the managers had a coordination rather than a control function. There were no job descriptions, no direction, monitoring, or evaluation by managers of work or workers, no records of individual workers or work group performance or attendance. Workers decided their own specific tasks and how to do them. It was the antithesis of Taylorism. Labour discipline came about in part due to the commitment of individual members and their identification with the purposes of the kibbutz. There is a common framework of norms, values and beliefs about the organization and the importance of work to which all members, as workers, consent and conform. At least one alternative form of organization and control is possible then, Warhurst concludes, in the workplace.

Yugoslav Self Management

Yugoslav workers enjoyed social ownership and worker self-management until that country's break up. For about three decades social scientists studied the Yugoslav self-management system, which was based on the assumption that organizations could be run by their employees operating through elected Workers' Councils. These had the right to hire and fire management and make major decisions. Theoretically, all decisions were made by workers; the role of management was simply one of implementation of those decisions. Technically, managers should not be members of workers' councils though they were able to attend and speak.

Research showed, however, that top management were members of the works council and tended to dominate discussions on strategic issues; they had most of their proposals accepted (Heller *et al.*, 1998). There was then a great gap between expectations of what self-management could achieve and what they did achieve. Much of this gap could be explained by differences in experience and knowledge of managers and workers. It may have been a mistake to expect all employees (most of whom came from peasant backgrounds) to take part in decisions on technology, marketing, and innovation, and to think that professional managers would carry out decisions without having a say. The Tayloristic scientific division of labour was widespread; democratic management was curbed. Self-management degenerated into little more than self-interest, a situation reinforced by the personal financial remuneration of workers within these enterprises (Warhurst, 1998).

There were, however, some successes. Yugoslav industries were the most participative of the industries studied in eleven countries. Self-management educated the workers and created a feeling of collective ownership and responsibility. It did much to transform a traditional hierarchical society. Self-management also trained a generation of managers (Heller *et al.*, 1998). Self-management disappeared when the Yugoslav state broke apart in 1990. Research by Pusic (see Heller *et al.*, 1998) shows that Croatian managers feel quite positively about self-management and in Slovenia a new structure has emerged based in co-determination. While Yugoslav workers' self-management has now largely disappeared, its experience provides some important lessons.

Employee Involvement—Profit Sharing and Share Ownership

Interest in employee participation in organizational decision-making peaked in the 1970s but continued interest in the subject is maintained by, for example, financial participation. One form of financial participation which is thought to foster greater identification among employees with their employer and a means by which employees can bear some of the risks and rewards of the enterprise is through profit sharing. In profit sharing employees are given the opportunity to take some of their income from employment in a form related to their employer's profits. Profit sharing was initially introduced in the mid-nineteenth century to prevent or inhibit union activity. Schemes were often withdrawn when profits declined along with the threat of union influence (Baddon *et al.*, 1989). Further surges of interest in profit sharing emerged just before the First World War, the inter-war period, and post-war. The fluctuating history suggests that the schemes were introduced for two main purposes: as an act of faith by employers towards their employees or as a means of securing employee compliance (Baddon *et al.*, 1989). Interest in profit sharing has grown again in recent years (Bhargara, 1995; Gomez-Mejia and Balkin, 1992; Morris and Pinnington, 1998). It is now estimated that 24 per cent of private-sector employees in the UK (3.7 million) currently receive profit-related pay (Robinson and Perotin, 1997).

Profit sharing can be effective in eroding the 'them and us' divide between owner and employees and in increasing commitment to enterprise goals and raising efficiency and profitability. There is very strong research evidence to show that profit sharing does act to increase company productivity (Robinson and Perotin, 1997). With profit sharing there is the potential incentive effect of a payment system which links workers' productive performance with their remuneration; it can also be seen as offering an incentive to employees to increase profitability as a group. One disadvantage is that it loses the directness of the effort-pay relation which can create 'free rider' problems (Kim, 1998) where workers do not put in the expected effort as they only receive a small part of the profits generated by their effort.

Share ownership means that employees are able to acquire a degree of ownership of the assets of the employer. The purpose is to allow employees to develop a sense of belonging to the company and to envisage a breaking down of the 'them and us' divide. In theory, employee ownership should generate more favourable attitudes towards the company and greater organizational commitment (Kelly and Kelly, 1991). This in turn will lead to changes in behaviour, such as greater personal effort, a reduced propensity to quit, and greater scrutiny of colleagues' work behaviour (Pendleton *et al.*, 1998). In time these changes should be reflected in improvements in collective performance as measured by productivity and profitability. Like profit sharing, employee share ownership schemes have become widespread in the UK (Millward *et al.*, 1992), some parts of the European Union (Uvalic, 1991), the USA

(Blasi and Kruse, 1991), the former Eastern bloc countries (Karsai and Wright, 1994), and Japan (Jones and Kato, 1995).

Although Robinson and Perotin (1997) say there is a link between profit sharing and productivity, others, like Baddon *et al.* (1989), have concluded that the evidence on increased profitability and productivity arising from profit sharing and share ownership schemes is mixed. Although employers and employees are potential beneficiaries of financial participation, there is surprisingly little hard evidence on what the benefits are or to whom they accrue (Baddon *et al.*, 1989). Baddon *et al.* (1989) surveyed about 400 employee share ownership and profit sharing schemes in companies. They found that companies commonly run more than one scheme of financial participation for more than one objective. The managers themselves had only a very general sense of what they were trying to achieve through these schemes. Case studies showed that there was a strong sense of unitary thinking in which share ownership (and to a lesser extent profit sharing) was seen as reinforcing employee loyalty and commitment, but there was no systematic attempt by the companies to measure the benefits of running these schemes. The conclusion is that the management objectives were not being achieved and that personal financial gain is a stronger motivating factor among employees than some of the loftier objectives. The benefits tended not to be seen by employees as an essential element of pay which would generate commitment, even where profit bonus benefits were quite substantial. They were 'just another kind of bonus' (1989: 275) which fell short of moving employees to a feeling of unity of purpose. No specific scheme held any significant advantage over others. Similarly Dunn *et al.* (1991) and more recently Keef (1998) have found that employee ownership does not result in expected improvements in attitudes. Two reasons are that employee equity stakes are too small in relation to total equity to bring about a pronounced sense of ownership and that few opportunities are provided for employees to translate ownership into increased control and participation in decision-making (Pendleton, 1997). It would appear that a 'sense of ownership' is important in bringing about attitudinal change. Opportunities for participation in decision making are more important that ownership *per se* in generating feelings of ownership. Feelings of ownership are significantly associated with higher levels of commitment and satisfaction (Pendleton *et al.*, 1998).

There are, then, alternatives to highly bureaucratic, hierarchical organizations which involve greater democracy, wider decision-making, ownership, and involvement. While Frederick Taylor, Henri Fayol, and Max Weber legitimated the managerial right to manage in the USA, Britain, and other parts of Europe, the managers' right to analyse the work situation scientifically and rationally, devising the most appropriate, efficient methods, this might not be the only way to organize. In Scandinavia, for example, there was a 'historic compromise' between capital and labour (Burnes, 1996) with government-backed approaches to industrial democracy and extensions of workers' rights. Rules, divisions of labour, and some bureaucracy will not be eliminated, but organizations could be more democratic, less hierarchical, and more collectivist. There are circumstances under which workplace democracy is possible (Joseph, 1989). As Joseph notes, what is striking about Britain is the extent to which alternatives to conventional management arrangements are non-issues. Greater moves could be made towards extending and renewing existing organizational forms. There are a variety of possible organizational forms of decision-making, ownership, and involvement to choose from that could result in 'a minimal bureaucracy' (Thompson and McHugh, 1995: 197). Would task sharing, egalitarian rewards, democratic controls, cooperative cultures, and participation appeal to you? Alternative organizational forms could offer solutions to the problems created by Taylorism, bureaucracy, hierarchy, and social inequality. You decide.

Questions for Further Research

1. The impetus and motivation for cooperatives comes from a number of different sources, according to the research. What motivation for the establishment of alternative organizations can you find in your reading?

2. Why would firms adopt profit sharing and employee ownership plans (see references above and Kruse, 1996)?

3. If share schemes improve productivity, why don't the majority of firms use them (see references above and Drago and Turnbull, 1996)?

Suggestions for Further Reading

Cornforth, C., Thomas, A., Lewis, J., and Spear, R. (1988) *Developing Successful Worker Cooperatives*. London: Sage.

Mellor, M., Hannah, J., and Stirling, J. (1988) *Worker Cooperatives in Theory and Practice*. Milton Keynes: Open University Press.

Whyte, W. Foote, and Whyte, K. King (1988) *Making Mondragon: The Growth and Dynamics of the Worker Cooperative Complex*. Ithaca, NY: ILR Press, New York State School of Industrial and Labor Relations, Cornell University.

References

Baddon, L., Hunter, L., Hyman, J., Leopold, J., and Ramsay, H. (1989) *People's Capitalism? A Critical Analysis of Profit-Sharing and Employee Share Ownership*. London: Routledge.

Bhargara, S. (1995) 'Profit Sharing and Financial Performance of Companies: Evidence from UK Panel Data', *The Economic Journal*, 104: 1044–56.

Blasi, J., and Kruse, D. (1991) *The New Owners: The Mass Emergence of Employee Ownership in Public Companies and What it Means to American Business*. New York: Harper Business.

Burnes, B. (1996) *Managing Change: A Strategic Approach to Organizational Dynamics*, 2nd edn. London: Pitman.

Cornforth, C., Thomas, A., Lewis, J., and Spear, R. (1988) *Developing Successful Worker Cooperatives*. London: Sage.

Drago, R., and Turnbull, G. K. (1996) 'On the Incidence of Profit Sharing', *Journal of Economic Behaviour and Organization*, 31: 129–38.

Dunn, S., Richardson, R., and Dewe, P. (1991) 'The Impact of Employee Share Ownership on Worker Attitudes: A Longitudinal Case Study', *Human Resource Management Journal*, 1/1: 1–17.

Earle, J. (1986) *The Italian Cooperative Movement*. London: Allen and Unwin.

Ehrenreich, R. C., and Edelstein, J. D. (1983) 'Consumers and Organizational Democracy: American New Wave Cooperatives', in C. Crouch and F. Heller (eds.), *Organizational Democracy and Political Processes*. New York: Wiley.

Gomez-Mejia, L., and Balkin, D. (1992) *Compensation, Organizational Strategy and Firm Performance*. Cincinnati: South Western Publishing.

Hacker, S. (1987) 'Women Workers in the Mondragon System of Industrial Cooperatives', *Gender and Society*, 1: 358–79.

Heller, F., Pusic, E., Strauss, G., and Wilpert, B. (1998) *Organizational Participation: Myth and Reality*. Oxford: Oxford University Press.

Jones, D., and Kato, T. (1995) 'The Productivity Effects of Japanese Employee Stock Ownership Plans: Evidence from Japanese Panel Data', *American Economic Review*, 85: 391–414.

Joseph, M. (1989) *Sociology for Business*. Cambridge: Polity in association with Basil Blackwell.

Karsai, J., and Wright, M. (1994) 'Accountability, Governance and Finance in Hungarian Buy-outs', *Europe-Asia Studies*, 46: 997–1016.

Kasmir, S. (1996) *The Myth of Mondragon: Cooperatives, Politics and Working Class Life in a Basque Town*. Albany, NY: SUNY Press.

Keef, S. P. (1998) 'The Causal Association between Employee Share Ownership and Attitudes: A Study Based in the Long Framework', *British Journal of Industrial Relations* (Mar.): 73–82.

Kelly, J., and Kelly, C. (1991) ' "Them and Us": Social Psychology and the New Industrial Relations', *British Journal of Industrial Relations*, 29: 25–48.

Kim, S. (1998) 'Does Profit Sharing Increase Firms' Profits?', *Journal of Labor Research*, 19/2: 351–70.

Kruse, D. L. (1996) 'Why Do Firms Adopt Profit Sharing and Employee Ownership Plans?', *British Journal of Industrial Relations*, 34/4: 515–38.

Lichtenstein, P. M. (1986) 'The Concept of the Firm in the Economic Theory of Alternative Organizations', in S. Jansson and A.-B. Hellmark (eds.), *Labour-Owned Firms and Workers' Cooperatives*. London: Gowe.

Mellor, M., Hannah, J., and Stirling, J. (1988) *Worker Cooperatives in Theory and Practice*. Milton Keynes: Open University Press.

Millward, N., Stevens, M., Smart, D., and Hawes, W. (1992) *Workplace Industrial Relations in Transition: the ED/ESRC/PSI/ACAS Surveys*. Aldershot: Dartmouth.

Morris, T., and Pinnington, A. (1998) 'Patterns of Profit-Sharing in Professional Firms', *British Journal of Management*, 9: 23–9.

Pendleton, A. (1997) 'Shareholders as Stakeholders', in A. Gamble, D. Kelly, and G. Kelly (eds.), *Stakeholder Capitalism*. Basingstoke: Macmillan.

—— Wilson, N., and Wright, M. (1998) 'The Perception and Effects of Share Ownership: Empirical Evidence from Employee Buy-outs', *British Journal of Industrial Relations*, 36/1: 99–123.

Robinson, A., and Perotin, V. (1997) 'Is Profit Sharing the Answer?', *New Economy*, 4: 112–16.

Rothschild-Whitt, J. (1982) 'The Collectivist Organization', in F. Lindenfeld and J. Rothschild-Whitt (eds), *Workplace Democracy and Social Change*. Boston: Porter Sargent.

Russell, R. (1995) *Utopia in Zion: The Israeli Experience with Worker Cooperatives*. Albany, NY: SUNY Press.

Thompson, P. (1983) *The Nature of Work*. London: Macmillan.

Uvalic, M. (1991) *Social Europe: The PEPPER Report*. Brussels and Florence: European Commission.

Wajcman, J. (1983) *Women in Control*. Milton Keynes: Open University Press.

Warhurst, C. (1998) 'Recognizing the Possible: The Organization and Control of a Socialist Labour Process', *Administrative Science Quarterly*, 43: 470–97.

Whyte, W. Foote, and Whyte, K. King (1988) *Making Mondragon: The Growth and Dynamics of the Worker Cooperative Complex*. New York: ILR Press, New York State School of Industrial and Labor Relations, Cornell University.

Yad Tabenkin (1997) *Kibbutz: Facts and Figures*. Efal: Yad Tabenkin.

Index